Feminist Spiritualities

SUNY series, Afro-Latinx Futures
―――――――
Vanessa K. Valdés, editor

Feminist Spiritualities

Conjuring Resistance in the Afro-Caribbean and Its Diasporas

Joshua R. Deckman

Cover image: Afro-Caribbean dancing in Cartagena, Colombia. Licensed under a Creative Commons 2.0 Generic License. (CC BY 2.0). https://creativecommons.org/licenses/by/2.0/.

Published by State University of New York Press, Albany

© 2023 State University of New York

All rights reserved

Printed in the United States of America

No part of this book may be used or reproduced in any manner whatsoever without written permission. No part of this book may be stored in a retrieval system or transmitted in any form or by any means including electronic, electrostatic, magnetic tape, mechanical, photocopying, recording, or otherwise without the prior permission in writing of the publisher.

For information, contact State University of New York Press, Albany, NY
www.sunypress.edu

Library of Congress Cataloging-in-Publication Data

Name: Deckman, Joshua R., author
Title: Feminist spiritualities : conjuring resistance in the Afro-Caribbean and its diasporas
Description: Albany : State University of New York Press, [2023] | Series: SUNY series, Afro-Latinx futures | Includes bibliographical references and index.
Identifiers: ISBN 9781438493404 (hardcover : alk. paper) | ISBN 9781438493411 (pbk. : alk. paper) | ISBN 9781438493428 (ebook)
Further information is available at the Library of Congress.

10 9 8 7 6 5 4 3 2 1

To Hayden, a constant light.

To Stephanie, for support in every sense of the word.

Para todas las brujas que ejercen sus poderes contra el estado asesino.

Para todes mis maestres y alumnes.

Esta poética de los altares no clama por una restitución ortodoxa de la religiosidad; no es exactamente eso, no. Clama por crearse un espacio liberador donde reconozcamos sin tamices de dónde venimos, quiénes somos, hacia dónde vamos.

—Nancy Morejón, *Poética de los altares*

We are not born women of color. We become women of color. In order to become women of color, we would need to become fluent in each others' histories, to resist and unlearn an impulse to claim first oppression, most-devastating oppression, one-of-a-kind oppression, defying comparison oppression. We would have to unlearn an impulse that allows mythologies about each other to replace knowing about one another. We would need to cultivate a way of knowing in which we direct our social, cultural, psychic, and spiritually marked attention on each other. We cannot afford to cease yearning for each others' company.

—M. Jacqui Alexander, *Pedagogies of Crossing*

Saquen sus rosarios de nuestros ovarios.

—Las Krudas CUBENSI

Diosa te salve, Yemayá
llena eres de ashé
la babalawo sea contigo
benditas tus hijas que toman la justicia en sus manos
y bendito es el fruto de tu Océano-río Oshún.

—Yolanda Arroyo Pizarro

Contents

List of Illustrations   xi

Acknowledgments   xiii

Introduction: Spiritual and Emotional Resistance to Empire   1

Chapter 1   Sacred Memories: Yolanda Arroyo Pizarro, Mayra Santos-Febres, and the Politics of Race in Puerto Rico   27

Chapter 2   The Path of Erzulie: Love, Vodou, and Counter-Imaginations of Hispaniola   59

Chapter 3   Afro-Latina Feminisms: Nuyorican, Domincanyork, and Afro-Latinx Political Resistance   85

Chapter 4   The Raw Ones: Ibeyi, Las Krudas CUBENSI, and Pedagogies of Resistance   109

Conclusion: Conjuring Paths, Points of Departure   137

Notes   143

Works Cited   155

Index   167

Illustrations

Figure 1.1 Santos-Febres responds to Mayra Montero in a post that draws hundreds of comments and even more shares. 31

Figure 1.2 Arroyo Pizarro responds to Montero in her own post, urging Montero—and by extension, Puerto Ricans—to take a long look at their own "hidden" racism. 32

Figure 1.3 Arroyo Pizarro comments on Santos-Febres's post, urging Montero to interrogate her own "hidden" prejudices. 33

Figure C.1 Caribbean Women Healers Project welcome portal. 138

Acknowledgments

This book is first and foremost the product of community, of a network of scholars, activists, artists, colleagues, and—yes—friends. I am indebted to the generosity and knowledge of those who offered me their most valuable resources: their time and their stories; who opened the doors of their homes; who traveled with me and accompanied me down the streets of Havana, smoke-filled bars of San Juan, and the shores of Veracruz; who opened archives, engaged in deep conversations in Harlem, and funded presentations; and who, when approached for advice, offered wisdom and warm coffee. It is a product of a compassionate and vulnerable kind of *uno múltiple*, that, when cultivated, becomes a transcendental space of productive knowledge creation. The imprints—*las huellas*—of this community are forever etched upon this text. They are my offering to be conjured upon opening its pages, a single point of departure leading to necessary future *lecturas*, engagements, and thoughts.

At Penn State University I was witness to the kindness and beneficence of many scholars whose critical eye and thirst for radical knowledge push academia forward. I thank Julia Cuervo-Hewitt, Marco Martínez, John Ochoa, Maha Marouan, Courtney Desiree Morris, Ariane Cruz, and Mariana Ortega. Other faculty of the Spanish, Italian, and Portuguese Department played various roles in the early stages of this manuscript, including Krista Brune, Sarah Townsend, Maria Truglio, Matthew Marr, Mary Barnard, and Nicolás Fernández-Medina. I am particularly grateful to have met, learned from, and collaborated with Judith Sierra-Rivera, who has been a teacher-mentor to me during the past eight years. Her tireless commitment to her research and her students, and deep reservoir of knowledge, is simply astonishing. She has guided me though the messy mangroves of higher education as a first-generation scholar and has been an unwavering example of integrity and scholarly excellence.

The research for this book was partially funded by the Africana Research Center at the Pennsylvania State University and the CUNY Dominican Studies Institute. In both of these spaces, I became part of an interdisciplinary community of scholars who greatly influenced the following pages. Specifically, Ramona Hernández, Sarah Aponte, Anthony Stevens-Acevedo, and Jhensen Ortiz. Each of these individuals were invaluable resources as I completed my library and research fellowship at the Dominican Studies Institute. The materials collected and insights into the histories of Dominican women in New York City served to construct parts of my third chapter. Sarah Aponte was also a key figure in organizing my interview with Josefina Báez, which guides the logics of the introduction, and who cannot be thanked enough for her wisdom. Without these amazing people, the book would not exist as it does today. At the Africana Research Center, I was provided with the space and time necessary to develop this work. I am indebted to Cynthia Young, William Dewey, Crystal Sanders, Alaina Roberts, Neelima Jeychandran, and Erin King.

My colleagues at Marywood University have supported me in so many ways. I have been fortunate to enter into a particularly caring and supportive academic community. While I was unable to take research release for this book, my department graciously assisted with advising duties, service requirements, and course assignments to make this possible. I must first thank Erin Sadlack, Ann Cerminaro-Costanzi, and Bill Conlogue, who read various iterations of book proposals and chapter sections. Their guidance and careful comments and suggestions are testimony to their outstanding mentorship. I am forever grateful for the dialogues, friendship, and pre-COVID trivia nights with Ann Cerminaro-Costanzi, Paola Marrero-Hernández, Helen Bittel, Lauren Esposito, Christa Irwin, Lindsey Wotanis, Adam Shprintzen, Yerodin Lucas, and Jeremy Rich. And my students. This wonderful group of young minds has provided me with the space not only to expand my archive (and share TikToks) but also to engage in rigorous debates and to discover texts anew. When the pressures of academia, at times, seem to be too much to bear, they offer hope and—on many occasions—laughter. I also thank my undergraduate professors of the Washington & Jefferson College Modern Languages Department, without whom I would not have embarked on this journey, particularly Katherine Ternes, Amparo Alpañés, Christy Shaughnessy, H. J. Manzari, and Maribel Manzari. Their dedication as educators is truly one of a kind.

I must also thank Rebecca Colesworthy and Vanessa K. Valdés, the editors of the Afro-Latinx Futures series as well as James Peltz, the editor in chief at SUNY Press for their support and enthusiasm. They offered reassurance and careful comments down this long journey. The text that you read now would not have been possible without these amazing people. I am also fortunate to have the following people in my personal, professional, and academic life: Odile Ferly, Tegan Zimmerman, Alaí Reyes-Santos, Yomaira Figueroa, Victor Miguel Castillo de Macedo, Alline Torres, Josefina Báez, Ariana Brown, Ana Ugarte, Stacey Mitchell, Anna Torres Cacoullos, Alejandra Gutiérrez, Victoria Jansen, Fernando Fonseca Pacheco, María Izquierdo, Michelle McGowan, and Emily Sterk. You have each, in your own way, offered time, support, guidance, conversation, and much-needed friendship.

I thank my parents and grandparents for their support of a journey they may not have always understood. From my youngest days, when Dorothy and Victoria would help me make my own "books" out of printed encyclopedia entries (yes, I was a cool child), they instilled in me a love of learning. I thank Hayden Rowan Deckman for continually reminding me what really matters. I hope to share this book with you someday, and I hope that it might offer a space to rethink and reimagine your world in relation to others. Stephanie, you have supported me in every sense of the word, shared triumphs and setbacks, traveled with me, listened to every complaint, and encouraged distraction and healthy time away from work. Words are not enough to express my gratitude. The joy and happiness we share is something that I hope will follow us for many years into the future. None of this would have been possible without you.

Introduction

Spiritual and Emotional Resistance to Empire

> You cannot look at a god that doesn't look like you and feel whole . . . so we must look to those spaces that keep our traditions of healing alive, because if you don't free your mind and soul you don't free the body.
>
> —Dr. Marta Moreno Vega, talk at the
> Caribbean Cultural Center and African Diaspora Institute

During my conversation with Josefina Báez, a Dominican-American author and performance artist who has published a wide array of literary works in New York, we spoke about the centrality of spiritual and emotional spaces in literary work by Black Latina women. Specifically, Báez outlined the restorative power that might be conjured by creatively engaging feelings of love and joy in this community, as well as occupying an open space of spiritual connection oriented toward those who share similar experiences. For her, these sensations felt by Caribbean women of African descent arise from the need to break through a colonial/imperial relationship not only with the United States but also with those island nations of the Atlantic to which the women can trace their roots. This is to say, these categories represent a possibility to overcome and to create reality otherwise. In our dialogue, Báez made an urgent call to embrace a politics that is "heart-centered" and proclaimed that by privileging the heart and deep spiritual connection, we might "make pain nothing." She defined this type of heart-centered politics as one that seeks to engage spirit and emotion in everyday life in order to uncover and center the histories of Afro-Latinx women, as well as the ways in which they forge alternative forms of solidarity, create knowledge, and take charge of the imaginary to envision other possible worlds.

Báez uses these narratives to also demonstrate how Afro-Caribbean women move together in difference, as she so eloquently explains in our conversation:

> [We need] a heart-centered community that is concrete, centered in the "is" and looking forward to a future that we have to create by taking care of ourselves and others. We all inhabit this Afro-diasporic body, and in that body each one of us has a work that will define it. Some of us are here [she holds out her hands] with fists clenched in the body, and these fists are needed. Others are in the heart, others are here [she gestures toward her throat] and are very vocal. And we all have cycled through all. And we move together in a dance, an amazing dance that is the walking of all of us together. A *ritmo* that includes pauses, silences, not knowing, knowing. But we are part of this body, and for me that is what is important. (Deckman 2018)

For Báez, this spiritual centering of the "heart," or those intimate stories that reach out and embrace the other in a mutual recognition, has a clear objective made apparent in the above passage: to empathize with the conditions affecting others, to recognize the other in one's self, to underscore the need to love Black bodies as a reparative gesture, and to pave the way into the future through spirit and joy. For the heart beats a life force throughout diaspora and connects in sinewy difference the disparate parts of the collective whole. Báez's advocacy for a coalitional politics of love in everyday life, then, urges Afro-Latinx women to share their experiences in such a way that this telling and retelling might perhaps move the community, as one body with many different functions, toward a future of liberation. The joy that this mutual recognition of humanity brings about, for Báez, is one that releases the body from the shackles of painful histories and creates a new *sense* of corporal sovereignty—a "ritmo" of spiritual and emotional wholeness that reclaims histories and bodies in order to create something new.[1]

Báez further declares that she is not interested in engaging with any traditional academic discourse or narrative in her advocacy for mutual support. In fact, she cheekily claims that the gravest violence one could do to her work is to "Foucault it," something that, for her, sounds too much like to "fuck it." She uses this language to underscore the fact that to impose another voice upon her art—especially that of a white male European intellectual—would be to smother her creation and limit the spaces she conjures on her own terms. Báez claims that this would be a type of intellectual rape that would steal her voice, spirit, and capacity to feel.[2] She is also clear to establish that her words are not to be understood as theory or metaphor; rather, the "centrality of the heart" should be engaged to build concrete and urgent spiritual, bodily, and emotional connections between women of color. In this way, her words stress a real spiritual connection shared by a collective "us" invoked repeatedly in her enunciations. This "us" composes the "we" of her statements, which binds together Caribbean women of African descent in a political community that marches through shared experiences of pain, historically rooted systems of violence, and the vestiges of colonial/imperial occupations that continue to manifest themselves in contemporary economic and political structures. The spirit that they share is a common but disconnected experience of dispossession and forced displacement, searching to create a world otherwise in their own way and on their own terms. This maneuver also serves to characterize "us" as an intimate diaspora of women who each dare to tell their stories in hopes of moving the collective body one step closer to liberation. Moreover, the urgency of locating these stories in the "is," as Báez defines the "present" filled with possibilities, breaks the barriers between past, present, and future, anchoring everyday experiences in an infinite connection with history and future potential. The "is" disrupts space and time in order to break through linear movements, allowing for other ways of knowing and connecting to emerge.[3]

This anecdote serves to open a more in-depth conversation into the ways that the spiritual, the bodily, and the emotional converge in the writing, artistic, and spiritual activism of Afro-Latinx women of the Caribbean in order to propose new ways of moving together in difference toward reparation, love, and joy. With a focus on contemporary literary and cultural productions, this book explores present-day manifestations of continuously shared economic and political circumstances of women of the African diaspora by examining five different contexts within the Afro-Latinx Americas: the Dominican Republic, Haiti, Puerto Rico, Cuba, and the United States (US). More specifically, each of the four chapters studies a particular spiritual need of the "Afro-diasporic body" manifested in the literary and creative works of Rita Indiana Hernández, Edwidge Danticat, Ana-Maurine Lara, Yolanda Arroyo Pizarro, Mayra Santos-Febres,

Nitty Scott, María Teresa Fernández, Elizabeth Acevedo, Ibeyi, and Las Krudas CUBENSI. The main questions that bind this archipelago of voices are, How do each of these authors reach out to a spiritual community to make sense of and work through the lingering pain of colonialism, slavery, and imperial projects? How do they engage feelings of love and joy to decenter this pain through their engagement with the entities of various spiritual systems, such as Espiritismo, Santería, Vodou, and other creolizations of these? And how do they link the spiritual and the emotional to *feel* their way through transformative, experimental processes—while productively considering their differences? How does the sacred become a way of embodying a self that is an intimate part of a historical community of movement and struggle? How does the sacred embody the ideals of decolonial love toward a genealogy of enslaved women as a system of healing? What lies at the crossroads of subjectivity and collectivity, spiritual knowing and power, memory, body, and emotion, and how might they move toward a decolonial future?

"We Are All in This Afro-Diasporic Body": African Diasporic Consciousness and Fractality

The literary and cultural producers in the following chapters engage with Afro-Latinx/Caribbean identities through their use of African diaspora spiritual practices and emotional politics. These religious beliefs include Dominican-Haitian Vodou as imagined by Hernández and Lara; Espiritismo and Santería as written by Arroyo Pizarro and Santos-Febres; creolized beliefs and self-proclaimed *brujería* wielded by Nitty Scott, Elizabeth Acevedo, and María Teresa Fernández; and Ibeyi's and Las Krudas's conceptualization of Cuban *orisha*. These works all highlight the interconnectedness of diaspora and the ways in which these imaginations of spirituality look toward a radical and urgent future world through building a genealogy of ancestral spirits and loving orientations toward one another.

Further, the emphasis on spiritual healing is a direct response to an inherited reality of violence, discomfort, and pain since all subjects in these works experience the lingering effects of colonization and the Middle Passage. The practice of spiritual healing becomes a necessary force for self-care, especially for women, in order to forge new futures that are untethered from the shackles of the past. Often these spiritual practices were written off as magic, witchcraft, or sorcery and were subject to restrictive laws set in place by colonizers (Olmos and Paravisini-Gebert 7). Historically, these spiritual practices and rituals acted as a collective space to protect the health of some of the most oppressed communities in the early colonies. They allowed enslaved African communities to preserve a sense of identity after suffering a violent cultural, social, and religious loss and even lent agency to African women who became the cornerstones of their new communities, as they were forced to create new modes of kinship (Murphy; Griffith and Savage; Olmos and Paravisini-Gebert; Strongman).

As Maha Marouan claims in *Witches, Goddesses, and Angry Spirits*, the criminalization of women's diasporic spiritual practices is clearly documented in the history of the Americas. She writes that this is due in part "because they provoked fear of poisoning and slave revolts . . . a result of racist ideology inherent in a European discourse of enlightenment that associates Blackness with evil" (9). Furthermore, she shows how African diaspora religious practices were often associated with magic, harm, and spells: "The knowledge of plants was seen as dangerous, because while plants are used to cure devotees, they also can be easily used to poison those in power" (9). The women in this book look to this history to rearticulate the way Afro-descendent women are represented, not as evil/demonic sorceresses but as cornerstones of their communities capable of reworking the order of things through an ephemeral connection in difference. For example, when Yolanda Arroyo Pizarro rescues the voices of enslaved women from the archives in San Juan, Puerto Rico, as part of her project Cátedra de Mujeres Negras Ancestrales, she charts active struggles by Black women against colonial forms of enslavement. She also converts the types of discourses that surrounded African religions, conceived as a force capable of disrupting the politics of Judeo-Christian respectability that guided colonial life, into poetic and literary creations that inform her vision of Afro-feminism in the Caribbean. At the same time, Ana-Maurine Lara immerses herself into the colonial history of the Dominican Republic and Haiti in order to communicate the violence of a self-righteous Christian male community when she describes the US occupation of Haiti (1915–1931) and the destruction of Vodou spiritual objects and persecution of practitioners of the religion in her own literary and academic projects. These are only two examples of the ways in which women of the Afro-Caribbean engage the spiritual and emotional residue of diaspora to reveal not only violent histories but also emergent forms of resistance and the radical potential of the imaginary in forging Afro-futurities.

The various spirits, ancestors, and orisha that operate in Santería, Espiritista, Vodou, and Santerista communities conjured in these creative and political works form a broad spectrum of beings that move between what Aisha M. Beliso-De Jesús calls diverse "Santería worlds" (6). These presences are oftentimes described as "felt" on the body and understood as "presences" within various spiritual networks that transcend space and time—inhabiting a space not unlike the "is" that Báez privileges in her own creative acts. Beliso-De Jesús employs the term "copresences" to refer specifically to this "complex multiplicity of racial spiritual embodied affectivity" that terms such as "presences" and "felt" imply (7). This means that sensations—emotions—can act as spiritual and religious subjectivities tied to a certain form of movement or bodily experience: "Dead African slaves, Yoruba diaspora oricha, and other racialized entities form part in a reconfiguration of practitioners' body-worlds . . . the various oricha, dead spirits (*egun*), energies of good (*iré*) or bad (*osogbo*) that influence practitioners' lives are copresences that haunt transnational spiritual interactions, inscribing themselves as historical affective archives" (7–8). This phenomenon is similar to what Avery Gordon terms a "seething presence," where ghosts and hauntings act on the present to call attention to "what has already past but is still very much existent" (Gordon 8). These feelings, knowledges, and otherworldly interactions conjure into existence certain spaces that "some know to be true but that others cannot fully see or comprehend" (Stoler 9). This demonstrates how embodied, emotional experiences can be understood as a type of spiritual locus of enunciation that may be crucial in uncovering the ways in which the structures of slavery and colonialism are still very much a part of the Afro-Caribbean experience—a locus that is at once singular and multiple, affecting the individual experience with ramifications for an entire community.

Rebellious Spirit/Against Western Modernity

Here it is important to describe this spiritual locus from which the authors in question speak. We must ask, What does this space look like and how does it allow for the politics of spirit to be renegotiated? How does it allow for lives to be rearranged and power to be shifted? Joseph Murphy writes that "to understand spirit . . . is to see that it is an orientation to a historical memory and to a living reality . . . the memory provides the precedent for all action. [For example in Vodou] things are done because 'cé commandment l'Áfrique.' Africa becomes the criterion of harmonious and moral action, and authority derives from fidelity to the traditions and spirit of Ginen" (38). But what is at stake when this historical memory is separated from the lived reality of a Black island? What type of "action" occurs when the "harmonious" "authority" of Africa is violently replaced with the imposed spirit of European whiteness and modernity? What type of turmoil does this cause a community that has been systematically cut from its collective memory, barred from the *uno múltiple* of ancestral communion?

Roberto Strongman reviews the boundaries between self and body in order to explore this rupture in the conceptualization of spirit, the boundaries between modernity and coloniality, with a markedly "decolonial attitude" (Maldonado-Torres 12). Through a brief study of philosophical thinkers such as Descartes, Bataille, Serres, Sartre, and Foucault, Strongman concludes that Western religious and philosophical systems continually entrap the soul. He claims this entrapment represents an internalization of the self that he contrasts with Afro-diasporic systems that have been historically and violently forced to the edges of the modern nation-state. This alternative understanding of how body, mind, and spirit are connected not only to the individual but also to the collectivity, he argues, may also permit a way to break through the imposition of Western philosophical discourses and ontological models upon the bodies, minds, and spirits of the historically colonized: "In fact, a thorough study of Afro-diasporic religions reveals how—unlike the Western idea of a fixed internal unitary soul—the Afro-diasporic self is removable, external, and multiple" (Strongman 10).

This multiplicity of the self observed in Afro-diasporic religious systems finds itself at home in the Caribbean and in the Caribbean diasporas and provides a locus from which to think from the periphery, the islands and their diaspora, and offer transformative approaches to thinking about modernity and its discontents. What Strongman reviews as "duality of the immaterial self" in African traditions becomes, in one cited example, the *tibonanj* and the *gwobonanj* in Haitian Vodou. In *Creole Religions of the Caribbean*, Margarite Fernández Olmos and Lizbeth Paravisini-Gerbert define these terms: "The head, which contains the two elements that comprise the soul—the ti bónanj or ti bon ange (the conscience that allows for self-reflection and self-criticism) and the gwo bónanj or gros bon ange (the psyche, source of memory, intelligence, and personhood)—must be prepared so that the gros bon ange can be separated from the initiate to allow the spirit to enter in its place" (118). Strongman summarizes the roles of these two aspects of the self by writing that the gwobonanj is consciousness, while the tibonanj is objectivity: "The gwobonanj is the principal soul, experience, personality. The tibonanj is described as the anonymous, protective, objective conscience that is truthful and objective, the impersonal spiritual component of the individual, whose domain also encompasses moral considerations and arbitration" (13). Thus, unlike the Western idea of the body as enclosure, Afro-epistemologies reorganize bodies and they become an open vessel—a ritual container that can be emptied, filled, and transported, what Strongman calls a "transcorporeality of being" that defies imposed logics of European thought. Thus, personhood in Africanized systems is tethered to multiple vessels, influenced by nonmaterial entities, and constructed in multiplicities. Even knowledge and the production of modes of knowing is something to be extracted, experienced, and conjured through bodily movement, ritual, and ethereal connections with spirits and ancestors. This radical (re)understanding of the body, spirit, and emotionality through spiritual ties aligns with contemporary archipelagic thinking and allows us to imagine new ways of mapping a geography of Afro-Caribbean feminist being. It challenges us to consider the limits of thinking from a Western perspective and to see time, space, and social relation differently.

As Strongman astutely notes tension between the Afro-diasporic concept of soul and the Cartesian understanding of its connection to the body, it is also worth noting that the conceptualization of spirit in Africanized religious traditions also conflicts with the modernizing and historical "spirit" of Enlightenment as understood by Hegel. In *The Phenomenology of Spirit*, Hegel describes a historical arc bending toward the Absolute—which he traces over the course of history through four empires ("Oriental, Greek, Roman, and Germanic"). According to Hegel, Spirit is developed in three stages. The first is in the form of self-relation, the Subjective Spirit composed of the minds of individual peoples. The second stage is that of Objective Sprit, or how individual minds come together and form communities. Here, Hegel argues that Spirit manifests itself through the laws of the state and that as history marches forward, all past stages are contained within the present "much like how a modern city is built on top of ruins of its earlier phases" (10). These layers are not separate or accessible but represent a series of steps taken in linear succession. These trajectories move toward what Hegel terms "Universal Spirit," as the past moves unilaterally toward enlightenment in a linear manner. For Hegel, Spirit is not something to be engaged or questioned, not something that travels between times, but instead is a descriptor of periodic and progressive movement forward. It is produced in an arc by an Absolute Idea, which leaves out certain areas of the world, removing them from the "progression of humanity."

This modernizing Spirit of Western Enlightenment has historically worked its way through the history of the colonies. In privileging certain ways of knowing and producing knowledge, it has supported political structures and nations that have emptied and alienated the inhabitants of Caribbean islands from their own stories, myths, and spiritual understanding of time and space. This has occurred in various educational missions—effectively zombifying in the name of the nation-state (Brodber 12). Thus, while moved by the Spirit of Enlightenment, the European gaze becomes predominant—the lens through which the colonized begin to view themselves. In this way, the Spirit of modernity works upon and *constructs* the colonized, who are punished and marked as deviant if they try to imagine themselves outside of this paradigm, outside of a linear progression toward a universal knowledge.

Caribbean Fractals and Space-Time Otherwise

Central to *Feminist Spiritualities*, then, is a rebellious type of spirit. It is a radical spirit that breathes into existence a united multiplicity that shatters linearity and purity, what Santos-Febres has begun to term *el uno múltiple* (taken up again in chapter 1). For Santos-Febres, who anchors herself in the Yoruban traditions of Western Africa and Puerto Rican Espiritismo, the knowledge that her body exists as a spatiotemporal crossroads bestows upon her and her literary production the power to forge other kinds of opportunities for connection and to imagine new futures while coming to terms with the past. I argue that the women of this collection all engage in an affective-spiritual conceptualization of the *uno múltiple*, a fractal understanding of Caribbean being that breaks through the colonial discourse of fracture and brokenness in linear time. If, as M. Jacqui Alexander argues, the legacy of colonialism in the Caribbean and the consolidation of modern nation-states implies an alienation from traditional indigenous and Africanized ways of knowing—fracturing the Afro-Caribbean spirit—then the women here become powerful healers who harness the multiplicity and transcorporeality of African diasporic spiritual systems to imagine a new system. This allows what Yomaira C. Figueroa-Vásquez terms "an examination of the varied liberatory strivings that rip the seams of foundational histories, and of the practices and fashioning of radical futures that do not rely on assimilation, dispossession, or coloniality" (23). This move carves an intimate spiritual space that connects racial and political projects across time and history and allows us to examine how historical processes of racialization, colonization, and imperial expansion play out in contemporary life.

On May 18, 2020, Santos-Febres laid out her emergent project of Afro-epistemology and fractality in a talk given at the Biblioteca y Centro de Investigación Social Jesús T. Piñero. In this talk, she speaks about Afro-epistemologies, the body as open vessel, and the productive utility that this thought has in terms of how we approach and think across various geographies of diaspora, cartographies of dispossession, and histories of forced displacements. She claims that following Afro-epistemologies allows us to address the lack of studies on testimonies of the enslaved, the lack of systematic studies on practices of *cimarronaje* and *cimarrón* establishments in Latin America and the Caribbean, and—her most salient point—a lack of the incorporation of the logics of Afro-diasporic spiritualities into academic discourses. While admitting that there does exist a history of sociological and anthropological studies that center race and Blackness in Latin America (involving what she says is an overreliance on data, fractions, and scientific approaches), she claims that not enough attention has been given to how these categories are engaged creatively or imagined by contemporary artists.

She states that "cuando hablo de fractal, estoy hablando específicamente de geometría fractal y de las organizaciones que comparten todos los seres . . . yo creo que el Caribe es fractal y que la identidad afrodescendiente es fractal por historia, pero también por esa continuidad extraña que es una tecnología de vida que hace que repliquen cosas en la memoria, en los distintos países y regiones a las que nos han llevado" ("when I speak of the fractal, I am speaking specifically about fractal geometry and the organizing structures that all beings share . . . I believe that the Caribbean is fractal and that Afrodescendent identity is fractal by history, but also because of that strange continuity, that technology of life that makes things replicate in memory, in different countries and regions to which they have forcibly taken us"). This conceptualization of space and time, again, stands in stark contrast with the linear progression of Enlightenment and the Cartesian understanding of body and mind. Here, memories seem to be passed down like genetic material, a "technology of life" yet to be uncovered that might tell "us" (her community of Black Caribbean women) where "we" have come from and recognize a similar pattern across the hemispheric Americas to perhaps forge connections of solidarity, mutual respect, and love beyond imposed geopolitical borders.

Santos-Febres argues that through the transcorporeality of Afro-diasporic being she is able to enter an "other" space in which her body is connected intimately to her past and her future. She becomes an open entity capable of disrupting the Western timeline to center the disparate histories of her people. As she continues to explain her understanding of fractality, she proceeds to display a photo of a silvery leaf on a slide and asks her audience to view the leaf as a map—an aerial view with rivers and mountains, oceans and landmasses that become more intricate and repetitive as she zooms closer. She declares that these rivers that course through the leaf have much to do with the ways in which we think spiritualities otherwise; that is, how many realities can coexist in what appears to be one singular image: "Lucen las capas de la realidad que no son lineales, sino se sobreponen, se multiplican" (The many layers of reality shine through. These are not linear; they overlap, they multiply). This is precisely where Santos-Febres locates the "logics of fractality," a term that she coins as *una provocación*, a pattern that repeats itself in difference across the Americas from the Dominican Republic, Puerto Rico, Mexico, and Cuba to the southern US, the Gullah Islands, and throughout the hemispheric context. The *uno múltiple* becomes a way of creating a view of reality that might perhaps suture the fractures of history in order to inhabit a fractal being—echoing Baéz's diasporic rhythm that moves through difference as one. It is the superposition of many layers that are at once one and multiple—a geometry of bodies and histories that repeats as each separate part is examined more closely.

Ultimately, she asks how we, as literary and cultural scholars, can use this pattern to step into the spiritual locus of enunciation and uncover truths that have for too long been kept silent: "Es algo específico. Es fragmental, NO fragmentado. Me pregunto siempre: ¿Qué tenemos que hacer [nosotres], los pensadores de esta nueva identidad o esta nueva configuración de la identidad afro en estos momentos históricos para discutir, para crear estas investigaciones? Porque les voy a decir una cosa, estas investigaciones hacen falta en el Caribe hispanoparlante para re-escribir el mapa de las presencias y de las negociaciones" (It is something very specific. It is fragmental, NOT fragmented. I always ask myself: What do we, the intellectuals of this new identity or this new configuration of afro identity in these historical moments, need to do in order to discuss and create these investigations? Because I am going to tell you all something, these investigations are lacking in the Hispanic Caribbean and they are necessary if we are to re-write the map of presences and negotiations (Santos-Febres "Afroepistemologías").[4] *Feminist Spiritualities* takes up Santos-Febres's call to map "presences" and "negotiations" across geopolitical boundaries, by grounding itself in an Afro-epistemology of spirit and embracing a logics of fractal being. In this way, the text does not seek to tell a coherent story of Afro-Latin(x) American and Caribbean colonization, enslavement, violence, and dispossession, nor does it seek to provide an in-depth overview of the spiritual systems mentioned. Rather, it attempts to evoke the ways in which those processes are disrupted when we center a Black spiritual resistance to imposed systems of (Western) knowledge. This, in turn, allows other modes of being to emerge and calls for a transformation in the ways we think of racialized belonging across and beyond Caribbean geographies. By centering the vessel, inhabiting the open fractal, each author takes on the spiritual locus of enunciation to claim for herself the crossroads of being and history in order to speak back defiantly. As the epigraph of this introduction by Dr. Marta Moreno Vega claims, the search for wholeness in difference must begin with an epistemology and spiritual understanding that is constructed from below, one that bestows its practitioner with power in identification where they become the powerful visionaries of a new tomorrow. To look at the world through someone else's lens, to "Foucault" (fuck) it, is to continue to ghost[5] histories, bodies, beliefs, and experiences that have the power to reshape reality and political structures.

"I Don't Want My People in More Pain": Feminist Emotional Politics through Spirit

As a logic of Afro-diasporic spirituality, transcorporeality, and fractals guide the organization of this book, the women studied also engage with the emotional impressions that these spaces and entities leave on their bodies—as well as the ways in which these feelings become opportunities for connection and knowledge creation in their own right. Thus, feminist thought from women of color and decolonial approaches give us the tools with which we can engage not only the spiritual politics of these works but also how these women invoke emotion within this spiritual connection. Returning to the opening anecdote, while Báez urges scholars not to "Foucault" the work of Black and Latinx women, she emphatically begs for us to "Anzaldúa" it. Here Báez means that she would prefer an exploration into the ways that her work addresses a type of "spiritual activism," invoking her own vision of the *uno múltiple*. However, she also considers Anzaldúa's teachings in *Light in the Dark* in order to question not only spiritual spaces but also how the emotions experienced within these spaces act as impressions left by social, historical, and political structures. For example, in *Light in the Dark* Anzaldúa remarks on the power of border dwellers—*nepantleras*—who engage emotional politics and embrace vulnerability to create new connections and imagine new futures. This type of thought or orientation echoes the drive toward creation that fuels the *nepantlera*, where the "thought" and creative act has the power to work on and change reality, reflecting also Édouard Glissant's transformative poetics: "[It] spaces itself out into the world. It informs the imaginary of peoples, their varied poetics, which it then transforms, meaning, in them its risks become realized" (1). These spiritual and emotional politics, then, are feelings that work not only on the mind but also on the body and the boundary between bodies, times, and spaces to forge an alternative cartography of meaning-making. Lara calls this a type of "potential map to Black sovereignty," that includes not only the spiritual but the emotional experiences of queer individuals and women "including the collapse of time in ceremony, including the manifestation of spirits through bodies, voices, and dreams, including the reconfiguration of gender and race through the corporeal-spirit body-land" ("I Wanted to Be More of a Person" 25). Here again, Lara reiterates the connectedness of spirit and bodily sensation, the importance that affect and emotion play in making sense of not only the world but also the nonmaterial, the temporal, and the spatial.

Emotional Politics in the African Diaspora and the Caribbean

In this sense, my study of emotional and spiritual discourses resonates with Katherine McKittrick's insistence on care as urgent feminist work for women of color and Black women. More specifically, both McKittrick and Sara Ahmed explore feminist methodologies of emotion as they are manifested in a multitude of literary and cultural productions in order to demonstrate that cultural and political structures impress themselves differently on different bodies, thereby creating publics and socials with different emotional textures and boundaries. Thus world-building within the united multiplicity of diaspora rests upon the ways in which "we" conceptualize nurturing relationships, build joy, and forge loving connections through a spiritual understanding of the self and the other. The foundations of this would mean the recovery of modes of life that have been subjugated and pathologized. This type of "familia from scratch" represents a radical fight to stay alive in spite of those who would see their way of life destroyed and a willingness to grow together in difference. *Feminist Spiritualities* will focus specifically on pain, love, and joy within a spiritual space of connection between past, present, and future as depicted by each author. It is precisely in the emotional refusal of empire that the women in this study claim for themselves positions of love and joy on their own terms—exactly what their bodies have been historically denied. Fractally together, they ask, How can we be and feel otherwise? How can we connect and share experiences of feeling otherwise? How is feeling alive, joyful, and loved a radical position in itself?

Specifically, the "affective turn" in Latin American and Caribbean cultural studies has emerged precisely from these questions. In their foundational collection of essays *El lenguaje de las emociones: Afecto y cutura en América Latina*, Mabel Moraña and Ignacio Sánchez Prado underscore the "work" that emotion can do in terms of opening up cultural and literary manifestations to further study: "El gradual e inexorable declive del poder explicativo de los vocabularios de los estudios culturales latinoamericanos en los últimos años ha dejado en claro la necesidad de nuevas formas de aproximarse a la cultura desde ese ángulo afectivo que, en la mayoría de los casos, ha sido leído como poco más que un síntoma de procesos políticos e ideológicos subyacentes" (12; The gradual and inexorable decline of the explanatory power of the vocabularies of Latin American cultural studies in recent years has made clear the need for new ways of approaching culture from that affective angle which, in most cases, has been read as little more than a symptom of underlying political and ideological processes).

The book's several sections, which span a vast cultural spectrum, include a variety of theoretical and thematic approaches, thereby deepening in an expressive interpellation of culture and underscoring what has been posed in the introduction—that affect and emotion are critical phenomena produced in post modernity and late capitalism and are effects in the processes of domination and marginality: "El impulso afectivo—en cualquiera de sus manifestaciones emocionales, sentimentales, etc.—moldea la relación de la comunidad con su pasado, las formas de lectura con su presente y la proyección hacia el futuro posible, deasedo e imaginado en concordancia o en opisición a los proyectos dominantes" (315; The affective impulse—in any of its emotional, sentimental manifestations, etc.—shapes the relationship of the community with its present and the projection towards the possible future, devised and imagined in accordance with or in opposition to the dominant projects). Thus, emotion—grounded in the historical processes of Latin America and the Caribbean—become essential sites of interrogation in order to open up cultural criticism to its liberating potential. In this book, emotional politics will be engaged with the spiritual to approach ways in which Black Caribbean communities and their diasporas have and continue to push toward possible futures—guided by radical spirit, joy, and love.

To speak about joy and love, we must first briefly understand how pain works politically and can even be taken on as a site of knowledge forged in the imperial order of things. In *Sister Outsider*, Audre Lorde—a Caribbean feminist scholar and intellectual in her own right, who spent the last years of her life on the island of St. Croix—describes her encounter with a white woman on a train to Harlem (124–33). In this memory, Lorde is a child and her mother spots what she terms an "almost seat" (one that is barely big enough for her to fit). Her mother pushes her into this seat, and Lorde spots beside her a white woman in a fur hat. With the woman's stare and the abrupt manner in which the woman jerks her coat closer to herself, Lorde senses a feeling of horror in the woman. Lord attributes this horror/disgust to a roach that the woman must have seen to have reacted in such a way. Suddenly, Lorde realizes that there is nothing crawling on the seat between them, it is Lorde the woman does not want her coat to touch. The bodies come together in the "contact zone," almost touch, and slide away. The sickening sensation that the white woman experiences becomes a rage or anger that the body of an "other" has gotten too close. The body of the young Black child is constructed as something that was sickening insofar as it has gotten too close and therefore ran the risk of "contaminating," the body of the white woman. Furthermore, this sudden recoil of the white woman "undoes" the young Black girl. It leads the Black girl to anger. This anger is then turned into hate toward the Black female body (her own body and the body of other Black women) as well as deep psychological and emotional pain. This is why, for Lorde, it is a political action to love the body of Black women. Lorde's conception of anger as a political force is full of information, energy, and the power to examine, redefine, envision, and reconstruct—especially for women of color, lesbians and gay men, and poor people.

Therefore, following Lorde's theorization transformed into anger and into valuable information for a politics of love, the term *pain* is used in this book to refer to specific moments of urgent physical discomfort exhibited in the examined productions. While the term has vast medical and psychological connotations, it is used here to communicate the "pain" of multiple forms of contact between the individual and the social and to demonstrate how these categories shape each other. In other words, I argue that we must consider the political, cultural, and historical work that pain does in uncovering the logics of empire that guide daily life. Thus, this book employs pain as a concept that enters into politics and opens a space from which we are better able to analyze complex relations of power. This politicization of pain requires that we take into consideration the ways in which painful experiences work in certain ways to affect themselves differently on various bodies. Through an analytical framework inspired by the texts in this book, just like Lorde's, my study will address the multiple border spaces opened by painful encounters and how we can and must move past pain to glimpse another type of spiritual-affective liberation.

Pain, and the multiple emotions with which it is usually associated (e.g., shame, anger, disgust, and hate), is defined by several scholars of the Caribbean as an intimate space of relation. I use space of relation to demonstrate how pain is bound up with how bodies inhabit the world. For example, Yolanda Martínez-San Miguel uses painful ethnic humor in Puerto Rico to demonstrate what she terms the island's "interethnic borders" when she writes in *Caribe Two Ways: Cultura de la migración en el Caribe insular hispánico*: "El chiste étnico funciona como otro de los discursos represivos contra las identidades minoritarias" (163; The ethnic joke functions as another repressive discourse against minority communities). Martínez-San Miguel goes on to refer to the *repulsión* that the national subject feels toward the racialized "other" (here: the Dominican immigrant or the dark-skinned Afro–Puerto Rican) and the hostile border that the joke produces (155). She underscores the fact that the border produced through this contact of the national subject's disgust and the "other's" shame is one that is particularly uncomfortable and filled with pain directed inward, as the subject is affectively removed from the comfort of belonging. What is more, the painful border is converted into a form of processing, articulating, and circulating hidden limits of what is considered appropriate or possible.

In *Our Caribbean Kin*, Alaí Reyes-Santos addresses a line of pain in the Caribbean that is intimately linked with national and transnational kinship models. Referring to Martínez-San Miguel's conceptualization of the ethnic joke, Reyes-Santos relates the painful experience of otherness to histories of colonial subjection and dependence, as well as US military interventions (107). Therefore, painful border spaces carry within themselves the power to act as a type of decolonial locus of enunciation—that is, the border allows one to speak at the margins of well-defined categories—and to make visible structures of power that have infiltrated the social and political experiences of Afro-descendent women in the Caribbean and its diasporas. It is in this specific context that I use the term *pain*: namely to address the ways in which these women who operate from the periphery of the European canon challenge—through their engagement with African diaspora spiritual practices—the cultural and racial hegemony of the center. To dwell in pain is to bring the conditions of "modernity" and the Eurocentric categories through which the modern nation-state is perceived to the surface. It is the pain that operates on certain bodies that makes these categories visible.

Moreover, in *Pedagogies of Crossing*, M. Jacqui Alexander writes: "Since colonization has produced fragmentation and dismemberment at both material and psychic levels, the work of decolonization has to make room for deep yearning for wholeness, often expressed as a yearning to belong that is both material and existential, both psychic and physical, and which, when satisfied, can subvert and ultimately displace the *pain* of dismemberment" (281, my emphasis). Within this framework, and following Alexander, the imprint that colonization has left on Caribbean society is one of a painful dismemberment and the yearning, desire, and constant search for ways to work through this painful inheritance toward a new form of wholeness. According to Martínez-San Miguel, pain in this sense acts as a way to identify and recognize colonial dismemberment or rupture in the present—that is the pain of the coloniality of diaspora (*Coloniality*). Here I follow Martínez-San Miguel's conceptualization of coloniality of diaspora, which is used "to refer to experiences of colonialism in the Caribbean that began in the sixteenth and seventeenth centuries and lasted, in some cases, until today, and that frequently include the coexistence of more than one colonial system (Spanish and US American in the Dominican Republic, Puerto Rico, and Cuba; Spanish, French, US American, and English in many islands of the Anglo- and Francophone Caribbean, such as Haiti and Martinique)" (22). Thus, my conceptualization of pain inserts these authors' productions into the colonial discourse to disturb its dynamics by calling attention to the ways in which colonial systems are at work in their everyday lives. Pain in these texts and cultural productions is a process that challenges the articulations of cohesive national identities; it expresses the often hidden and violent social, cultural, and political realities hidden behind the "happy fantasies" (Ahmed *The Promise*) of the modern nation-state.

It is important to note that although I discuss the Black body in pain as a site of knowledge in the context of racism and xenophobia, this pain does not condemn these bodies to hopelessness and erasure—nor should it ever become the focal point of individual or community identification. Rather, it may constitute a rupture with a present that oftentimes fails to acknowledge racist and xenophobic (anti-Black) practices. I connect pain with the disruption of modes of knowledge or ignorance regarding race and oppression in order to point to coalitional possibilities across experiences and histories throughout the Afro-Caribbean. Therefore, one of the important contributions of my conceptualization of pain in this archive is to illustrate the power that emanates from dwelling in the borders created through painful encounters and the type of decolonial knowledge that this dwelling-in-pain communicates and how it often moves bodies toward a powerful spiritual and emotional experience filled with knowledge. This move toward community, pushed by a painful past, also represents the movement toward a love that may perhaps wipe away this pain and a joy that asserts bodily autonomy and self-sovereignty.

"We Need a Heart-Centered Community": Decolonial Love, Joy, and Ethical Relations

By taking into consideration decolonial theory, my analysis focuses on how pain performs as a kind of colonial wound—gesturing toward an interstice that is found at the borders between Western and non-Western knowledge, the one that the assumed norm of modernity marginalizes. Therefore, to study this kind of pain within decolonial thought demands a rethinking of knowledge beyond Western concerns—and dwelling in these interstices brings us closer to overcoming and embracing joy. Specifically, Walter Mignolo illuminates how this kind of "border thinking" provides a liberating energy from which "local decolonial 'I's'" may "speak their truth" (xiv). That is, he explores the strategies that we may employ to imagine a landscape and knowledge belonging specifically to those traditionally left outside of modernization projects.[6] Furthermore, I take up Mignolo's challenge to not dwell within one disciplinary territoriality but instead intend to "dwell in the borders" of literary and cultural studies by using the tools that these disciplines provide to go beyond them and analyze those discursive, political, aesthetic, and cultural practices aimed at dismantling those residues of slavery and coloniality.

In this sense, illuminating pain as a kind of "counter knowledge" speaks back to what Aníbal Quijano, Mignolo, and José Buscaglia-Salgado have theorized as the coloniality of power. This concept can be understood as the asymmetry of power based on a racial and geopolitical classification that establishes the differences between Europe and its former colonies (Mignolo xvii). Thinking and doing decolonially means painfully and consciously unveiling the logic of coloniality and "delinking from the rhetoric of modernity" (Mignolo xviii) to engage in a knowledge from specific loci of enunciation, in our case from the emotional/spiritual experiences of Afro-Caribbean women both in the islands and beyond. Mignolo then argues for the need to decolonize knowledge and being and advocates that the "decolonial humanities" will have a fundamental role to play in this process (Epistemic Disobedience 3). Also, as Mabel Moraña, Enrique Dussel, and Ben Jáuregui have noted, "the study of coloniality implies . . . the challenge to thinking *across* (frontiers, disciplines, territories, classes, ethnicities, epistemes, temporalities) in order to visualize the overarching structure of power that has impacted all aspects of social and political experience in Latin America since the beginning of the colonial era" (17). Santos-Febres's conceptualization of Caribbean fractality and Afro-epistemologies extends this line of thought, and the women in this book engage in their own extension of this mindset: a politics of anti-colonial power that emerges from the interstices of the spiritual locus of enunciation.

Decolonial Love

It is in this sense that Chela Sandoval's work becomes fundamental to my study. In her *Methodology of the Oppressed*, Sandoval argues for the "emancipatory potential in women-of-color formations and strategies precisely because, unlike traditional conceptions of diversity, difference is embraced in these formations and strategies not as an objective in itself, but rather as a point of departure and a method for transforming repressive and colonial social circumstances" (xi). Thus, she creates the possibility and strategies for decolonization through what she calls "love in the postmodern world," which represents a way of deeply understanding each other that establishes an intimate collective movement of women. Against the exclusionary politics of national love, decolonial love functions in the materials I examine here as a critical methodology that looks to the past to enact a present of hospitable possibility for those marginalized from the national promise of a love associated with national identity. Through this type of love, Sandoval exposes the underlayer of modernity by showing those historical/colonial forces that have (not so) silently influenced the history of US-European consciousness.

In "Uses of the Erotic: The Erotic as Power," Lorde theorizes from a Black feminist standpoint this decolonial loving attitude toward the other. In this particular essay, spirit and emotion take central importance as a force that works to move bodies toward each other in an intimate coalition. Lorde describes the erotic as source of knowledge that is spiritual in nature and lies in those unknown or unexpressed feelings. It takes the form of an episteme that disrupts masculinist "rational knowledge" (53). Lorde writes that it is particularly the space of the erotic that has been perverted by the "male world," which fears the depths of this knowledge too much to examine it within themselves. She claims that too often the erotic is confused with the pornographic. But the pornographic represents the unknowing of this erotic knowledge: "pornography emphasizes sensation without feeling" (54). When intimate connection is flooded with feeling, a void is filled and knowledge emerges.

Thus, feeling and emotion become central components of the spiritual locus of enunciation. Power and connection come from "sharing deeply." Lorde writes, "The sharing of joy, whether physical, emotional, psychic, or intellectual, forms a bridge between the sharers which can be the basis for understanding much of what is not shared between them, and lessens the threat of their difference" (56). This is to say that once one experiences the liberation and happiness that one is capable of experiencing, one can then go on to speak back to systems of power that restrict the body from the ultimate joy of life. These political and emotional categories are not separated from the spiritual. Lorde erases the border between the spiritual and the political by claiming that what connects these two categories is precisely the deepest meaning of love (55). This passionate connection is conceived of as true knowledge, true desire that emanates from within outward. When we are able to dig down into ourselves: "In touch with the erotic, I become less willing to accept powerlessness, or those other supplied states of being which are not native to me, such as resignation, despair, self-effacement, depression, self-denial" (58). The potential for coalition comes precisely from this same recognition. For we must recognize the erotic feelings in ourselves to share the power of the feelings of others.

M. Jacqui Alexander also proposes her notion of "the crossing," which, like Mignolo's border thinking and Lorde's erotics, represents the breaking through of imposed categories to make different conversations and solidarities possible. For Alexander, *pedagogies of crossing* refers specifically to those knowledges that are produced in the experience of marginalization that might be used to "destabilize existing practices of knowing and cross the constructed boundaries of exclusion and marginalization" (7). Likewise, the message of the crossing (derived from the memory of the Middle Passage) is to understand how transgressing boundaries might better instruct us to define new ways of being in the world (8). More importantly, Alexander expands on the importance of these border positionalities of the crossing in the analysis of feminist thinkers, such as Anzaldúa, Moraga, Mohanty, Lorde, and bell hooks, and their engagement with "spiritual work." According to Alexander, all of the elements of feminist thought can be addressed within a line of analysis that uses spiritual knowledge as the mechanism of making the world intelligible, especially for women. Alexander highlights "the paradox within a feminism which has become so secularized that it has paid little attention to the ways in which spiritual labor and spiritual knowing is primarily a project of self-knowing and transformation that constantly invokes community and collective change" (291).

Alexander charts the migrations and displacements of these cosmological systems to demonstrate how the sacred becomes a web of interpretive systems that are grounded in meaning and imagination; that are "ancient," taking place in a different time yet constantly manifesting; and that make a place through the active participation of community. This is to say, that the sacred in African diaspora religious practices is found in the interactions with everyday life and bodies through which the divine manifests itself. This concept is demonstrated as Alexander quotes an *espiritista*: "Yo soy mis santos; mis santos soy yo" (293). This quote is important to my study because it echoes the *uno múltiple* and shows the ways in which the body is constructed as a border space, a dwelling in the border, between European and African systems, and as a way to mediate between the living and the dead.

Thus, I conceptualize love—an emotional locus of enunciation[7]—as a space that is grounded in a deep connection not only to the self and the other but also to a site that is linked to the past and the future. It is a matrix of connection that takes in information from historical processes that have produced the current moment, the demystification of the processes in the mutual recognition of humanity in the other's gaze, and the coming-together with the other in an urgent union, forged in the yearning for a future otherwise. It produces a space in which present times are reconfigured and aspire to redirect—if only for an instant—gendered and sexed violence, racial fractures, and economic dispossession. While these fleeting spaces of emotional potential represent an impermanent utopian force, the knowledge that is gleaned from the feeling is one of pedagogic significance. It is a type of emotional space of "crossing," which makes the one multiple—that is, love—the tool by which the *uno múltiple* may emotionally make itself known and thus intervene and push bodies toward action.

These emotional and spiritual feelings, as we have seen, are rarely taken seriously in a broader academic context. They sometimes exist as almost an afterthought, anecdotal, a kind of escape from the "real work" of critical thought. However, in engaging these categories to manifest racial(ized), gendered, and sexual(ized) histories, the women of this book forge a bridge between research, creation, and feeling. The documented, felt, and fantastic stories taken on in this study all point toward something that floats outside the "center" but is still worth paying serious attention to. These writings perform acts of conjure and manifestation to make feelings a space of spiritual connection—they manifest solidarity and demand action. These insights into disparate processes of world-making and creating kin point toward what Solimar Otero describes as the archives of conjure, which can be understood as "the limits of certain genres of expression in explaining the 'structures of feeling' that go into creating communities like Afrolatinx spiritual families" (52). This is to say, these archives express how the very real realities and sociohistorical structures that undergird affective relationships and ritualistic engagement of spiritual systems drive practices of solidarity and alternative sovereignty. Otero argues further that "shared beliefs, experiences, and especially alliances and identifications with nonmaterial beings are difficult to express if one relies solely on academic discourses" (54). The tensions inherent in the discourses of the academy, emotional experience, and spirituality offer a unique opportunity for the reinvention of self and community. For example, the tensions in Arroyo Pizarro's poetry that are gendered and sexualized ask the reader to reconsider how Puerto Rican-ness has been produced historically to center those elements privileged by a white, Eurocentric project. Tshanwe, Arroyo Pizarro's protagonist through the slave trade and early colony, acts as a defiant reaffirmation of Black womanhood—invoking the certain aspects of Santería and other creolized religious systems to defy the erasure of her sense of selfhood through the imposition of the church. These stories are ones that seek not to place Black bodies in more pain but to heal and negotiate the hostilities and violence shown them and their kin. They rework an affective geography of the *uno múltiple* through an imaginative and radical spiritual locus that regenerates, remembers, and recreates. This book takes these considerations seriously, as Santos-Febres pleads, in order to make room for complex solidarity across geopolitical borders—a spiritual, feminist, and emotional call to engage the imaginary and rethink the human.

Each of the chapters in this book represents a small part of the *uno múltiple* of the Hispanophone Afro-Caribbean and its diasporas. In each section, I read a series of literary and cultural productions linked by a central theme. The book embraces the fractal spirit, with each chapter reflecting a similarity in difference and each chapter engaging political concerns to show how literature and culture have the potential to radically change how we view the human and how these women think themselves and their communities into existence.

Chapter Outline

Feminist Spiritualities invokes the idea of conjure as it is understood by Solimar Otero and Roberto Strongman. This is to say that the texts engage distinct geographies, temporalities, and spatialities to look at the ways in which rituals, the dead, ancestors, deities, and material objects are engaged, as Otero writes, "as actors in multiple forms of kin and worldmaking" (2). In this way, I do not look at officially sanctioned discourses as they emerge from institutionalized religious spaces—which, in their own ways, exert a certain level of social control over bodies, sexualities, and emotions. Otero argues that it is in following nonmaterial, spiritual beings and popular imaginations that we may be able to address affective histories of racism, patriarchy, and colonialism, as well as the sticky residues that these histories have left behind (3–4). In order to inhabit multiple geographies, temporalities, and spatialities at once, each chapter is conceived as a conjuring of a specific historical moment—each one an embodiment of residual energies that push "us" to move in diasporic unity. Together, these chapters "work" to call forth a new type of existence: a call to arms for Black resistance located in knowledge that had, for centuries, been kept hidden, criminalized, and punished. I am following Otero in my understanding of "conjure . . . [which] is to make manifest a desired reality through *trabajo*, work . . . [and to create] by incorporating, subverting, and rendering the energy available at the moment" (4). Thus, the chapters represent a convergence of past, present, and future political trajectories in hopes to inspire a unified front—in difference—against intolerance, white supremacy, patriarchy, and homophobia to be called upon in any order, at any time, for any reason. Each chapter "renders" those historical imprints left upon bodies, emotional marks engraved by history, and deep yearnings for liberation in order to ultimately foreground healing and fractal community building.

In chapter 1, I analyze four narratives written in the early 2000s in Puerto Rico. I propose a comparative reading of Arroyo Pizarro's *Saeta: The Poems* (2009) and *Los documentados* (2005) and Santos-Febres's *Fe en disfraz* (2009) and *Boat People* (2005) to underscore how these texts interrogate colonial and imperial historical narratives and migration networks in the Caribbean. Specifically, this chapter will center on the experience of displacement between the island of Hispaniola, Puerto Rico, and the US. In *Saeta* and *Fe en disfraz*, Arroyo Pizarro's rewriting the historical narrative of *las crónicas de conquista* from the perspective of the female slave is the central motivation behind the articulation of a series of narrators who exercise alternative spiritual and sexual practices for concrete, painful, *and* liberatory experiences that they document.

In chapter 2, I engage in a close reading of Rita Indiana Hernández's "Da pa' lo' do'" and Ana-Maurine Lara's *Erzulie's Skirt*. These works represent radical cultural and political sites of contestation to moments of violence and exclusion in Haitian and Dominican history. Danticat dedicates her story to "the brave women of Haiti, grandmothers, mothers, aunts, sisters, cousins, daughters, and friends on this shore and other shores," that have "stumbled but . . . will not fall" (ix). In a similar manner, Lara's text tells the story of Miriam and Micaela, two women from Haiti and the DR, respectively, who embark on a journey from Haiti to the DR, to Puerto Rico, and ultimately back to the DR. They profess a love for each other, invoking both Changó and Erzulie, that leads them to a place of rest in the *bateyes* of the Dominican sugarcane fields.

In chapter 3, I follow Urayoán Noel's conceptualization of "counter-publics" to study Elizabeth Acevedo's and María Teresa Fernández's slam poetry produced in New York. I examine not only the poems themselves but how certain experiences that these women narrate circulate between poet and audience. I demonstrate how everyday forms of racism in the US Latinx community painfully remember a long history of colonialism and slavery. Through a discussion on beauty, I argue that the body of Afro-Latinx women becomes the spiritual locus from which a new knowledge may be forged.

In chapter 4, I focus on the Afro-Cuban feminist hip-hop group Las Krudas CUBENSI and Cuban-American group Ibeyi. I argue that more attention should be placed on the religious discourse in Las Krudas's and Ibeyi's song lyrics, as African diasporic religious practices (Santería or Regla de Ocha) are employed in order to express their call for the liberation of Black Cuban women. This chapter calls on the memory of Lydia Cabrera to construct these *raperas* as powerful santeras that call upon the orisha. I examine the possible futures that are imagined through this engagement with nonmaterial and spiritual entities and how resistance to patriarchal forms of being are conjured through these maneuvers.

The conclusion opens a space for reflection and posits additional questions. Here, I demonstrate how Afro-diasporic spiritual systems and the fractal/emotional spaces they conjure open lines of further inquiry. I call for more studies that invoke the decolonial attitude, the divine as well as the diabolic, to continue to push against the boundaries of Western modernity and the systemic white supremacy that undergird Caribbean spaces.

This project provides a way of reading a diaspora that has been pushed to the edges of belonging[8]—as Vásquez-Figueroa would argue, "not from the perspective of the underside, but from an approach that sees difference as consequential . . . as an archive of overlapping histories and incommensurable differences" (29). To continue this mode of analysis, *Feminist Spiritualities* embraces the spiritual locus of the *uno múltiple* to bring together Afro-Caribbean subjects who speak from a space of openness and mutual recognition, across time and space, and in multiple mediums. The historically dispossessed are given space to speak back to the violent processes of colonial/imperial rule that have worked to draw limits on their movement, bodily autonomy, and world-making potentialities—to reject the order into which they have been bound and to create their own.

Chapter 1

Sacred Memories

Yolanda Arroyo Pizarro, Mayra Santos-Febres, and the Politics of Race in Puerto Rico

> Ay ay ay, que soy grifa y pura negra; / grifería en mi pelo / cafrería en mis labios; / y mi chata nariz mozambiquea (Ay ay ay, that I'm kinky-haired and pure Black; / kinky hair, Kafir lips / and my flat nose Mozambiques).
>
> —Julia de Burgos, *Poema en veinte surcos*

In 2016, when the Cuban author Mayra Montero, residing in Puerto Rico,[1] published her controversial article "El entierro de Chianita: Un complot chino" in *El Nuevo Día*, she tapped into visceral memories of slavery and anti-Black racism that have endured throughout the Antilles since the nineteenth century. This particular article, penned ferociously by Montero, focused on a racial dispute following Angela Meyer's November 2016 revival of the character Chianita, a Blackface performance that was originally developed by the actress in the 1990s to parody the election cycle. For example, Chianita's famous slogan, "Voten por yo," is intended as an aberration of the phrase "Vote for me." Here, the character deliberately mispronounces the correct slogan ("Voten por mí") to ridicule elected officials and their capacity to govern. While this character may represent to some a harmless act of mockery during election time, Chianita draws upon deeply ingrained racial stereotypes such as the inability to speak what is deemed "proper" Spanish in order to promote her "comical" content. The racial stress that this character brings out makes visible long histories of structural racism in Puerto Rican society, as is evidenced by the passionate response of island activists.[2]

The return of Chianita was met with a group of protestors who stormed the Univision headquarters and proceeded to symbolically bury an effigy of the character, coffin and all—boldly claiming that the practice was outdated, was a blatant form of racism, and would no longer be tolerated. Montero reacted to the protest by writing in her article: "[Un grupo de manifestantes] exigió que lo eliminaran [al personaje], cosa a la que el canal accedió. Eso es lo peor: que el canal accediera. Una vergüenza que doblara las rodillas ante la estupidez" (1; A group of protestors demanded that they eliminate the character, to which the channel acquiesced. That was the worst part: that the channel would agree to these terms. A shame that they would bend their knees before such stupidity). Montero goes on to argue that the real victim of the protest was not the Afro-descendant community in Puerto Rico but one of "los más vulnerables," the aging actress who would no longer be able to perform her character. The author concludes the article dramatically by engaging in a fearmongering monologue, envisioning an angry Black mob that would restrict the civil liberties of Puerto Ricans across the Island: "[Y] en cuanto a Univisión, que canceló el segmento, sepan que mañana irán a por otro personaje, y luego por otro. . . . Todo será como el teatro de Mao Tse Tung, donde los oficiales enemigos, cuando tenían que retirar sus tropas, no decían, como cualquier general: ¡'Retirémonos!', sino '¡Huyamos como ratas, que se acerca el glorioso ejército de Mao!" (3; And to Univision, who canceled the segment, know that tomorrow they will come for another beloved character, and then for another. . . . It will be like the theater of Mao Zedong, where the official enemies, upon their retreat, didn't proclaim as would any general: "Retreat!," but "Flee like rats, the glorious army of Mao is upon us!"). Montero makes this comparison between the protest and Mao Zedong's Cultural Revolution in China to further ridicule Univision's decision to cancel the program, implicitly critiquing Maoist thought and the seemingly mindless adulation of Mao's ideology represented in the Little Red Book, as *Quotations from Chairman Mao Tse-tung* is known in the West. In the Puerto Rican context, the cultural revolution would be one in which the masses would act to condemn those images that damage their well-being—that is, hate speech mistaken for free speech—and overthrow the structural oppression that years of imperial/colonial histories have solidified for the Island's Afro-descendent community. This type of cultural revolution is threatening in the context of Puerto Rico, and to the white fragility of Montero, because it jeopardizes the fantasy of a *mestizo* nation born into racial harmony between Spaniards, *Taínos*, and Africans; that is, the cultural revolution complicates history and shifts power away from a comfortable (guilt-free) whiteness and its Eurocentric conceptualization of identity.

Among the hundreds of people throughout the Caribbean and North America that reacted to Montero's article were two of the most prominent voices in contemporary Puerto Rican literature: Mayra Santos-Febres and Yolanda Arroyo Pizarro.[3] Both authors have historically been celebrated for their literary, academic, and activist work—through their countless appearances, articles, short stories, novels, and poetry productions, as well as their demands for full recognition and equal rights for African peoples in the Caribbean. Moreover, both have taken a fierce initiative to connect the contemporary experience of being a Black woman in Puerto Rico with a sacred memory of enslavement beyond merely their literary production. On the one hand, Santos-Febres has mobilized the artistic and writing community on the Island around the Festival de la Palabra.[4] On the other hand, Arroyo Pizarro has created the Cátedra de Mujeres Negras Ancestrales as a forum to collect and preserve the voices of Afro-descendent women on the island.[5] These Black intercultural initiatives and narratives emerge to describe other possibilities of Puerto Rican-ness that take form through complicated histories of colonization and slavery—focusing not on the pain of the passage but on the joyful force of creation as resistance.

Santos-Febres was quick to responded in a Facebook post (see figure 1.1) to several of the remarks made by Montero by centering three main arguments: (1) the question of humor and parody in the depiction of Chianita as a satirical device, (2) the public spaces the Black body can comfortably occupy, and (3) the media's role in shaping public opinion and perception of Afro–Puerto Rican individuals. She questions and denounces Montero:

> Un grupo de ciudadanos que exigen respeto de representación por razones de raza se enfrenta a Univisión y tú nos acusas de abusadores y comunistas de la talla de Mao Tse Tung. No presupongas que entre nuestras filas se desconoce lo que ocurrió en la Revolución Cultural China; los encarcelamientos, ejecuciones, quemas de libros que se condonaron. Tu comparación es exagerada, tremendista e históricamente errada. Evidencia

> racismo. Es la misma lógica que tuvieron los esclavistas cuando peleaban en contra de la abolición. . . . El humor es siempre un lente que exagera las cualidades o defectos humanos. Y ese es el problema, que, cuando un actor se disfraza de negro erige al color de piel (y la supuesta ignorancia que lo acompaña) como DEFECTO social.
>
> A group of citizens demanding respect for reasons of race confronts Univision, and you accuse us of being abusers and communists the like of Mao Tse Tung. Do not think that among our ranks we are unaware of what occurred in the Cultural Revolution of China: the jailings, executions, burnings of books that were condemned. Your comparison is an exaggeration, crude and historically flawed. It evidences racism. It's the same logic that those in favor of slavery employed against abolition. . . . Humor is always a lens that exaggerates human qualities or defects. And this is precisely the problem. When an actor dawns Blackness (and the supposed ignorance that accompanies it), they take on the color as a social DEFECT.

By underscoring ethnic humor, specifically *who* is able to share in the laughter of the racialized joke, Santos-Febres astutely points to the underlying power structures that allow Montero, as a white woman, to overlook the fact that representations such as Chianita reiterate the Black body in terms of poverty and a lack of education and technological knowledge (see figures 1.1a and b).[6]

Moreover, in Santos-Febres's post, the multiple geopolitical and cultural "borders of *puertorriqueñidad*" become visible though the author's use of her own racialized body.[7] Through personal experiences as a Black Puerto Rican woman, Santos-Febres views painful experiences of ethnic humor as a locus from which stories of exclusion can be recovered and used to contest hegemonic visions of what it means to be a member of the Puerto Rican nation. As the author writes: "Crecí toda mi vida con todos esos personajes 'pintados de negro' acrecentando mi sentido de vergüenza, de sentirme inapropiada en lugares públicos, de incomodidad, de ver que soy el hazmerreír de los demás" (I grew up my whole life with those characters "painted Black" heightening my sense of shame, of feeling inappropriate in public places, of discomfort, of seeing that I am the laughingstock of the country). Here, Santos-Febres addresses not only removal of the Black body from a sense of a Puerto Rican family

Mayra Santos Febres
November 6, 2016 ·

CONTESTACION A MAYRA MONTERO POR SU COLUMNA RACISTA "ANTES DE QUE LLEGUE EL LUNES".

Para los que siguen la rucha antirracista en Puerto Rico, sucedió el pasado miércoles 2 de noviembre que un grupo de ciudadanos negros fueron a Univisión a exigir que no se permitiera revivir el personaje de Chanita en su programación. Chanita fue un personaje desarrollado por Angela Meyer durante los años 70 en que la actriz se pinta de negro. Desapareció como han desaparecido de las pantallas televisivas ese tipo de personajes en casi todo el mundo. Pena que otros personajes pintados de negro no desaparecieran con ella.

Mayra Montero, la escritora cubana residente en Puerto Rico, escribió una columna en contra de la manifestación que fue a reclamar a Univisión que no revivieran a Chanita.

Me sorprendió profundamente la columna de la escritora. Tildaba a los manifestantes de vagos, de abusadores , de ignorantes de la tradición humorística del blackface, de asimilistas que queremos copiar a los gringos y a la vez (!!!qué disparate es ese!!!) de comunistas a la usanza de Mao Tse Tung.

Aquí mi respuesta:

Ay, Mayra... Entre los que apoyaban esa manifestación estaba yo, que soy feminista, de otra generación y trabajo mucho. Estaba Marielba Torres, profesora, Rafael Febres, profesor , estábamos muchos que sí trabajamos, que no somos unos vagos ignorantes y que estamos buscando cohesión para armar desde Puerto Rico, SIN ASIMILISMOS FACILONES una lucha contra el racismo nativo. Había abogados, pintores, relacionistas públicas, maestros, estudiantes, ingenieros y mucha gente que trabaja por un país mejor.

Crecí toda mi vida con todos esos personajes "pintados de negro" acrecentando mi sentido de vergüenza, de sentirme inapropiada en lugares públicos, de incomodidad, de ver que soy el hazmereir de los demás. Los medios de comunicación sí moldean la opinión pública. Los lugares de la risa, el deporte, el crimen, la hipersexualización y el folclore son todavía los únicos lugares permitidos para lo negro (y sí, te lo concedo, también para la mujer, los gays y otras mal llamadas minorías). El que sea negra no me frena de acusar machismos, coloniaje, ni otros atropellos que veo. Pero tengo que pelear por lo mío, por mi dignidad, por la de mis hijos, por la de mi gente evidentemente negra que sigue recibiendo atropellos (y ahora el tuyo) sin parar.

Un grupo de ciudadanos que exigen respeto de representación por razones de raza se enfrenta a Univisión y tú nos acusas de abusadores y comunistas de la talla de Mao Tse Tung. No presupongas que entre nuestras filas se desconoce lo que ocurrió en la Revolución Cultural China; los encarcelamientos, ejecuciones, quemas de libros que se condonaron. Tu comparación es exagerada, tremendista e históricamente errada. Evidencia racismo. Es la misma lógica que tuvieron los esclavistas cuando peleaban en contra de la abolición. "Estos nos harán a nosotros lo que nosotros les hemos hecho"- pensaron. Se dio en Haití, y todavía el mundo occidental se los esta cobrando. No, muchos de nosotros no buscamos ni creemos en la venganza, en la persecución ni en la marginación de los diferentes. Creemos en la justicia , que es otra cosa. No buscamos erradicar el humor en el mundo, ese humor- que solo es un tipo de humor - que opera a costa de reírse de los esclavizados, los minimizados, los históricamente vejados. Queremos otra cosa. No nos midas con tu misma vara.

Tampoco presupongas que no sabemos lo que ocurrió en el semanario Charles Ebdo. De hecho, hace unos meses, volé a Nicaragua a un foro organizado por Sergio Ramírez para hablar de humor y terrorismo. Estuve allí para denunciar ese acto asesino. No me parece que matar a alguien es la mejor manera de silenciar sus ofensivas representaciones. Otra comparación tuya exagerada y desacertada.

El humor es siempre un lente que exagera las cualidades o defectos humanos. Y ese es el problema, que, cuando un actor se disfraza de negro erige al color de piel (y la supuesta ignorancia que lo acompaña) como DEFECTO social. Y eso no estaría mal si viviéramos en una sociedad donde lo negro se respeta. Dónde a políticos no se les llama "Yuyo" porque quieren ocupar un puesto público, dónde a escritoras como yo les llegan emails cada año diciéndonos "negras sucias, tú no eres digna representante de nuestra literatura" como me ha pasado. O "vete a Loíza", como también pasa.

Es raro, tan raro ver esta columna salir de ti. El asunto que aquí nos compete es muchísimo más complejo. Es un asunto entre los límites de la risa, de la libertad y de la representación de la raza en los medios de comunicación pública ya en franca decadencia, intentando lo que sea por mantenerse a flote ante el embate de las redes sociales. Aquí está Univisión, que botó a toda su plantilla de periodistas locales, queriendo darle un chancesito a una "artista local" en tiempos de elecciones, para no seguir pasando programación barata y enlatada. ¿Y qué es lo que escogen? Revivir el personaje de Chanita.

¿Y los comunistas, los perseguidores, los abusadores somos nosotros?

Ya veo por dónde vienen los tiros.

Yomaira C. Figueroa-Vásquez and 1 mil others 218 Comments 503 Shares

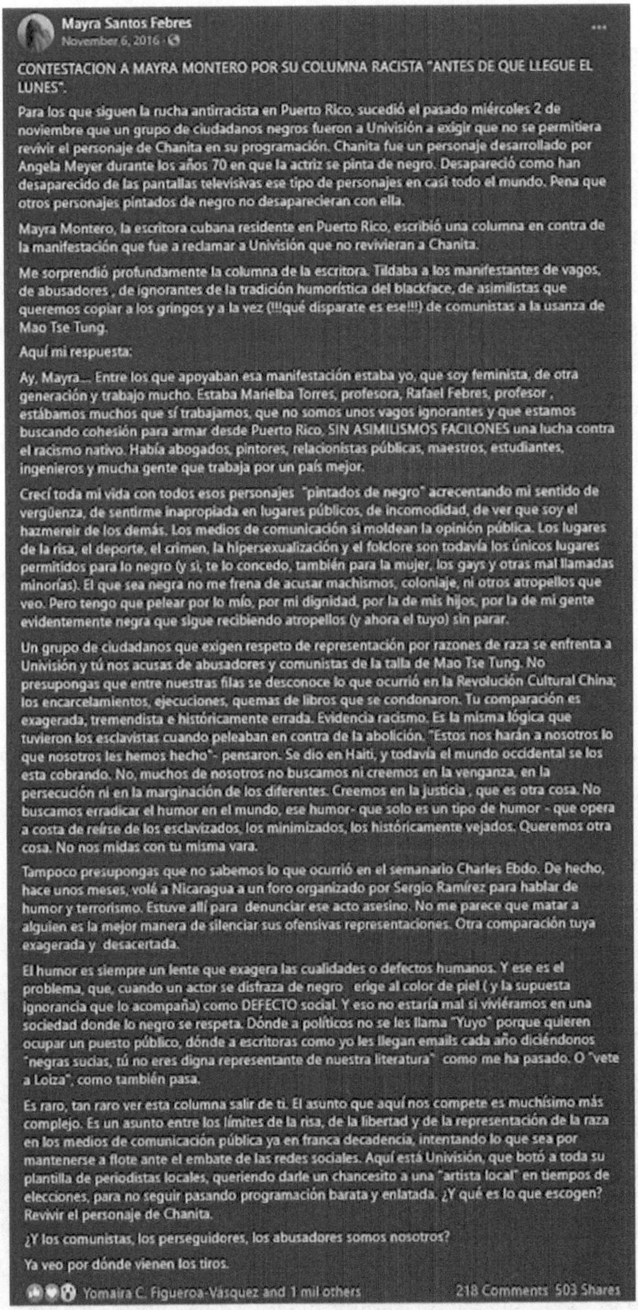

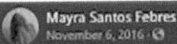

Figure 1.1. Santos Febres responds to Mayra Montero in a post that draws hundreds of comments and even more shares. Courtesy of Myra Santos Febres.

or nation through the shame of Blackface but the violence and *painful* experience that racial humor emotionally and physically exercises upon the Black body. This painful spatial reduction is also captured when she further presses on that a new society is urgent, "Donde a escritoras como yo no les llegan emails cada año diciéndonos 'negras sucias, tú no eres digna representante de nuestra literatura' como me ha pasado. O 'vete a Loíza,' como también me pasa" (Where emails do not arrive to writers like me each year telling us "dirty Black women, you are not a worthy representative of our literature" as has happened to me. Or "go back to Loiza," as has also happened).[8] At the internal racial borders of Puerto Rico, the Black body is torn apart, caught up in the wake of slavery and colonization, relegated to the margins and to those spaces of Puerto Rican geography that have traditionally become associated with Blackness and poverty (Torres-Robles; Reyes-Santos).

Arroyo Pizarro—also a voracious user of Facebook to convey her political messages to vast audiences—commented on Santos-Febres's post to express her own reaction to Montero (figure 1.2). She refers to Montero's subtle racism and the manner in which the author equates those fighting for social justice to lazy vagabonds with nothing better to do and no job to sustain themselves.

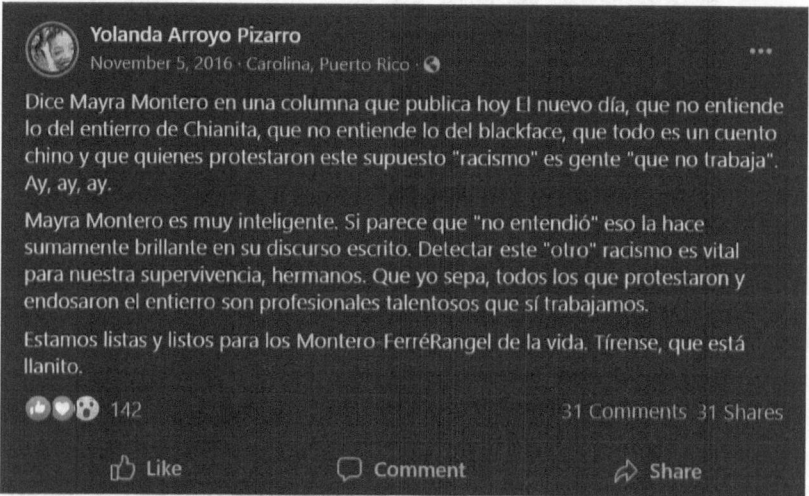

Figure 1.2. Arroyo Pizarro responds to Montero in her own post, urging Montero—and by extension, Puerto Ricans—to take a long look at their own "hidden" racism. Courtesy of Yolanda Arroyo Pizarro.

This comment underscores the urgent necessity for the community of Black Puerto Ricans of the island—the "we" of the comment that shares the same experiences and feelings of exclusion—to recognize racist behavior in what is left unsaid. This is to say that the community brought together through (not so) hidden racial violence must be ready to confront those voices that work to keep the current system of racial oppression in operation. Arroyo Pizarro creates the cluster Montero-Ferré Rangel to call out the editor of *El Nuevo Día* and his complicity in the diffusion of Montero's article. Luis Alberto Ferré Rangel—current editor of the newspaper—is the brother of celebrated writer Rosario Ferré and the son of former governor Luis A. Ferré. The Ferré Rangel family is one of the richest on the island and has extended its influence over a variety of business and cultural enterprises. Not only does Arroyo Pizarro demonstrate the ways in which prominent families are able to contribute to the ongoing whitewashing of Puerto Rican identities, but she also gestures toward a neoliberal economy that upholds certain ways of being Puerto Rican.

Pizarro's comment not only confronts Montero's criticism of the event involving Chianita but also implicitly targets a silencing of painful racist interactions and whitening projects that embrace a type of mestizo nationalism in the hidden prejudices that lay beneath the surface. In the following screenshot of another comment made by Arroyo Pizarro, these ideas come to the fore (see figure 1.3).

By referencing a type of "closeted prejudice," Arroyo Pizarro effectively echoes the first post by Santos-Febres in her ability to uncover a racialized border in Puerto Rican identity that separates the Afro-descendant, the fat, the prostitute, and the Dominican immigrant from achieving full status as a member of the Puerto Rican family. Furthermore, Arroyo Pizarro addresses the urgency of recognizing this subtle racial violence as a type of

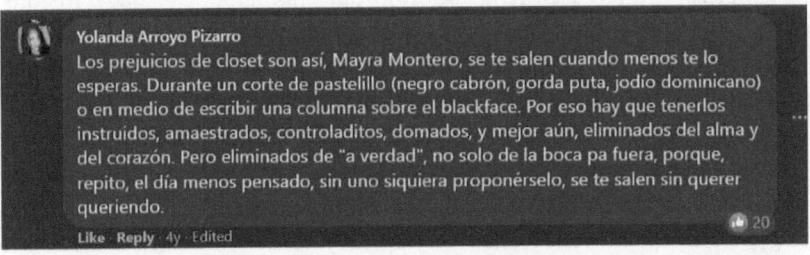

Figure 1.3. Arroyo Pizarro comments on Santos Febres' post, urging Montero to interrogate her own prejudices. Courtesy of Yolanda Arroyo Pizarro.

survival mechanism. By this I mean that by recognizing "hidden racism," the body made uncomfortable and othered by these acts can intervene and demand change.

Therefore, if, as García-Peña demonstrates in her analysis of Dominican national identity, the limit of such a geography is exemplified by "the body that carries the violent borders that deter them from entering the nation, from access to full citizenship and from public, cultural, historical, and political representation" (4), then in Santos-Febres's and Arroyo Pizarro's reactions to Montero's piece, the Black body resides in the painful border torn open by racialized humor and serves as a bridge to uncover those voices from national exclusion across history and generations. It is from this problematic locus of enunciation, in the cracks of Puerto Ricanness, that another type of knowledge can be found that emerges from the everyday emotional experiences and spiritual inheritance of Black Puerto Rican women. Precisely, by analyzing Santos-Febres's and Arroyo Pizarro's reactions to Montero's criticism of Chianita's cancelation, we begin to see a line of thought in both public intellectual figures that points to the cultural, social, and political borders of *puertorriqueñidad* that bend and fray under the duress of colonial sedimentation. We begin to see the crossroads that are opened when simultaneously inhabiting a Black body, looking to the past for guidance, and looking toward the future for change.

This deeply emotional and spiritual response echoes the epigraph of the chapter in which Julia de Burgos expresses the cultural/historical torment that her body carries—an "ay ay ay" that emerges also from Arroyo Pizarro's post on November 5. The mulatta poetic voice in de Burgos's "Ay ay ay de la grifa negra" expresses her fears of *mestizaje* and speaks back to the years of oppression experienced by Black Puerto Ricans. This anxiety is captured in the last line of the poem in which the author ironically claims that the racial mestizaje will represent "the future fraternity of América." Moreover, the anaphora of an onomatopoeia that transmits the poetic voice's pain, "Ay ay ay," accompanies the thought of "la raza" (Blackness) moving toward the white race and eventually mixing. As the repetition of the painful "ay" in the poem undoes a triumphant reading of mestizaje and mourns the loss of Blackness, so too do Santos-Febres and Arroyo Pizarro mourn the hypervisualization of Blackness—and thus its removal from official conceptualizations of puertorriqueñidad—through the joke. To speak back to this silence, they choose to straddle the racial borders of the nation and reside within those painful spaces that make their bodies uncomfortable in order to communicate a new type of oppositional knowledge, thus carving space for those who are all too often left on the margins of the nation.

Historical Hauntings

Before attending to the literary analysis, I find it important to trace a brief account of Puerto Rican racial politics. The processes of slavery and emancipation, as well as the nature of colonialism (Spain, 1492–1898, and the US, since 1898) in Puerto Rico, resulted in various racial discourses at different moments on the island. Many scholars have demonstrated the discursive absence of slavery in Puerto Rico (Findlay; Duany *The Puerto Rican Nation*; Martínez-San Miguel *Caribe Two Ways*; Figueroa; Hoffnung-Garskof; Rodríguez-Silva; Godreau *Scripts*; Alamo-Pastrana). These scholars often argue that the official historical narrative surrounding slavery reflects nineteenth-century concern for consolidating a cohesive national identity (Godreau *Scripts*). Following Isar Godreau, the process of historical narration and representation of this moment in Puerto Rican history "entails silence, trivialization, and above all, a simplification of the history of slavery in the dominant registers of Puerto Rico's national culture" (69). This is to say that official historical accounts reveal the often-repeated myth of a "benevolent" or "soft" brand of slavery in Puerto Rico, which is then juxtaposed with a "harsher" system in the US, for example. This fantasy was constructed on the idea that whereas the US was home to a state-sponsored racial segregation, Puerto Rico had not implemented such laws and therefore treated its Black population well, relatively speaking (Rodríguez-Silva; Godreau *Changing Space, Scripts*).

Furthermore, as Ileana M. Rodríguez-Silva traces it in *Silencing Race*, the dominant discourse on the island posited Puerto Rico as a unified nation that reinforces the narrative of a harmonious racial mixture (*Taíno*, African, and Spaniard)—a narrative that also surrounded the comments made by Mayra Montero. This same passive discourse renders the act of questioning racial tension as anti-national; that is, racial body politics is understood as something imported from outside of the national sphere and thus disrupts and impedes a cohesive national unity: "Most Puerto Ricans, however, do not recognize their everyday references to racialized markers of difference—mostly derogatory remarks about Blackness—as a product of and form sustaining racialized domination" (3–4). This history of harmony in mestizaje has worked to erase long and painful histories of racial oppression and even to deter some Puerto Ricans from critically examining racialized spaces and bodies on the Island.

Specifically, since 1898, the nationalist attitude in Puerto Rico has oftentimes excluded racial and ethnic minorities—such as Dominicans, Haitians, and dark-skinned Cubans—from its nation-building project (Duany 24). These exclusions run through a variety of literary texts, political speeches, essays, journalistic articles, paintings, and other cultural material aimed toward the construction of a cohesive national identity[9] (Duany; Negrón-Muntaner and Grosfoguel). According to Reyes-Santos, throughout the early twentieth century, new narratives of "national kinship" emerged as a strategic, rhetorical move against ongoing colonial structures of the island. However, Reyes-Santos warns that this turn to national kinship as a cohesive way to imagine national sovereignty was "in stark contrast to nineteenth-century transcolonial narratives of mulatto alternatives," which "reassert the subjectivity of the propertied, educated, white-identified, and heteronormative man as bearer of the political agency of the citizen" (64–65). Here she refers to the *Confederación Antillana* movement proposed by Ramón E. Betances and Eugenio María de Hostos—both staunch advocates of Puerto Rican independence. Jossianna Arroyo argues that Betances, in particular, "appealed to transnational mulatto/Black solidarities in an effort to critique institutional racism" (71). This critique looked to forge alliances between the islands of Puerto Rico, Cuba, and Hispaniola, thus forging new definitions of political solidarity that foreground Haiti and Black resistance—without engaging Hostos's and José Martí's insistence on "a raceless society that would consolidate a Creole elite that would negotiate with local metropolitan powers" (71). This transnational imagination was grounded in revolutionary solidarity recognizing the need to understand, on a grand scale, the long histories of colonialism and anti-Black politics.

However, in an attempt to be "good neighbors," and as a result of US occupation, Latin America and the Caribbean often adopted US concepts of civilization, which often included "their racial exclusions and . . . the regulation of kin relations through the institution of marriage within their structures of governance" (Reyes-Santos 65). Arroyo also demonstrates that belonging in the Hispanic Caribbean at the beginning of the twentieth century could also be imagined as being part of a *family* of Spanish nations "where nationalist traditions relied on ideologies of *mestizaje* as a narrative of biological or cultural whitening" (34). In this type of cultural nationalism in which Puerto Rico would align itself with an inheritance of mestizo, Hispanic being became a rather safe response to US imperial occupation: "A variety of sectors—upper-, middle-, and working-class intellectuals, suffragists, labor activists, and radical independence movements—participated in the conceptualization of Puerto Rican nationalism" (Reyes-Santos 74). It is from this fraught cultural milieu that produces narratives of what many scholars have called "the Great Puerto Rican Family," as well as other iterations of racial democracy myths in Latin America. All of these in one way or another proclaim a multiracial ideal in which "Latin American societies are nondiscriminatory and that their deep economic and social disparities have no racial or ethnic component" (Nobles 1). As a consequence of this type of thought, discussions on Blackness, sexual orientation, gender, and nonhegemonic cultural practices are often pushed to the periphery. They are not considered productive for the preservation of the status quo or for those who are able to comfortably inhabit national spaces without having to question that comfort. In blindly defending mestizaje as the category into which all iterations of Puerto Rican-ness can be found, we fall into the same type of racial trap—where the mestizo norm works to silence and police other bodies that do not easily fall into line.

We can say, then, that Puerto Rican nationalism throughout the twentieth century has been characterized by Hispanophilia and anti-Black structures. Here it is imperative to make a distinction between nationalism as a political, anti-colonial movement and state nationalism. The former, political nationalism, was inspired by a Black man, Pedro Albizu Campos, whereas the latter was institutionalized by Luis Muñoz Marín through the 1952 Constitution and the Estado Libre Asociado to combat Albizu Campos's radical nationalism as a political force of change. The institutionalized state nationalism gave the mythical figure of the white *jíbaro* preference. This also reflects a racialized conception of the island's geography because, until the middle of the twentieth century, the island's center was often portrayed by the image of the white peasant who grew mostly coffee and tobacco. According to the most conventional and conservative meanings, this symbol would be converted into a sign of national identity. As a result, while the island's interior developed its identity, Black and mestizo communities came to be associated with the borders, the coastal plains that were historically dominated by the growing of sugar: "[Thus], a cultural dichotomy was established in Puerto Rico—coast versus mountain, sugar against coffee, negro or mestizo against white *jíbaro*" (Torres-Robles 214).

Those frontiers also remit the political imagination to the body of the immigrant, particularly the Dominican body. Though studies about anti-Black racism and Dominican immigration have begun to dominate the bulk of intellectual and literary inquiries about Puerto Rico, attention is rarely given to how these borders are ritually and spiritually made intelligible by their inhabitants. Furthermore, many scholars have studied the migration networks that exist between Puerto Rico, the Dominican Republic, and Haiti (Martínez-San Miguel *Caribe Two Ways*; Duany; Méndez). In accordance with studies realized by Jorge Duany, César Ray, Luisa Hernández Angueira, and Yolanda Martínez-San Miguel, the Dominican community that currently resides on the Island started to migrate after 1961, following the assassination of Rafael Leonidas Trujillo. By the 1990s and early 2000s, Dominicans in Puerto Rico had become the new limit against which the boundaries of puertorriqueñidad had begun to press. Moreover, just like the Haitian becomes the dangerous symbol of Blackness in the Dominican Republic (as we will see in chapter 2), Blackness in Puerto Rico is associated with the Dominican threat to puertorriqueñidad. Within this racial history, scholars, artists, and community activists have collaborated to bring recognition to the Black history of Puerto Rico. These efforts include important social, political, and cultural movements; a cultivation of Black consciousness; and the developing of solidarities and coalitions that move beyond the island.[10] Both Arroyo Pizarro and Santos-Febres place the Black body in a central position in their literature and address the historical marginalization and silencing of Blackness in Puerto Rico.

An Island in the Wake

In the remainder of this chapter, I examine these ideas by studying how several protagonists and poetic voices in the works of Santos-Febres and Arroyo Pizarro inhabit "the wake," that is, how they grapple with the multiplicity of violences and painful experiences sustained by the dominant narratives of the nation deeply rooted in ongoing histories of slavery and colonization—that is, how their literary production reflects and extends their lives as public intellectuals to take on the whitewashing myths of the modern nation-state. To do this work of speaking from the wake—what I will refer to as dwelling in the borders of puertorriqueñidad—I look comparatively to two works by Arroyo Pizarro (*Saeta: The Poems* and *Los documentados*) and two by Santos-Febres (*Fe en disfraz* and *Boat People*).

In each of these four books, the literary voices engage with Afro-Caribbean spiritual practices to address racialized notions of belonging and to chart new visions of Puerto Rican futures. Precisely, my reading argues that by drawing upon Afro-Caribbean religiosity, these texts construct a diasporic Afro-Puerto Rican identity that intervenes in the reigning discourse of a harmonious history of mixture.

Generally, when critics cover Arroyo Pizarro's and Santos-Febres's writing, they usually focus on their more well-known novels and collections of short stories, such as Arroyo Pizarro's *Ojos de luna* and *Caparazones* and Santos-Febres's *Pez de vidrio*, *Sirena Selena vestida de pena*, and *Nuestra Señora de la noche*. Further on, most critical work uses as an analytical lens the authors' self-proclaimed identities as Black, feminist, warrior, women writers (Hidalgo de Jesús; Mosby) or the ways in which their novels communicate a particularly Caribbean identity (Castillo; Moreno; Grau-Lleveria). Following the recent acclaim for *Saeta: The Poems*, however, Arroyo Pizarro explains on her blog a different type of force that drives her creative work: "Es una memoria de la esclava que fui, de la esclava que fue mi abuela. . . . No es artesanal, ni es un libro/objeto. Es un performance/libro concebido a partir de un recuerdo, real o imaginario, de mi trascendencia. Fui la esclava, la capturada, la rebelde, la incitadora, la cimarrona. Soy la esclava que va aprendiendo la lengua del amo torturador (asimilo el anglo de a poco). Soy Tshanwe aprendiendo español, Yolanda aprendiendo inglés" (It is a memory of the slave that I was, of the slave that my grandmother was . . . it is not fabricated, nor is it a book/object. It is a performance/book conceived of a memory, real or imagined, of my transcendence. I was the enslaved, the captured, the rebel, the incitor, the cimarrona. I am the slave that continues to learn little by little the language of the torturous master [I assimilate English now and then]. I am Tshanwe learning Spanish, Yolando learning English). By centering her own body alongside the spiritual bodies and memories of "las ancestras," Arroyo Pizarro seeks to uncover and remember histories that have long been silenced. Her stories and poetry give a life force to those Black women who fought hard for their freedom but who have been silenced by the archive that favors the rebellions of men. She writes in a paper delivered at the Conferencia Magna of the Centro de Redacción en Español at the University of Puerto Rico: "De esas inspiraciones nacieron mis heroínas, las protagonistas de 'Las negras': Wanwe, Ndizi y Tshanwe. Acaso avatares de ficción coladas en el trance de mi memoria ancestral, que se convirtieron en las mujeres negras esclavizadas y hechas libres por ellas mismas y sus propias confabulaciones. Mujeres subversivas, transcorpóreas, que pidieron voz, cuerpo, armas y venganza" (88; From these inspirations my heroines were born, the protagonists of "Las negras": Wanwe, Ndizi, and Tshanwe. They are fictional avatars brewed in the trance of my ancestral memory, transformed into Black women enslaved and made free by their own efforts, their own imaginations. Subversive women, transcorporeal, that demanded voice, body, weapons, and vengeance).

With these assertions, the author clearly posits that the source of her poetic inspiration is not solely a product of her own intellect or experiences but rather an ancestral knowledge that guides her writing. Particularly, she states that these entities represent "transcorporeal women," that is, a line of ancestral insight that is multiple, diasporic, and external to any one body—which is understood here as only a receptacle of knowledge and energy. This understanding of the *ancestras* underscores a truly Afro-diasporic cultural representation of being, that her work represents an open vessel calling out to be possessed and inhabited by a variety of rebel hosts. This same ancestral remembrance allows Arroyo Pizarro to draw parallels through space and time to theorize her own coloniality of being as it radically pushes against the limits of coloniality/imperialism that would render Black bodies as soulless and empty.

In the same way, Santos-Febres demands that scholars work to destabilize and decolonize how we understand the self in relation to others, as well as a host of ancestral women who have come before her. In a talk given at the University of Minnesota, Santos-Febres declares that "we must embrace a Caribbean fractality; that is, we must create another framework of thought that escapes binary oppositions in order to point at the existence of knowledges or conceptual frameworks that do not rely on contradictions, that are *organic*" (February 19, 2021). For Santos-Febres, this "organic" knowledge that works to break through modern-colonial understandings of bodies, space, and time comes from a deep knowledge and metaphorical assimilation of Afro-Yoruba theology. In particular, she points to the *uno multiple* that extends from the Ifa divination system and the cult of ancestors in Afro Caribbean thought. Santos-Febres remarks that as Afro-Caribbean women "we must return to the discourse as is said in Yoruba: *yo soy yo y mis ancestros.*" In this way, aligning with how Arroyo Pizarro has positioned her own creation and activism alongside a line of *ancestras*, Santos-Febres also deconstructs the idea of identity that stems from modernity. For both women, there is no "true" self, unless the self is understood as a vessel that is connected in a nonlinear way to both the past and the future.

Thus, Arroyo-Pizarro and Santos-Febres demand that Black Puerto Rican women partake in the plural communion of their past, inviting inside the rebellious spirits of Black women who fought for their freedom, to once again welcome them into a shared national space and reimagine Puerto Rican sovereignty. For both of these women, writing the self and the collective always implies the question, How do we write in ways that unsettle? How might we produce knowledge or create discourses that displace the primacy of light and linearity?

First, I will analyze Arroyo Pizarro's *Saeta: The Poems* and Santos-Febres's *Fe en disfraz* to study how these authors work to understand painful experiences in the present by invoking a spiritual connection to a line of enslaved African women. This genealogy of women serves as an archive of power, perseverance, and resistance that orients Black women's bodies toward a future of radical change. This framework, along with the spiritual trajectory of the chapter, helps me link how the authors produce spaces through intimate-spiritual connections to the Middle Passage and those souls that have been lost to the waters of the Atlantic. I will pay particular attention to how those African diaspora beliefs challenge dominant notions of borders, Blackness, and historical memory in Puerto Rico.

Slavery, Ancestors, and Racial Play

Arroyo Pizarro's collection of poetry *Saetas* engages *el uno múltiple* of *las ancestras* and firmly establishes itself in the wake of Puerto Rican racial politics. The text is about the memory of the Middle Passage and the experience of dismemberment that accompanies it. The anthology exhibits the struggle for liberation and what must be given up to achieve it. Spirituality in this text is used in several distinct ways, often as a symbol for a type of knowledge found by engaging and taking seriously painful experiences of Afro-descendant women. The main poetic voice/protagonist, Tshanwe, guides the reader through a series of events that include forced capture in Africa, the loss of her name in the Atlantic passage, and the re-memory of the ancestors that she conjures in diaspora. This spiritual memory becomes a symbol of her transformation to someone in control of her destiny. In this way, religiosity and ancestral figures not only become empowering forces in the characters' struggle for liberation, but they also represent a political aperture to discuss the ongoing victimization and cultural exclusion of Afro-descendent populations in Puerto Rico, as well as their simultaneous movement toward self-sovereignty and joy. At the end of the collection, Arroyo Pizarro offers her own addition to this alternative archive. The author reflects on painful racist experiences as a child and demonstrates that her body carries with it the memory and knowledge of those that came before her, forces that carry her into the future.

Arroyo Pizarro constructs her collection in the form of an intimate cycle of menstruation—a sacred ritual itself, pointing to the divine feminine energies that inform her poems. Each section of the collection is entwined with those feelings and processes at each stage of the cycle, moving toward the birth of a new woman. The text is a multilingual production, as it incorporates Spanish, Swahili, English, and French, tongues that remit the reader to a long history of colonization. The first section of *Saeta*, "menstruo/hedhi"—composed of twenty-nine poems—deals with the pain of forced dislocation and cultural fragmentation suffered by those ancestors captured in Africa and forcibly transported to the Americas. Not only does the title of this section represent a type of linguistic border, as both *menstruo* and *hedhi* (Spanish and Swahili) mean menstruation and exist together, signaling a section written mostly in English, but the title also refers to menstrual blood itself as the in-betweenness of a cycle. Menstruation is a painful end and also a new beginning, much like the crossing that the text conjures.

In the poem "I Remember Middle Passage," the poetic voice writes: "I recall the waves / the saltwater vomits / the excretory pains / while mi fingers play with the maderos of the boat / I remember *el tumbaquetumba*" (Arroyo Pizarro, *Saeta* 25). Taking into consideration the environment and historical silences surrounding slavery on the island, the poetic voice expresses the need for memory, for a deeply spiritual connection that might heal her relation with her island. For the poem's protagonist, this spiritual link is a question of a mystical promise between women, between those who survive the violence imposed upon them by the slave trade: "Those two women / friends from the same village / glitter in four pupils / magic in four eyebrows / they make a promise to each other / *barabtubembón*" (25). The reader detects a gesture toward the need for intimacy and love between those bodies that have survived the harsh and forced fragmentation imposed by the European colonizer, as the following poems "He Gets Rid of the Boots" and "I Am a Hostage" document the poetic voice's negation of self and loss of identity at the hands of her white master.

In the first poem, "He Gets Rid of the Boots," the poetic voice—Thanswe—documents a moment in which her master forcefully rapes her. The scene opens with the slaveholder slowly taking off his boots, holding down Thanswe's body, and repeating a name that is not hers, Teresa, which she does not fully recognize to be associated with her life and her experiences. In the second poem, "I Am a Hostage," the poetic voice again asserts the need to recover an identity that was stripped from her in the passage from Africa to the island. This is perhaps an identity that can be found through intimate collection or a type of spiritual memory that invokes community and comradeship: "I can't touch the *cachetes* of my people / until we arrived at the boat / the dark clouds are forbidden / the sweet late water is banned / . . . / I miss my face / my tears / nobody is caressing my arms / nor my hands / brothers are crying all night / asking for mamma / they told us we have a new name" (27). With the use of intimate imagery grounded in the connection of bodies and spirits that have been violently ripped apart, the poetic voice expresses the need for an alternative system in this new land. She asserts that this system will be characterized by the memory of pain that her ancestors have experienced and the strategies employed to come into intimate relation with them and other Black bodies in Puerto Rico. This is further emphasized by the use of *cachetes* in the poem ("cheek" in English). The word in Spanish is more intimate to the author—who feels a deep connection with Thanswe—and carries at its root etymological links to verbs such as "to capture," "to take," and "to grab" and also "capacity" with references to certain parts of a sword (Real Academia Española). At once this word is being used to refer to intimate physical contact between Thanswe and her lost people, to a violent history of capture, and to the revolutionary capacity hidden in connection and love through memory and spirit.

The first lines that speak of West African spiritual systems in this section of *Saeta* are with the poem "Today, Catholic Church Teaches Us Dignity," which opens with a scene of slaves forced into the Catholic Church: "The Church insisted that every slave be baptized / I can choose my name / Maria, Teresa, Isabel, Juana / the Catholic faith, they say, is pretty / the church's doctrine will make me better / not a beast" (50). There is an intimation of the colonial imposition of Catholic doctrine upon those deemed "savage" by European powers. It is through the Judeo-Christian tradition that the body of the slave—stripped of all significance—through the passage to the island acquires new meaning and humanity symbolized in the taking of a name ("Maria, Teresa, Isabel, Juana"). However, the spiritual powers of the ancestors remain hidden in the poetic voice's prayer at the end of the poem, a silent rebellion of the enslaved against the powers of the church: "*Padresnuestros / padre Orulah / virgen Yemayá* / I am not supposed to escape / because now I am someone" (50). With this verse, the text merges African religious practices in the diaspora with opposition to colonial rule. While the poetic voice is obligated to acquiesce to the teachings of the Catholic Church, she keeps with her the teachings of her culture, her kin, and the beliefs of her ancestors as a type of cultural/social collective memory.

For the next two poems in the first section of the collection, "Fatalities" and "Speak with the Dead," spiritual blending of religion and belief—along with the spirits of the ancestors—become the central paradigm by which the speaker is able to express her desires for freedom. This is to say that these poems demonstrate a move toward religious creolization[11] as a way to insert memories of the past into the present. The poetic voice emphasizes necessity that her people have to tell their stories through the bodies of their ancestors and in the light of their gods. In both poems, this desire is communicated in response to "sea salt vomits," "suicides," "torture," and "pain in the bones" (57–59). The poems relate the spiritual experience of communicating with the dead, spiritual healing, and religious practices such as Santería, Santerismo, and Espiritismo. What is more, these practices become a kind of haunting that not only refers to the clash between living bodies and the spirits of those who have perished on slave ships and in bondage, but it also describes the link with conceptualizations of nation and racial difference.[12]

In the first one of the two, "Fatalities," creolized religious practices are experienced as a source of power and resistance when faced with the death of loved ones: "*Santería* blending / *santerismo* adoption / our angels / our virgins / our saints / tainted by our Black identity / segments / nothing is genuine / my form of religion is stained by *Regla de Ochá* / spoiled by rosary prayers / *y el credo, los sacramentos* / I embrace resistance" (58).[13] The poetic voice lists the loss of her loved ones, the suicide of her brother who could no longer endure the conditions of the slave ship, and the connection that she feels to other slaves who have been recaptured, transported to the Caribbean, and shipped off again to other points throughout the Americas. The invocation of religious mixing becomes a way for the fragmented communities to preserve a sense of collective identity. Furthermore, these religious systems go beyond the cultural and also speak to the intimate connection that is needed to undo modern-colonial domination. As these religious practices were often looked upon as "magic" and associated with cultures of premodern societies, their very essence emerged out of relations of inequality and oppression in colonization—the pain of the colonial project—that contributed to modernity's achievements. In this way, articulating Santería and Santerismo as a type of resistance or retaliation implies embracing the pain of dwelling in the borders of imagined modern nations and questioning the discourses of national belonging and citizenship by defining an African inheritance as a central part of Puerto Rico, as a mode of gaining a sense of security and empowerment through those beliefs that were written off by the modern nation-state.

The last poem of the first section, "Speak with the Dead," references the *orisha* (gods) of the Santerismo tradition in Puerto Rico as a type of counternarrative to the colonial project of the slave masters. The poetic voice incorporates the stories of the African gods into her narrative of resistance and subversion of the colonial project. The orisha are able to work their influence in the daily lives of humans through the vital force of *aché*.[14] By invoking these forces that connect human struggle with the divine through aché, the poetic voice taps into the communal power of the ancestors. In the African context, Moreno Vega reminds us that "the ancestors are always present and influencing the lives of the living" (340).

By the end of the first section, we are shown the way to heal the dismemberment of the first poems: ancient spirits are convoked to mend the fragmentation of slavery and colonization. Moreover, spirituality and ancestor worship constitute a strong force that awakens rebellious attitudes, as they carry the stories of those who refuse to be silenced, and the driving force toward bringing about healing and liberation. In these ways, Arroyo Pizarro infuses new meaning into spirituality, herbal healing, and religious practices so that they constitute one of the main sources of knowledge and power in her poetry. A poetry that resides in the borders that have split open the painful experience of modernity.

The poetic voice lists deities such as Elegba, Oggun, Oshun, Yemayá, and Orula. First, the voice invokes Elegba and Oggun. All ceremonies begin with Elegua, spirit of the pathways and crossroads. This deity also acts as the messenger between humans and the orishas. Elegba opens a space for change and new beginnings. Ogun is then invoked as an important figure related to war, iron, and metalworking. Ogun not only signifies strength in the rebellion but was also venerated by those slaves who looked to overthrow their masters. Oshun and Yemayá are water deities that are connected to the ocean, rivers, running waters, and gold. These goddesses connect the poetic voice to the sea, which represents a pathway back to Africa and freedom in the motherland. Orula represents the sacred knowledge learned from Iroko—the ceiba or silk-cotton tree— and is a master of divination. His prophesies are always fulfilled and he works to guide the poetic voice to a new space. The poem mentions these deities to underscore the ways in which the poetic voice carries these legends with her. Each entity reveals a different aspect of the collective move toward liberation and the ongoing pain that must be embraced to open a new society.

Haunting and spirit communication can thus be taken from the religious experience narrated throughout these poems in order to demonstrate the ways in which those deemed "other" by the imperial and colonial powers relate to one another. These relations create spiritual intimacies of different characteristics that mediate those border spaces of puertorriqueñidad, that is to say, the liminal spaces produced by discourses that construct Blackness as "other" in the Puerto Rican national imagination. By spiritual intimacies, I mean the knowledge communicated through African spiritualties, which places the practitioner into intimate contact with a history that is still unfolding. The poetic voice, in invoking the spirits, brings these entities into intimate and familiar boundaries. Upon inhabiting this spiritual boundary occupied by the presence of those who have passed on, the poetic voice communicates a new type of community intimately linked with historical violence. The haunting brings the past into the present and displaces temporal boundaries as well. Not only are the spirits a source of community and rebellion within the poem, but the text also forces the reader to recognize the ghosts that accompany colonization, those victims left in the pervasive wake of the enslaved African community both on the Island and beyond.

In the second and third sections of the collection ("Óvulo/Yai" and "Pre menstrual/Kabla ya hedhi," respectively) the violence of the slave trade erupts in armed resistance and is transported to contemporary Puerto Rico. In "Óvulo/Yai," meaning ovulation in both Spanish and Swahili, the text again mirrors the menstrual cycle. It is during ovulation that much of the pain of menstruation subsides and the possibility of new life unfolds. In this section, the text changes from English to Spanish and the use of

Swahili is limited. As the poetic voice nears the abolition of slavery and the construction of a modern nation-state, Spanish becomes the language that is most prominent. This linguistic change reflects not only the colonizing project in Puerto Rico but also the author's own experience with those languages that have constructed the way she moves and inhabits the world. With the intermixing of the three languages, the text offers a complex and multiple world of faith and magic in which the secrets of rebellion and colonial tension are rescued in writing for posterity. It also represents a textual performance of the complexity of cultural exchanges and negotiations that make up Puerto Rican society.

In the poem "Las negras esclavas se sublevan," in the second section, the poetic voice documents the ways in which the Black woman was constructed as an object of fear in the eyes of the slave owner: "Mecen a los chiquillos / en los brazos amorosos / y endulzan el pon aprendido / de los fogones en Sínsoras / Yacó hechizo maleficio / eso creen las dueñas" (104). The poem refers to Black slaves working as nannies who would care for the children of their masters. The references to *fogones* (fires) and *hechizos* (curses) of the Black women underscore the Judeo-Christian discourse and colonial construction of African diaspora religious and spiritual beliefs as dangerous and demonic. However, the poetic voice subverts this paradigm by interjecting at the end of each stanza "eso creen las dueñas" (104). The empowering potential behind this subversion lies precisely in the political implication of the poem—the author is providing an alternative space for women of the African diaspora to defy those hegemonic constructs that reduce those spaces to very limited and limiting practices of spiritual expression. By stating that the fear is unfounded in a rather sarcastic tone, the poetic voice reclaims the space and power of her cultural inheritance.

It is not by coincidence, then, that this poem, which evokes fear of ritual, spiritual, and medicinal beliefs of enslaved African diaspora women, appears prior to those poems that describe revolts, rebellion, and slave codes of the mid-1800s precisely because this fear had solidified into political documents that intended to restrict the movement and space of the Black body. The author closes the second section of the text with the poem "Code Noir," a poetic rewriting of the Reglamento de la Esclavitud de 1842 and the Code Noir, which remained in place until 1848 in Puerto Rico and all European colonies in the Antilles and which integrated various articles that regulated almost every aspect of the life, religion, and daily conduct of slaves.[15] The text begins by stating that "a consecuencia de los últimos decretos del Gobierno / sobre la emancipación de los esclavos /

por la ferocidad estúpida de la raza Africana / que no sabiendo apreciar la gracia / que su gobierno les ha concedido / responde con el incendio" (Arroyo Pizarro, *Saeta* 118). The poetic voice of the text strikes a harrowing critique of those laws put in place to control and police the movement of Black bodies on the island.

The poem is a parody, which Arroyo Pizarro inhabits in order to open a type of parallel world to compete against humor such as Blackface and the racial joke (like the ones examined at the beginning of this chapter). By hyperbolizing the many ways in which the Black body may potentially disrupt public order, Arroyo Pizarro enters into a conversation with the types of humor discussed in the first section of this chapter with an ironic critical difference; that is to say, the text satirizes the expectations of the Code Noir while at the same time ridiculing the over-signification of the Black body. This poem acts as a type of counter-discourse used at once to confront the past and to move beyond it.

Again, for the voice in the poem, African religious practices fall under scrutiny and run up against those barriers put in place by the Code Noir. The act of naming "hechizos" as acts that "atentan el orden / y tranquilidad pública" and as "chispas del incendio que devorarán / el bien común / los buenos modales / los mandamientos y sacramentos católicos," as well as warning against the inevitability of "delitos que puedan cometer / los precitados individuos / contra las personas blancas," traces a line of Black criminality and otherness in the Caribbean (118). The anxiety that the Black body incited in the French and Spanish colonies manifested itself in a type of respectability politics in which even those slaves who had gained their freedom were subject to beatings, whippings, or incarceration if found in violation of the various statutes surrounding behavior and belief on the Island. These codes concerning the possibilities of movement and occupation of space of the Black body were embodied in the concrete practices of people in their everyday lives in nineteenth-century Puerto Rico. These discourses worked to racially order society, doing so in constant defense against the disorder—as noted in the poetic lines above—that the Black body came to represent and threaten. These legal discourses act as the sediment that has hardened into walls that the Black body must constantly come up against, delimiting those social, cultural, and political spaces that it is "allowed" to inhabit within the nation. The last lines of the poem demand attention to these ordinances as a legacy of Blackness in Puerto Rico. The poetic voice exclaims that these policies constitute a "maldición de mis ancestros" (122).

This *maldición* of the ancestors hinted at in the last poem of the second section in Saeta becomes the organizing principle that drives the message of the collection's final part. It is in "Pre menstrual/Kabla ya hedhi" that the true force of the archive of pain and spiritual intimacy between the poetic voice, a history of enslaved African women, and those uncomfortable experiences in everyday life on the Island truly come together. The cycle begins to intensify and repeat itself in this section, resulting in a direct parallel between the violence of the slave trade and everyday violence experienced by Yolanda for being a Black woman in Puerto Rico. As the last stage in the menstrual cycle, this section hints at a repetition of the violence of the past. Here, the poetic voice becomes a fictionalization of the author and the text becomes autobiographical. The form of the collection changes as well in that Yolanda utilizes prose to recall exceptionally painful experiences of her childhood, including her experiences as a child in class. When the teacher would mention Africa, the author writes, young Yolanda had to fake stoicism and actively demonstrate that the word had no effect on her body or mind: "No faltaba el grito jocoso que proclamaba, ¡Yolanda, africana!, mientras la maestra regañaba el alboroto" (125). These subtle acts of racism—as Arroyo Pizarro wrote in her response to Montero in her Facebook post—had a painful impact on her life as a child: "Todas las noches rogaba por amanecer blanca al otro día. Todas las veces fallaba el pedido y se ponía de manifiesto el embuste de que 'aquel que pide con fe todo se lo concede.' Todas las mañanas volvía a ser negra" (126). To calm these anxieties, Arroyo Pizarro writes that her grandmother recounts a story in which Yolanda as a small child falls from her grandmother's lap into a cup of coffee. Yet because of this, Arroyo Pizarro writes, "Al sentarme a escribir no me siento todo lo negra que debería, o todo lo blanca que debería, o todo lo mujer que debería, o todo lo humana que debería. Algo falta, me percibo de otro planeta" (127). This reflection ends with Yolanda claiming that, while she feels a deep connection with her ancestors, the racial discourses that surround her and the colonial history of mestizaje and *mejorando la raza* force her to feel as if she were a body without race, caught in the racial border of puertorriqueñidad. This last section serves also as Arroyo Pizarro's own cry, which mirrors Burgos's lamentation captured in the epigraph to this chapter. Both women experience the pain of being a Black women on the island and demand to be seen in their entirety.

As she ends the collection, Arroyo Pizarro constructs the Black female body not only as an ontological site of pain, as the bearer of a history of racist practices, slavery, colonization, and ultimately contemporary confusion, but also as much more—a space of spiritual power and resistance. Her construction of this history of pain as it is associated with the Black body in Puerto Rico and throughout the diaspora does not represent an essentialization but intends to make visible the historical violence associated with the slave trade and colonial occupation that so many do not want to see. The post-racial discourse and the national fantasy of harmonious coexistence act simultaneously as a machine of forgetting and a path toward a fiction of racial equality. In this way, the recovery of a past that is lost and often forgotten works to expose a present that is equally broken. This poetics and politics of pain thus aids in the construction of a counter imagination of Puerto Rican-ness and also serves as a spiritually intimate project that lays the groundwork for a more political coalition that may reach out beyond those Afro–Puerto Rican bodies inhabiting the island space to include other traditionally marginalized sectors of the island—such as Dominicans, prostitutes, and queer-identified individuals—and recognize them as central components of what it means to be Puerto Rican.

Ancestras and the Erotic Space of Self

Whereas Arroyo Pizarro inhabits the painful border space of puertorriqueñidad in her *Saeta* through a personal reflection of her lived experiences with racism and an imagined intimate-spiritual connection with her ancestors, Santos-Febres engages in a fictional narrative that performs the painful history of the perverse rape of the Black female slave. Likewise, Santos-Febres creates an imaginary archive of resistance carried out by enslaved African women throughout Latin America and the Caribbean in her novel *Fe en disfraz*. The main character, Fe Verdujo, conjures this connection with their histories through the sexual dynamics of domination and submission. Here again, the Black body is constructed as a site upon which historical violence is reenacted and performed in an attempt to overcome a history of trauma and exercise a certain amount of agency within this violence. Santos-Febres locates a liberatory pleasure as the central axis around which her story revolves in *Fe en disfraz*. The type of pain that she describes is spiritual and intimate; that is, the pain is one closely associated with sexual acts.

As an epigraph to this novel, Santos-Febres quotes Roman poet Lucrecio's "La herida oculta": "Y estrechan codiciosamente / el cuerpo de su amante, mezclando aliento con saliva / con los dientes contra su boca, con los ojos / inundando sus ojos, y se abrazan / una y mil veces hasta hacerse daño. / Hasta tal punto ignoran donde se oculta / la secreta herida que los corroe" (qtd. in Santos-Febres 11). This quote references a frenetic type of love, passionately ferocious, that causes physical pain to its practitioners. The "hidden wound" that bursts open and destroys the lovers ("corrodes them") emerges from the sexual act. As Arroyo Pizarro describes the hidden wound of slavery in terms of the slime that is passed on in the "maldición" of the ancestors, so too does Santos-Febres articulate a similar type of hidden wound located in interracial sexual violence and pleasures—a spiritual act in its own right that transports the Black female body and bestows upon it agency and memory. This memory of an absent past recovers a history of failed dreams and patriarchal violence toward the Black female slave. Sexual intimacy acts as that spiritual link the present has to the past and locates the Black female body as the painful border space between a wounded and wounding history and an equally fragmented and wounded present. In performing these painful memories through the practice of BDSM, the protagonist of Santos-Febres's novel locates the Black female body in pain simultaneously as a site of resistance by revisiting and remembering a long history of sexual trauma.[16] By forming an intimate connection with those women who have suffered the violence of slavery at the hands of their white male masters, the protagonist's controlled painful experience in the present interrupts a post-racial discourse and reminds the reader of pain that usually remains hidden from view and a worthy tool of social analysis.

Another important detail to highlight is that Santos-Febres's novel—like Arroyo Pizarro's collection of poetry—represents a destruction of time and a cycle of violence that opens with the performance of the pagan ritual of Sam Hain on the eve of All Saints Day.[17] The narrator declares that Fe is about to be offered "la carne de Martín Tirado, historiador, quien intentó descifrar, cada vez con menos éxito, los signos de esta historia de la cual quiero dejar constancia" (14; The body of Martin Tirado, historian, who tried, each time with less success, to decipher the signs of this story, of which I now write to give testimony). This work then, serves a type of ritualistic function: the white male historian is put forth as an offering to the Black female protagonist and the ritual cycle is intended to record their story. Within this world of ritual, and ravenous sexual contact that bears pleasure, pain, and memory, Santos-Febres includes entities of the African diasporic religion of Regla de Ocha and communes with the *ancestras* through the *uno múltiple*. In the text itself, this intimate-spiritual connection is accessed through the practice of painful sexuality, which becomes a source of knowledge within her community of Puerto Rican peoples of African descent that share a history of colonization by the US. Indeed, while the protagonist of the story places herself as a member of the Puerto Rican community, she is also politically conscious of her membership in a larger African diasporic experience throughout Latin America, as evidenced through the various references to slavery in South America and Brazil. In *Fe en disfraz* the spiritual experience of pain takes on new connotations in the rescuing of a past that is too often forgotten.

The beginning of the novel represents an urgency to document and preserve histories that are not traditionally given adequate attention within academia and even the public sphere. Santos-Febres tells the reader of Fe's efforts to save the Department of Latin American Studies at the University of Chicago where she is employed as a researcher. Her project involved an exposition of freed female slaves throughout Latin America. However, the department had other priorities and intended to organize an exhibit concerning peninsular immigration to the city—a project that would have caught the attention of the University's "ex-alumnos ricos" (Santos-Febres 27). The opposition to Fe's project—a project that will ultimately bring her fame and save the school—sets the ground for a more nuanced investigation into colonial relations that will haunt the story. Fe's body and project juxtaposed with the desires of a white, affluent public and the anxiety, pain, and physical, emotional, spiritual work that the project represents reflect the stories of the slaves that guide Fe's actions and destiny. To fully acquire a voice in her department, Fe must delve deeper into a history of female slaves that fought to free themselves from their bondage.

The stage has been set for a project of decolonizing knowledge, as Fe must constantly face the walls of the neoliberal university that does not work for people who look like her. This echoes Santos-Febres's own project of creating the first Afro-diasporic and race studies program at the University of Puerto Rico. She comments:

> Our program is inspired by the legacy of Arturo Schomburg, but also dialogues with the United Nations proclamation of 2014–2024 as The International Decade for People of African

Descent. We worked in close contact with many Caribbean, Latin American, and African American organizations that are acting locally against racism, but with an Afro-global perspective. One of these institutions is the Mellon Foundation, which has given us the funds that the University of Puerto Rico has denied us for decades in order to develop this program. You don't know how many excuses we have received to argue against the need for academic diversification and decolonization in our institutions! But the work of many Afro–Puerto Rican intellectuals has the chance to be recognized. (Dávila)

Here Santos-Febres, like Fe, ties academic scholarship to much larger social and political movements, fiercely claiming that the histories of white supremacy and colonial/imperial dispossession are played out each day in the courses, faces, and administrations of the modern university. For Fe, it is imperative to displace the cycle of silence and rape—symbolized through the university's preference for studies that engage Iberian, European studies in the hopes of appeasing its donors and affluent neighborhood. When Fe takes control of her project and launches herself, body and mind, into the past, she is able to take up the call to be inhabited by *las ancestras* and thus conjure their rebellious spirits to push against her oppressors. Her project seeks to bring to light other voices and create knowledge that has been long hidden. In this way, as Fe seeks to change the narrative of her own space. She also seeks to bend reality and open it up to the cracks of its existence.

Martin and Fe begin as colleagues working on a public exposition of Black women during colonial Latin America. Fe feels very strongly about her project, and after discovering an archive in Brazil and several countries in South America, she takes it upon herself to create a new exhibition of Black female slaves' forceful petitions to several governors after sexual violence. For Fe, this project represents a milestone in her career. She compares the collection of documents of slaves written in English with those that have been written in Spanish. In the US, there exist hundreds of documents in which slaves give their testimonies against slavery. But in Spanish, apart from memoirs by authors such as Juan Manzano or Miguel Barnet, there exist very few slave narratives, even fewer from women.

The protagonist's name—Fe—and the title of the work, which implies that Fe ("faith" in English) is caught in a disguise, reflects those religious and spiritual practices of the African diaspora that often employed a type of Catholic disguise to conserve their faith and religious beliefs in a hostile environment. The disguise that Fe dons in this text is a metal harness, which was gifted to her during one of her research trips to South America. Fe is told that the harness once belonged to enslaved African women and graciously accepts the gift to put on display during her exhibit of formally enslaved women. Upon visiting a convent of las Macaúbas in Brazil she is told that this particular harness was once worn by Francisca da Silva de Oliveira (Xica da Silva), who is known for overcoming slavery and making herself rich and so gained the title of "the slave who became a queen."[18] Fe's connection to this woman represents her own transformation experienced throughout the novel. Fe will ultimately liberate herself through an aggressive role in her sexual relationship with Martin, her white research assistant in the US.

Fe enlists Martin to help her digitalize the documents of women's voices and build the presentation and archive. As Martin reads these narratives of sexual violence, he becomes sexually aroused: "Entonces, como en medio de una revelación, veía a las esclavas siendo poseídas por dedos, lenguas, vergas metidas entre sus piernas abiertas, tiznadas apenas por un brillo de humedad sobre un rosa profundo. Tiradas entre un montón de paja, dejaban entrar el cuerpo del amo o del capataz, hasta que ardían ella, él, ellos, el asco y el deseo, la repulsión, el odio y un gemir, todo unido" (45–46; And then, a revelation, I was seeing the slaves being possessed by fingers, tongues, dicks forced between their open legs, stained like a glimmer of humidity upon a profound rose. Thrown on a pile of hay, they let the body of the master or foreman enter them, until she burned, he, them, disgust and desire, repulsion, hatred and a moan, everything at once). He also begins to think of other women such as Malitzín, La virgen, and the Hottentote venus: "Aparecían centenares de indias, negras y mulatas paridoras de hipogrifos mestizos, abiertas desde sus carnes más secretas, exponiendo la flor de su tormento" (46; Hundreds of Indians, Black and mulatta women bearing hippogriff mestizos, open by their most secret flesh, exposing the flower of their torment). These narratives evoke a history of pain and suffering of the Black female body and others such as the Indigenous, the mestizo, and the mulatto, a pain in which they are constructed as objects with no agency, forced into motherhood, objects of pleasure by their masters. Martin, as a white man, is swept up in the movement of history and overtaken by the sexual urge to exert dominance over the Black body.

However, this illicit eroticization of violence and power in the privacy of Martin's home is later inverted and transmogrified into something else. As Martin and Fe continue their sexual relationship, Fe slowly becomes the dominant partner, oftentimes mimicking the slaving documents that she had read. Throughout the novel, Fe reenacts historical scenes of brutality upon Martin in order to make herself feel closer to the women she has studied. However, while the BDSM in this novel may not fully heal the historical wound of slavery, it becomes a stage to replay and reimagine these same scenes of Black/white sexual intimacy and the imbrications of pleasure, power, race, and sex. When Fe puts on her metal harness, she forces Martin to ejaculate in her mouth by holding him down and licking his body. Martin is given very little agency in this encounter: "Sentí miedo y vergüenza. Había sido yo el penetrado, el desnudo. Yo, el venido. Los ojos de Fe, su silencio, me lo hicieron saber. Mientras me vestía en el salón de nuestro encuentro, aquel silencio me obligó a escapar" (59; I felt fear and shame. I had been the penetrated, the naked. I, forced to cum. The eyes of Fe, her silence, told me so. While I got dressed in the room of our encounter that same silence forced me to escape). In these encounters, Fe is always in a position of power—even if this position still causes Fe pain (the metal harness cuts into her skin as she engages in sexual activity), she decides when and to what degree she will feel her pain. Pain delivered can be read as a release of pain carried in the flesh. Fe feels that the pain from her harness is lost when she is forcing Martin to also feel the pain of her scratching his back and forcing him to become submissive. The combination of anger and pain in the text reveals, if not a keen awareness of the historical legacy of Black female sexual violence, then an intimate understanding of Black women's ambivalent positionality in the realms of sexual pleasure.

These dynamics of reproduction and subversion of the imposed sexual violence of slavery are compounded with the equally "slimy" vestiges of colonialism that haunt the narrative. Fe, in the last article that she sends to Martin for revision, includes her own history in the archive of slave abuses. This text is one that she herself wrote and it tells the story of her life in Puerto Rico and her move to the US. In this personal history, Fe reflects on the legacy of colonialism and how it has changed the connection that her ancestors have with history and spirituality. She claims that with Catholicism and the forced conversion of her ancestors came the colonization of the spirit—a type of slavery and violence that parallels the stories that she has collected throughout her life. The effects of this colonization, according to Fe, are seen in the forgetting of the cult to the ancestors. She says that something terrible had also happened with the concepts of time and history at the hands of the oppressor:

> El tiempo no existe y todo lo que existe es tiempo. Tan solo se materializa a través de ritos que sacralizan ese inmenso vacío, lo vuelven fijo, fijado con sangre. . . . Los ancestros son lo que nos fija en el tiempo. Esas largas genealogías de muertos intentan trazar una línea que, atravesando una masa informe de cuerpos, se desplaza por el espacio infinito. Eso es la Historia, una tenue línea que va uniendo en el aire a los ancestros—a esos pobres animales sacrificados en la pira del tiempo. (97)

> (Time does not exist and all that exists is time. It materializes through rituals that make sacred that immense void, they make it fixed, fixed with blood. . . . Ancestors are what fixes our time. Those long genealogies of the dead that attempt to draw a line which, moving through a formless mass of bodies, charges through infinite space. That is History, a tenue line that unites our ancestors in the air—to those poor animals sacrificed upon the pyre of time.)

She describes her own skin as the map of her ancestors, marked by forgetting or tribal scars and chains. When she puts on her metal harness, when she dawns her "disfraz," she is invoking and taking control of a history that has relegated the stories of the women in her past to silent submission to the masculine and European concept of history.

Finally, their acts of pain and pleasure play with the concept of race itself. They cross boundaries of what each body historically has come to represent. In one of his last comments in the novel, Martin declares: "La haré sudar su vergüenza hasta que brame sin palabras desde el otro lado de su miedo, desde el otro lado de su soledad. Me hundiré dentro de ella hasta que gritemos juntos. Hasta que olvidemos juntos quienes hemos sido. Abandonarse es, a veces, la única manera de comenzar" (115; I'll make her sweat in shame until she groans words from the other side of fear, from the other side of solitude. I'll dive so deep into her until we scream together. Until we forget together who we have been. Abandoning oneself is, sometimes, the only way to begin again). This search for not only pleasure but emotion and abandonment of the body is also a space in which racial power and hierarchy can be reformulated and rearticulated. This *abandonarse* of the two bodies speaks of a new beginning in which Fe is released from her bondage through an embrace of her sexual desires. In this moment of ecstasy, both bodies lose their racial markers and exist together on a new plane that has been separated from the long lines of racialized sexual violence that each individual has inherited and repeats.

Embracing the Wake, Sacred Memories

Both Arroyo Pizarro and Santos-Febres deploy narratives of spiritual intimacy alongside experiences and memories of pain, violence, and colonial/imperial forces (from Spain and the US). Academic and religious understandings of both pain and spirituality must be considered within the rubric of decolonial and anti-imperial projects that underscore the legacy of Afro–Puerto Ricans. Colonial notions of belonging and the tendency to celebrate Hispanic legacies have always been considered in studies of nationalisms and citizenship in Puerto Rico. However, not many analyses have noted how uncomfortable experiences and sacred memories of enslavement emerge out of a collective Puerto Rican imaginary to complicate and disrupt the borders of puertorriqueñidad. The texts studied in this chapter dwell in those painful intra-national border spaces to demonstrate the ways in which traditional nationalist narratives fail not only because of their inability to reconcile racial and class differences or because of US imperialist encroachment on their desire for autonomy but also because of an awareness of the anti-slavery and plantation-based labor practices that are often ignored. Moreover, intimate-spiritual ties and sacred memories of the ancestors are not simply alternatives to whitened, elite, mestizo nationalisms but make a direct intervention into a narrative of Black personhood on the Island that stems directly from colonial/imperial projects of difference. These narratives employ pain as a new epistemology to underscore the position of the Black body within the nation and to open an imaginary border space from which to articulate an alternative historical imagination.

What we also find in these texts, as well as other cultural materials currently being produced on the Island,[19] is that paying attention to painful and spiritual intimacies requires entering the intimate domain of romantic and sexual relations. When reviewing an archive of fictional female slaves, the protagonist of Santos-Febres's *Fe en disfraz*, for example, revives their stories through her engagement in interracial acts of bondage and submission. These acts also negotiate the reality of racial mixture, miscegenation, cross-racial sexual encounters, and trying to conceptualize an intimacy that would ideally legitimate her political and racial claims as subject. Therefore, the painful experience of the intimate act exposes the sacred memory of enslaved women. This serves to construct ways to imagine and recognize other intimate relations that imbue agency upon the Black woman.

Arroyo Pizarro and Santos-Febres provide an opportunity to reflect on the position of the Black body within the Puerto Rican national imagination in the past and today. Though anti-colonial movements were integral to decolonization efforts in the mid-nineteenth and early twentieth centuries (Reyes-Santos), in the twenty-first century their value has been interrogated and the attention to racial-ethnic difference has been overlooked. Thus, Arroyo Pizarro and Santos-Febres propose that we pay attention to those painful border spaces in everyday life to think of the Puerto Rican nation otherwise. The authors remind the reader that to better address puertorriqueñidad we must attend to those areas that are often left untouched: its heteronormative, patriarchal, racial, class, and ethnic hierarchical structures.

The texts studied in this chapter and the struggles they represent have the potential to speak to the present moment, providing a possible tactic for addressing contemporary racial struggles and neocolonial policies in Puerto Rico, as Montero's text—analyzed at the beginning of this chapter—demonstrates. They remind the reader of the ongoing wake of slavery in which the Island is caught. They show that the ways Black bodies were imagined within the systems of enslavement continue to shape the status of Afro–Puerto Ricans on the island and in the diaspora. This chapter has suggested that dwelling in the painful border spaces of Puerto Rico opens a space from which to articulate the sacred spiritual memory of a line of enslaved women in order to intervene and question political agency and citizenship in Puerto Rico today.

Chapter 2

The Path of Erzulie

Love, Vodou, and Counter-Imaginations of Hispaniola

> Haiti is a very spiritual place. I model my faith after the people I grew up with, not as a prescribed belief but an ability to envision a hopeful future even after facing extraordinary obstacles.
>
> —Edwidge Danticat, *Breath, Eyes, Memory*

In late September of 2013, the Dominican Republic's Constitutional Tribunal Court decided to take back the citizenship of a Dominican woman of Haitian descent, Juliana Deguis Pierre.[1] This decision created a precedent to strip the citizenship of all other children of Haitian migrants, who have been integral to the economic history of the Dominican Republic since the beginning of the twentieth century. These same subjects are now labeled as persons "in transit," with a policy that reaches as far back as 1929 and potentially affecting over two hundred thousand people. According to the 2015 Inter-American Commission on Human Rights report, this particular *sentencia* and its implementation represent "a situation of statelessness of a magnitude never before seen in the Americas" (4). The policy relegates migrants to a type of political and legal limbo, suddenly considered foreigners by the law and unable to return to Haiti—a country in which many have never set foot. Moreover, many of these migrants do not consider themselves Haitians, as they were born and/or have resided in the Dominican Republic for generations. This contemporary legislation was supported by a racial discourse that constructs Haitians as racially "other" and potential contaminators of Dominican national identity.

In early October of 2013, Rita Indiana Hernández published an article in *El País* in response to this particular September ruling of the Dominican Republic's Constitutional Tribunal Court. As a rather well-known author, public intellectual, and musician on the island, her creative works, such as the novels *La estrategia de Chochueca* (2003) and *Papi* (2012), and the song "El castigador" (2017), all address questions of homosexuality, masculinity, political corruption, and racial tensions in the Dominican Republic. Apart from her academic work, Hernández has published many pieces as a public intellectual in newspapers such as *El País* and other academic outlets such as *Contratiempo*, an academic and political review published in Chicago and widely read by the Latinx communities in the US. In her response to the *sentencia*, she took the opportunity to criticize current racial tensions and citizenship debates that had taken the Dominican Republic by storm. Though Hernández has a long history of critiquing the treatment of Haitian migrants and Dominicans of Haitian descent, she was particularly adamant to inscribe Blackness and African cultural and religious practices into the Dominican imaginary with this piece. Specifically, she draws from a historical rhetoric condemning religious practices such as Haitian Vodou to talk back to the discriminatory laws and anti-Black sentiment incarnated through the September court order. First, Hernández reminds the reader of the spiritual/religious discourse that emerged from the earthquake, mostly stemming from US-based evangelical Christian organizations. Since the 2010 earthquake, evangelical Christianity has been growing in Haiti and has represented Vodou as a backward and satanic religion[2] juxtaposed with a *mestizo* and Catholic Dominican Republic. For example, Hernández writes that Pat Robertson, a famous American televangelist, argues one needs only to compare the fates of the two nations in order to prove his point: "Según Pat, [la República Dominicana es] un ejemplo de 'prosperidad,' gracias a que la nuestra no es una república de satánicos" (2). The "pacto con el Diablo" that Hernández references in her article alludes to the birth of the Haitian Revolution in 1791. She invokes the Vodou *lwa* Oggún, the god of iron and war, stating that this particular deity "adorado en ambos lados de la isla, no generó más maldición que la del bloqueo al que las potencias imperiales sometieron al pequeño país y la indemnización de 150 millones que exigió Francia en 1814 para reconocerles su independencia" (2).

In writing this, Hernández reminds readers of the revolutionary and anti-colonial beginnings of Vodou. This is to say that Vodou enters Haitian history as Boukman (an *oungan* or priest) along with a *manbo* (priestess) conducted the ceremony that began the fight for independence. Those in opposition to the independence struggle described the revolts as accompanied by "sorcerers" and "magicians," their homes filled with elements of "African superstitions" (Dayan 29). However, Hernández reformulates the accusation of devil worship to claim that the Dominican Republic has, indeed, harnessed the power of "artilugios más potentes, siniestros y escurridizos que los que se hacen acompañar del tambor" (2) in once again engaging with a rhetoric that works to erase Blackness from the Dominican national identity to embrace a Hispanicized vision of the nation. The "dark things" that the Dominican conjured are the discriminatory laws passed against Haitian immigrants, including those born in the country. The demons that have been raised, then, are not the "satanic devils" invoked by Catholic and Protestant priests alike but instead are the old anti-Black and anti-Haitian prejudices that have haunted Hispaniola since the conquest. This is to say that the Dominican national identity is constructed as an identity closely tied to the Spanish language, the Catholic religion, and a mestizo racial imaginary. The "nigromantes" of the Junta Central Electoral work their magic to close "el ciclo letal (como son cíclicas las maldiciones) en el que orbita el espíritu de la violencia y la muerte, portal de sangre abierto en octubre de 1937, cuando fueron asesinados en territorio dominicano más de 30.000 haitianos" (3). In this way, Hernández demonstrates how centuries-old discourses of magic and devil worship can be reversed to be used against the coloniality of power displayed in contemporary social and political structures.

Hernández's engagement with Africanized spiritual systems serves a dual purpose. First, it brings attention to those beliefs and practices that have been systematically marginalized across both island nations throughout history. Second, it is a direct attempt to push against what Ana-Maurine Lara terms the *Catholic Hispanic nation state*, whose historical consolidation of power can still be felt today. Lara writes in *Queer Freedom*:

> While protective laws are often ignored or not enforced, repressive laws are enforced quite heavily against and through those deemed undesirable: homosexuals, trans people, Haitians, dark-skinned people, women, and the poor. Proof resides in

> the redefinition of life in the Dominican Constitution, the ongoing criminalization of abortion, the cardinal-sanctioned deportation of thousands of Haitian people, the denationalization of Dominicans of Haitian descent, and the tactics of sexual terror used to intimidate LGBTQ people, whose presence is not illegal, but is configured as an affront to *la moralidad pública* (public morality). (59)

Thus, Hernández implicitly engages these ideas in her response to the *sentencia* and draws attention to the colonial/imperial wound gouged by the church and Christian-colonial processes. Here, Hernández opens a space to contemplate those bodies, desires, and orientations that do not align with "Christian colonial morality" and the "bifurcation of flesh and spirit" that isolates the human body and abolishes the *uno múltiple* of a collective remembrance (Lara 60).

By invoking the *lwa* Oggún and Vodou ceremonies, Hernández seems to perform her own ritual of remembrance to remind the presumed Dominican reader of several points that have been erased by prior histories and literary imaginings of the two nations: that the two parts of the island share one common geographic space and their future depends upon their coexistence. Spirituality becomes a space in which to redefine personhood, rethink sexual and gendered roles, and demand a more inclusive and open conceptualization of what it means to embody full citizenship on Quisqueya. Moreover, throughout this relatively short critical piece on the 2013 *sentencia* by the Tribunal Court, I detect a certain gesture toward the need for a deeper spiritual connection between Haitians and Dominicans. In this sense, by outlining a history of pain between the two island nations (by invoking those bodies who have been historically expelled from both Haitian and Dominican national imaginations) Hernández points toward an intimate-spiritual connection of bodies that transcends and complicates both history and officially established geopolitical borders and subjects. In this way, a joy and intimacy with the capacity to unite take center stage.

Invoking the Spirits

It is within this critical line that this chapter will analyze the ways in which spiritual practices are invoked not only to link contemporary painful experiences with a history of enslavement and colonization but also to open a space in which we can uncover hidden histories and the multiplicity of margins within the nation-state. This chapter is also an attempt to continue to frame Vodou epistemologies as ways of knowing not easily recuperated by Western or Eurocentric knowledge systems. While fully explaining how Vodou and other Afro-Caribbean religions function in local epistemologies is far beyond the scope of this particular chapter, I will trace some of this system's basic outlines in order to demonstrate how the sacred energies/memories become subversive revolutionary forces in Hernández's song and music video "Da pa' lo' do'" (2013) and Ana Maurine-Lara's novel *Erzulie's Skirt* (2006).

More specifically, this chapter follows the many paths of the *lwa* Erzulie (female spirits) in order to open a space to consider how—as Karen McCarthy Brown argues—they are both "mirrors and maps" for imagining the nation otherwise (3). Thus, I ask, How might engagements with Vodou not only remember lost histories of slavery and sexual violence against Afro-descendent women in Haiti and the Dominican Republic but also serve as a creative space to produce a new vision of nation and belonging beyond imposed geopolitical borders? This choice to follow the path of the *lwa* Erzulie throughout these texts and cultural productions, then, performs Black feminist intellectual work. If Omise'eke Natasha Tinsley says in "Songs for Ezili" that "[we] people of color have always theorized . . . in narrative forms, in the stories we create, in riddles and in proverbs, in the play with language, since dynamic rather than fixed ideas seem more to our liking" (419), then in listening to the stories and narratives surrounding Erzulie, I aim to situate these spiritual writings within a lineage of women of color feminisms and decolonial politics.

My discussion in this chapter argues that the cultural productions and literary texts I analyze here are all about how the *lwa* Erzulie are taken up by women to (re)imagine their way of being in the world and as a reparative force beyond a history of imperial/colonial subjection. My argument will first examine how Hernández employs the symbols of Haitian and Dominican Vodou practices to perform a kind of spiritual healing that sheds the European clothes from the bodies of the two protagonists and brings them together in a decolonial embrace of spiritual intimacy. I then move to analyze Danticat's and Lara's works to study the ways in which Erzulie moves, employing decolonial love that, remembering Sandoval's conceptualization, is an oppositional kind of love that operates against exclusionary forms of love (e.g., the imaginary of the national family). Also, my reading of Erzulie as a decolonial space of contestation follows closely Alexander's ideas on the spiritual as a feminist epistemology, as discussed in the introduction.

Therefore, I propose a study that unifies Erzulie's power and potentiality within the framework of decolonial love. That is, I follow the desires and passions that work to undo how the notions of kinship,[3] filiation, and national family are officially wielded by the nation-state to imagine a closed community tied by feelings of solidarity that reinforce homogeneity. My study will demonstrate how the force of Erzulie works as a decolonial love that pushes bodies to migrate away from the nation and toward a collectivity that may act as a form of heterogeneous resistance. In turn, I argue, this movement articulates alternative spatial imaginations of a nation that includes racialized bodies in its representations—addressing also a central question of this volume and one that Lara begs us to consider in her *Queer Freedom*, that is, how Judeo-Christian colonization and the drive of modernity produce a temporal dissonance: "Whose time is more legitimate? Valid? Central to life and personhood?" (7). While Lara argues that the state pushes toward what she terms linear "Christian colonial futures" and legitimates "specific corporalities." Erzule, then, provides the decolonial lens through which the uno múltiple can locate itself to disrupt this imposed timeline and open it up to other realms of being and possibility.

The Feminist Politics of Erzulie's Decolonial Love

The *lwa* Erzulie within Haitian/Dominican Vodou systems represents not only a singular spiritual entity but also a plurality of spiritual paths. Erzulie embodies the divine forces of love, sexuality, pleasure, femininity, maternity, creativity, and fertility (Tinsley, "Songs for Ezili" 420). The paths of Erzulie include Erzulie Fréda, the seductive mulatta who prefers perfume, flowers, and luxurious items; the fierce protector Erzulie Dantò, who first appeared during the ceremony of 1791 at Boïs Cayman, which eventually began the Haitian Revolution, and Lasyrenn, the mermaid who inhabits lakes and rivers where she seduces other women to join her and instructs them into mystical—erotic—knowledge (Tinsley "Songs for Ezili"; Deren; Brown). According to Randy P. Conner and David H. Sparks, Lasyrenn may also be described as bisexual or pansexual in nature, and while her male companion is Agwe, her female lover is Labalèn (58–59). Erzulie Dantò is yet another manifestation of Erzulie that has queer undertones.

Dantò is often portrayed as a dark-skinned advocate for the poor and oppressed and has fought for her children during the Haitian Revolution (D. Brown 42). Brown further writes:

> Ezili Dantò has not married any of the spirits who are her sexual partners. Being a single mother who raises her children on her own is an important part of her identity. Dantò is, however, a frequent participant in marriages with vivan-yo (the living). In these rituals, individuals pledge loyalty, services, and even sexual fidelity for one night each week (sleeping with no human on that night and waiting to receive the spirit in their dreams) in return for the spirit's increased care and protection. . . . People in Alourdes's [Mama Lola's] community admit that some of these marriages are with women. Thus the portrait emerges of an independent, childbearing woman with an unconventional sexuality that, on several counts, flouts the authority of the patriarchal family. (228–29)

Thus, we come to understand that Erzulie and the many paths that this deity follows come to represent not only the many iterations, tensions, and historical violence but also sexual possibilities of Haitian and Dominican women that act as radical sites of contestation. That is, the type of spiritual epistemology that Hernández, Danticat, and Lara weave with their texts is one in which the spiritual locus of enunciation holds space for those histories that are too often forgotten, left unspoken, and misunderstood. These same spaces also serve as creative sites from which to imagine new futures outside of ordinary time, space, and national identifications.

Furthermore, some critics have linked Erzulie with Caribbean women's histories and stories, too. For example, Joan Dayan argues in "Erzulie: A Women's History of Haiti" that through various discursive practices (such as song and stories), the many paths of Erzulie offer a more nuanced view into Haitian and Dominican womanhood and the daily experiences of women on the Island than other types of feminist thought (21). Erzulie, then, becomes the story of Haitian women, "a principle of Caribbean gender, a femme queen, a mermaid, and a theory" (Tinsley, "Songs for Ezili" 424). However, beyond this conceptualization of Erzulie as a feminine/feminist epistemology, Maya Deren writes of Erzulie as "that which distinguishes humans from all other forms: their capacity to conceive beyond reality, to desire beyond adequacy, to create beyond need. . . . In her character is reflected all the élan, all the excessive pitch with which the dreams of men soar, when, momentarily, they can shake loose the flat weight, the dreary, reiterative demands of necessity" (138). In this way, Deren proposes that it is precisely Erzulie who embodies the creation of other realities, an imaginative realm that is intimately linked to the embodied experience and history of Haitian and Dominican women.

Likewise, the work of imagination and futures otherwise is a central component of Black feminism: "It remains a Black feminist necessity to explicate, develop, and dwell in realities other than the secular Western empiricisms that deny Black women's importance in knowing, making, and transforming the world" (Tinsley, "Songs for Ezili" 400). Therefore, Black feminist scholarship points toward the many alternative possibilities for Black women. In Saidiya Hartman's words: "To imagine what cannot be verified . . . to reckon with the precarious lives which are visible only in the moment of their disappearance" (12). Grace Hong further argues that the imaginative can be a particularly political and powerful space for Black women: "Calling for a Black feminist criticism is to do nothing less than to imagine another system of value, one in which Black women have value" (424–25). I consider that, following this particular kind of Black feminist theory as well as a need to subvert Eurocentric histories, knowledges, and futures within their works, the authors throughout this chapter all take up this spiritual path of Erzulie to communicate histories of violence, pain, and displacement but also of pleasure and futures not confined to imposed ideologies of the modern-colonial world (Tinsley, "Black Atlantic" 201).

Specifically, if Erzulie is often invoked in connection to strong feelings of love between women, a bond that at times functions as a forbidden source of power and history, throughout the discussed materials, each protagonist must come to terms with broken relationships, national affinities, and kinship connections. Oftentimes, strong emotional responses accompany references to the practice of Vodou and the invocation of the spiritual realm. This intimate-spiritual connection and the emotions that such connection conjures communicates a knowledge that is otherwise hidden from view. I argue here that love in these texts—as it emerges from the spiritual knowledge communicated through references to Vodou and ancestral memories—constitutes, as Sandoval teaches us, a radical emotional response to the coloniality of power and gender and a vital force in the creation of alternative imaginaries. I want to explain this idea better in the following paragraphs by engaging in a discussion of the role of emotions in the political complexity that inhabits the Dominican/Haitian relationship.

In many studies on Dominican and Haitian conflicts, scholars (García-Peña *The Borders*; Fumagalli; Chancy; Shemak; Martínez-San Miguel *Caribe Two Ways*) have generally ignored how Haitian migration has also been constituted into an emotional object in such a way as to accentuate a national love for the Dominican Republic and the constructed Dominican identity. Further on, another emotional aspect worthy of analysis is how Haitian migrants decide at key points to reject the promise of belonging to the Dominican nation, which may never come, and turn instead to more intimate terms of a loving community than what national love offers. This is why I consider that a study on emotional phenomena lends itself to a better understanding of Haitian-Dominican boundaries and frontiers.

According to Ahmed, emotions function as historical and political markers, which touch bodies according to their position within the officially imagined nation and, in this way, reinforce or adjust a sense of belonging. These emotionally-impressed bodies become "objects of feeling," and through their circulation, "boundaries and borders" are also reinforced or relaxed (*The Cultural Politics* 133). In particular, happiness and love are two concepts that Ahmed analyzes in terms of the impressions left by movement toward a promised familial ideal and the creation of a *sense* of "national character" (134). Ahmed defines national love as the ways in which various bodies are affected by and move toward the nation. More specifically, she posits that love can be conceptualized as an exclusionary politics (closely tied with hate), which aligns some subjects with others and against *other* others. Narratives of national love work by generating a national body that is put in danger by others who will eventually take the very position of the subject within the nation. This type of emotion is particularly social in that "it circulates between signifiers in relationships of difference and displacement" (*The Cultural Politics* 120). This is to say that a loving orientation must circulate through bodies, creating an outline of others who are constituted as a "common threat" (121). This form of intimate love and a hate directed toward those who can never be fully relegated to the "outside" ultimately involves the "negotiation of boundaries between a self and Others and between communities where the Others are brought into existence as a threat" (122). We can thus claim, with Ahmed, that in "hating" others, the subject or collectivity is also proclaiming a self-love: "Hate structures the emotional life of narcissism as a fantastic investment in the continuation of the image of the self in the faces that together make up the 'we'" (123). It is precisely this national love/hate that is invoked in official nationalist narratives of the Dominican Republic. Nationalist fantasy is to create a community in which those who appear as if they do not share the same Hispanic origins, sound as if their first language were not Spanish, or practice the Catholic religion are constituted as the silent invaders whose sole purpose is to dilute and overthrow the mythical mestizo race of Dominicans. The official narrative is employed to move others away from the national ideal of Dominican identity.

Those subjects who are not aligned with the "promise of happiness" (Ahmed *The Promise*) of the Dominican family/nation are thus cast as the "unhappy" or the objects of national hate. Ahmed demonstrates that unhappy meant "causing misfortune or trouble" and later "wretched in mind" (17). Here wretched comes from "wretch, referring to a stranger, exile, or banished person. The wretch is not only the one driven out of his or her native country but is also defined as one who is sunk in deep distress, sorrow, misfortune, or poverty," "a miserable, unhappy, or unfortunate person," "a poor or hapless being," and even "a vile, sorry, or despicable person" (17). Thus listening to the wretched may offer us an alternative view of happiness. Those cast from the structures that engender a happy existence within the nation might "make room" for a counter-discourse that undoes official nationalist narratives and offers new possibilities of connection beyond happiness and love associated with the official national subject (18).

Decolonial love allows us to disconnect from the dominant, "happy" perception of reality to make possible an other space of possibility through coalitions configured as lines of affinity through difference. We can thus conclude that loving Blackness as political resistance has the power to transform ways of being in the world and works actively to create the conditions necessary to move against the forces of colonization and dominant nationalist discourses to reclaim Black lives and say that they matter. As I will demonstrate, the protagonists move toward a spiritual space opened by the loving presence of Erzulie, a border space that serves as a stage from which an intimate love for the racialized body can disarticulate the forever indeterminate national promise of belonging.

Additionally, Reyes-Santos looks toward kinship and family metaphor as a productive site from which we might consider the fraught processes of identity-making, as well as the limitations of "national family" structures. She introduces what she terms the "decolonial affective matrix" to show how power differentials are written into "transnational neoliberal and foreign aid projects on the islands" and also the legacies that colonial policies and histories have left upon the emotional psyche of the region (106). Through a close reading of the novels *Solo falta que lleuva* and *The Farming of Bones*, Reyes-Santos underscores the ways in which family relations and conceptualizations of kinship have always rested within the "heart" of Haitian-Dominican politics. Specifically, she uses the rhetorical device of the "unrecognized sibling" to demonstrate the historical lifeblood that has entwined both nations for centuries. It is also a device that can be used to "temporarily forget, ignore, or hide" a "secreto a voces," that is, to discursively evade a "secret" that is known by all.

These narratives of kinship and emotional ties between the two island nations extend beyond the academic and theoretical circles. For example, in recent responses to the Constitutional Tribunal Court's ruling, literary figures such as Junot Díaz and Danticat have specifically addressed Haitian-Dominican tensions in family metaphors and have been outspoken members of the diasporic community in acknowledging the importance of shared experiences in recent legal disputes on the island. In a 2014 conversation moderated by *Americas Quarterly*, Díaz and Danticat met to dialogue about conflict, colonialism, and race in the two countries. Díaz is quoted as stating: "[Neither side understands] we're sisters and brothers, that we share a poor, fragile island, and that without true solidarity we won't make it." This comment invokes the trope of Haitians and Dominicans as (un)recognized siblings separated by national origin. Both authors criticize the generalizations made by Dominicans of Haitians and state that understanding and unification can only emerge from the recognition of shared historical struggles and experiences. The authors propose a kinship model that subverts the narratives of the nation as a "happy" family, suggesting that this model is exclusionary and limits imaginations that may cross the nations' frontiers. Furthermore, they suggest that the shared vulnerability of racialized subjects on both sides of the border may in fact be a catalyst for solidarity.

This loving bond between bodies who have been dismembered and made invisible by the coloniality of power and gender coupled with the healing and memory of African diaspora religious practices represents a radical response to a history of violence, erasure, and anti-Black sentiment. Love and spiritual healing guide the examined narratives as well as their protagonists toward a new future in which the bonds between women of color are powerful reminders of their presence and connection in and beyond Hispaniola.

Opening Paths

I turn now to Hernández's music video for the song "Da pa' lo' do,'" in which the artist takes up the role of Erzulie to bring both sides of Hispaniola together, represented by two brothers. While the lyrics to the song verbally create a narrative of two siblings under one common father, the video itself—steeped in African diaspora religious symbols—articulates a more complicated relationship. Just as Hernández employs religion as a space to uncover hidden relations of coloniality in contemporary Dominican legislation through her journalistic production, her music video narrates the painful history between the two island nations, while at the same time looking into the type of relationship that the two nations still maintain today. The artist's vision makes visible those silences and gaps long perpetuated by the Hispanophile hegemony of the Dominican national imaginary. Spiritual figures (such as the Virgin Mary and Erzulie Danto) appear to be blended as one, what might have the potential to become, as Alexander would argue, "an antidote to the coloniality-of-power that engendered and sustained anti-Haitianism for over a century" (14).

The video begins with a large tree in bloom located in the middle of an open field, which becomes reminiscent of Loko in the Vodou tradition, that is, a giant tree with its roots in the waters beneath the earth, which draws the spirits from beyond the sea in Genin.[4] The silence is broken by dramatic drum beats and a Black man wearing the uniform of the Spanish infantry in the Dominican Republic (red jacket and white pants), running toward an unknown destination. The man carries a rifle and two pouches strapped across his shoulders. The music begins to mimic his movement as Hernández starts to sing: "Había dos hermanitos / compartiendo un pedacito / porque eran muy pobrecitos / y no tenían ni mamá. / Ellos se preguntaban, / ¿Por qué si somos dos gente / nos hacen comernos uno nada más?" As the last line of the stanza is uttered, the man wearing the red uniform stops and stares ahead at a hill covered in grass, rifle at his side pointing toward the earth. Hernández's voice echoes in the foreground: "Su pai se la buscaba / trepaó en una patina, / repartiendo plátano / y patá y trompá." The words *patá y trompá*, or "kick and punch," introduce a second man, running through the opposite side of the same field toward the tree in bloom. The uniform of this second man (blue jacket and a straw hat) suggests an affiliation with the French infantry, signaling a connection to Haiti (Jaime 90).

Lorgia García-Peña argues that the first way in which the video pushes against colonial visions of Dominican society is that it presents us with a metaphor of the Dominican Republic as an orphaned child: "Nineteenth-century Dominican intellectuals, battling with their desire for sovereignty and their yearning to maintain a link to 'Mother Spain,' lamented the loss of Hispanic cultural values" (157). Hernández rescues this metaphor of orphanage, but rather than apply it solely to Dominicans as García-Peña argues, she recasts both siblings as colonial "orphans" (157). She argues that this move also works to dismantle the foundational myth of the Dominican Republic that has historically cast Haiti as a colonizer-invader, as the song invokes a shared memory of colonial history: "Siéntelo / el abrazo del mismo abuelo / Desde Juana Méndez hasta Maimón / y desde ahí a Dajabón."[5] For García-Peña, then, in providing us with a vision of a historically unrecognized kinship connection under the abusive hand of one grandfather, Hernández suggests that perhaps Haiti is not the enemy of the Dominican nation but rather that the problems that both nations faced were caused by another (foreign) force.

Nevertheless, while García-Peña focuses more intently upon the metaphor of orphaned siblings in Hernández's video, I would like to tease apart the representation of the singer herself as simultaneously the Virgin Mary and Haitian vodou *lwa* Erzulie, which opens a line to talk about a politics of decolonial love. Beyond kinship, this spiritual metaphor (Mary/Erzulie) connects each sibling on a much more intimate level and mends the colonizing discourse that keep them separate. Hernández enters into the scene of the musical piece on the back of a motorbike draped in a turquoise satin shawl. As she lifts her head to reveal her face, we see that she has painted her face a darker shade of brown/black. While this appearance may seem at first offensive and problematic, I agree with Karen Jaime when she argues that, in reappropriating the imagery and iconography of Blackface/Brownface, Hernández forges a powerful social and political critique: "She does not reinforce the ways Blackface and minstrel shows operated as a way to lampoon Black people and situate them as ignorant, lazy, joyous, and musical . . . [Rather] she challenges the ways Catholicism functions as a form of whitening within the Dominican Republic" (91). Also, Jaime contends that Hernández's representation of Blackness goes against the whiteness and purity of Catholicism versus the syncretism represented by Haitian Vodou (92–93).

I want to focus my analysis not solely upon the Africanizing of the Judeo-Christian tradition represented by the Black Virgin Mary but extend this reading to include the representation of Vodou *lwa* Erzulie and the ways in which she is invoked as a type of spiritual healing of an island broken by a line of colonial/imperial wounds. Hernández as Erzulie appears first in the video to the brother in red, representing the Dominican Republic. As she approaches this man—who is found lying under a large ceiba tree—the camera focuses on a golden "M," which hangs from a chain around her neck. Under Erzulie's gaze, the man begins to take off his red jacket identifying him with the Spanish colonial infantry to reveal clothes of pure white. Although this "M" has been interpreted by both Jaime and García-Peña as a symbolic reference to the Virgin Mary, I propose that this particular object acts as a type of crown, a symbol of both luxury[6] and a reference to African diaspora religions in which the head is a sacred space of knowledge, the space where ordinary men and women commune with the divine.[7] Both brothers are resignified in the video through the power of the divine crown that Erzulie bears. In removing the garments that link each brother with his colonial father, under the golden figure, the men symbolically enter into a new divine order removed from the inherited and ongoing racialized colonial oppressions. Now they wear a white robe, which is associated with those initiated into the Vodou community, white being the color of divine knowledge and community that "saves" the two "unrecognized siblings" (Reyes-Santos).

The crown also offers an alternative symbol of sovereignty. After all, within Vodou cosmology, the concept of "belonging" becomes a matter of participation in a spiritual community beyond any national or regional allegiance.[8] Being part of the Vodou community is defined by service to the *lwa* or to fellow initiates. It is important to note that one is never a "member" of the Vodou community but rather a servant of the *lwa*. This means that each member is in the service of a certain divine entity and follows certain rituals and practices to ensure the entity's contentment. Furthermore, the community—represented in Erzulie's crown—is strengthened through a gradual cleansing of the "heads" of the *serviteurs* so that their eyes may be opened. This process follows a path known as *konesans* (a new knowledge) based on intricate ritual knowledges and sacred memories of ancestors and the spiritual realm (Clifford et al. 25).

For these reasons, when Hernández appears to the two brothers born into familial chaos in the video of "Da' pa' lo' do," she does so as Erzulie, bearer of a spiritual knowledge and alternative sovereignty—in an attempt to work through the racial anxieties and violence of the brothers' past. As Erzulie gazes over the Haitian brother, her image is reflected in the very water that he uses to wash his head. The Dominican brother repeats the process. This moment represents a symbolic *lave tèt* (a "washing of the head") as the means of entering into the sacred community. It is worth remembering here that motivation to enter into the service of the spirits usually follows a call from the *lwa* (Dunham; Murphy), which is reflected in Erzulie's interest in the two men throughout the video. This ceremony allows the initiates to enter into a psychological and social state in which radical changes become possible.

The outcome of the ceremony is to receive the *lwa* as a *mèt tèt*, the master of one's head, which transforms the individual from leading an ordinary life to allow the divine to intervene in all aspects of one's existence. Both Joseph M. Murphy and Katherine Dunham describe the importance of discomfort and pain as a necessary ingredient in this period of transition to clear the receivers' heads. Deren explains the special meaning of the head in Vodou as a comingling of the visible and the invisible. This is to say that the physical head is understood as a type of container for two invisible elements, which in Vodou are called "angels." This effectively replaces individual intelligence and memory with that of spiritual knowledge, a knowledge that allows the spirits to intervene in the initiates' lives. More importantly, *memory* is restored and a deeper connection between both brothers is revealed. Once again, the intimacy of the uno múltiple as outlined by Santos-Febres in chapter 1 opens a space for an alternative collective of transtemporal Black sovereignty. Here, the alliance between the spirits, ancestors, and the brothers pushes back against the colonial imaginations of the modern nation-state, which only seeks to separate and promote Black death.

Going back to Hernández's music video, both heads of the two men begin to glow with alternating colors, reflecting the ones that appear in the head of Erzulie. These pulsating colors bind the brothers and the *lwa* in an intimate relationship. Through this spiritual process, Erzulie has eradicated the histories of colonial rule and has reminded them of their common inheritance under Africa. The final shot of the video shows each man walking toward one another bare-chested—rid of even their white garments—and so, vulnerable toward each other. Inhabiting this vulnerability, their faces display the colors, growing more pronounced, that Eruzlie had given them, showing divine knowledge of their shared history and a loving orientation toward each other.

In the last frame of the video, as the two men draw near to each other under the shade of the tree, Hernández repeats the phrases: "Es que somo' hermanos" and "da pa' lo' do." Hernández emphasizes the connection that the brothers share on the island in repeating that there is enough, of what I interpret to be love, for each of them. The men finally end in an embrace that is at once erotic and spiritually intimate. They stand in their embrace bare-chested as the colors that Erzulie imbued upon them intensify. These colors move from one body to the next and Erzulie is seen dancing with children under the tree. Thus to partake in Erzulie's love and to dance in service of the spirits is to recognize a historical memory of the ancestors and their lands of origin. Once this memory has been embraced and the other can be loved as an equal, new futures may be enacted that derive from harmonious and loving actions made together.

The dance, the embrace, and the love shared at the end of the video are not done solely on a personal level but also done for the benefit of the community. The sticky nature[9] of Erzulie's spirit—represented in the shared colors—and the path down which she has taken the two protagonists serve to empower her children in their struggle. Erzulie's presence in the video is one that is shared in an economy of love that inhabits those bodies who inherit a history of pain and violence. In embracing Erzulie's love and recognizing the shared humanity and historical trajectory in each other, a new future is made possible at the end of the video—one that may bring together both sides of Hispaniola.

Erzulie's Spirit and Political Imaginations of the Borderland

I would now like to extend the decolonial love/spiritual framework to analyze the ways in which female protagonists subvert long histories of colonial/patriarchal violence to forge a new space for themselves between the national boundaries of Hispaniola. Lara's *Erzulie's Skirt* narrates Miriam and Micaela's journey from Hispaniola to Puerto Rico and back again in an attempt to make room for themselves and their love somewhere between the three nations. Their journey ultimately ends in the *bateyes* (plantations) of the Dominican Republic where their knowledge of herbal medicines and spiritual healing is used to help the women living and working in the sugarcane fields, a place associated with Trujillo's 1937 Haitian massacre[10] and the historically contested border. Lara's novel becomes, then, a tale that employs spiritual practices and beliefs to articulate alternative modes of being in the world outside of the coloniality of power and gender. Further on, this book transforms feelings of pain and shame into a source of celebration and agency for the protagonists while also reworking the geopolitical borders of the island and the Caribbean.

Lara is a member of the Haitian and Dominican communities, and she uses her belonging to validate her role as cultural intermediary and practitioner of Vodou for the production of a new episteme. She has been an active advocate of Black Dominican women's rights and cultural inheritance both on the island and in the US, as demonstrated by her recent work with the CUNY Dominican Studies Institute and her project to rescue the voices of Afro-Dominican women from the historical archive. She is currently an assistant professor of anthropology at the University of Oregon and continues to write as a form of political activism. In her *Queer Freedom*, Lara takes on the border space as a power site of knowledge production. She writes that she occupies the "center of knowledge," quoting Anzaldúa to elaborate on the "spaces between." In this way, Lara conjures a vision of nepantla to frame her decolonial trajectory, citing that nepantla "averigua el conflict. It provides associations and connective tissues. . . . [It] interweaves multiple, superimposed strands of thought" (qtd. in Lara 25). Here, Lara occupies the spiritual locus of enunciation of the uno múltiple and uses the language of Anzaldúa to draw a "potential map to freedom" (25).

Lara's *Erzulie's Skirt* is one of the only literary productions to represent Erzulie as a spirit implicated in a same-sex relationship between women, according to Tinsley ("Songs for Ezili" 12). The text begins with an emotional conversation between Agwe and Erzulie on a peaceful morning in the Atlantic Ocean. Agwe is known as the protector of ships at sea, of marine life, and of fishermen. He is the companion of Erzulie and inhabits the bottom of the sea. Agwe Tawoyo is said to be the captain of the ship *Immamou*, which carries the souls of the dead back to Guinee. In the scene, the ocean is calm and the sun has yet to rise until the two spirits begin to speak; then, the ocean begins to roar. Agwe comments that his bones hurt due to the souls that walk through him in the sea: "They are lonely down here. They don't see each other, but I see all of them. They just wander about" (Lara xiv). Erzulie tells of how it brings her no joy either to pull new souls down to Agwe: "You think I do so much work to help these heads be born only to have them back so soon? . . . It breaks my heart sometimes" (xiv). This ceremonial invocation of Agwe and Erzulie at the beginning of the text summons the transatlantic slave trade and the souls that have been lost in the long and lingering histories of colonialism, slavery, and other forced economic and political migrations in the Atlantic. When the two spirits finish briefly discussing the shipwrecked souls who have perished in the sea, Agwe asks Erzulie to tell him a story. Erzulie's story, centered on Miriam and Micaela's lives, provides a spiritual mapping of history onto both the present and future that, in turn, generates alternative sites for the production of knowledge and post-national imaginations. In this mapping, everything begins and ends with the water.

Chavel, Miriam's mother, dreams about an "old witch" that sits by the sea, sifting through the sand for cowry shells. The witch chews tobacco and spits the juice into the ocean and then proceeds to look at Chavel. Miriam's mother searches for answers to this vision in the women from her village, and they say that the witch "[has] been alive since we Africans arrived from Africa. They say she eats men to feed her blood" (10). Finally, the women tell Chavel that she must go right away to the river and find out what the old witch has to say. When Chavel arrives, the witch tells her that she is pregnant: "Your daughter, you will call her Miriam. She needs to live. . . . You must promise her to Changó—god of rain and thunder" (12). After a moment of hesitation, Chavel promises it. The witch thanks her and declares that she must never forget where they have come from and that the ancestors thank Chavel for this promise. The witch leaves and "it was only when she was already climbing the mountain that she realized the woman had no feet" (13). This last line of the first section of the novel alludes to Erzulie's form as Lasyrenn, the siren, the protector of the seas and of those souls who are lost at sea.

Micaela's story begins in a similar way. She is born into a Dominican family of devout Catholic women; however her father secretly practices Vodou without the permission of her mother. On the day that Micaela is supposed to be born, her father ventures near a river, lays down, and falls asleep. He is approached by a woman in his dreams who informs him that his daughter will be named Micaela and that she will be promised to the goddess Ochún, the divinity of fresh water, sexuality, and love. This woman also takes the form of a siren and wears a necklace of cowry shells around her neck, remitting the reader to Erzulie Lasyrenn. When he wakes up, he finds that his wife is struggling with her labor and eventually dies in childbirth. He follows his vision and names the child Micaela. Here it is important to note that each child has been promised to Changó and Ochún, male and female deities paired together in sexual and loving relationships in Santería.

The reference to Erzulie, the siren, marks the life of Miriam and Micaela as one that was foretold by the Vodou goddess and that imbues upon their lives a particularly spiritual component. This suggests that to engage in the cultural memories that both women experience is also a type of remembrance of a *spiritual* identity. As Miriam and Micaela are both marked spiritually by Haitian and Dominican Vodou practices, it provides an instance to explore more fully the diversity, histories, and futures of African women in diaspora. While acts of spiritual remembering might open spaces of resistance to political, cultural, and social problematics, intimate-spiritual relationships can also draw attention to contested cultural spaces and locations, such as the borders between modern nation-states, that are also deeply spiritual, situated, and embodied (Dillard; Alexander; Anzaldúa *Borderlands*; hooks). Remembering, then, becomes a type of radical response to historical fragmentation at the cultural, political, spiritual, and bodily levels in response to colonialism, slavery, and patriarchy.

Not only is this form of Erzulie one that protects and exhibits a certain amount of love for Miriam and Micaela, but this form is also a particular manifestation of Erzulie known as Lasyrenn. This love that connects the two women is one that mends their fragmented lives at different points of the novel. For example, when Miriam, Antonio (Miriam's son), and Micaela apply for a visa in the Dominican Republic to travel to New York, they are stopped at the consulate. Miriam is approached by a guard and told that "Haitians have to go to Haiti to apply for visas" and that this line "is only for Dominicans" (Lara 137). The guard immediately marks Miriam as Haitian because of the color of her skin and refuses to help her. Micaela, on the other hand, is able to easily secure her visa (138–39) and holds Miriam as she cries. Micaela's love toward Miriam moves her forward and works to ultimately sooth the moments of racial violence.

When the two women are unable to acquire a visa to travel to New York, they are forced to contract a *yola* in hopes of reaching Puerto Rico. This journey represents the thousands of Haitian and Dominican migrants that cross the Mona Strait (where the Atlantic and Caribbean clash violently together) each year and perish in their desire to reach Puerto Rico. The journey proves to be lethal for other members of their *yola* who are forced to throw children overboard and die of dehydration in the hot sun. It is in this violent and perilous space filled with pain and loss that both Miriam and Micaela begin to see visions of the past.[11] The *yola* is also a space in which both women forge an intimate-spiritual connection with their own archive of ancestral spirits. Specifically, this is the space in which the past and the present come together in the novel: Lara utilizes ancestral memories of transport from Africa that appear to Micaela in her dreams (200–1). The text presents this history of oceanic slave routes as accessed through the "other side of the water." This "other side" of the sea is particularly important in Vodou cosmology as it represents that space in which the ancestors and *lwa* reside. This haunted space where Atlantic meets Caribbean speaks to Micaela:

> Micaela looked out at the ocean, at the churning waters at her feet, closing her eyes to the cool night air. La Mar had always been there. She knew from dreams that it was from there that she had arisen. That sometime long ago she had entered her waters and emerged on this side, whole and broken. That somewhere in her depths was the key to her death and to her living. As Micaela prayed, La Mar appeared before her dressed in silver and jewels and the rosy shells of lambí. She lit up the sky so that even the moon hid behind Her brilliance . . . La Mar told her of a place where two people lay with irons on her ankles. They gazed at each other across the darkness, despite the darkness, and their eyes shone like the stars. In the unending Blackness that covered them, that suffocated them, they spoke: "Amor, I long for your kisses, your arms around me, along my hips. Amor, I love you." All this they whispered without moving their lips, in languages that escaped the trappings of sound. (159–60)

While Tinsley argues that this depiction of La Mar is dripping with fluid desire and offers the reader a type of fractured "queer mirror" that bends language, time, and couple, I want to extend the reading of this passage to focus specifically on the spiritual aspect of La Mar's appearance, the significance that this spiritual figure has in terms of Atlantic/Caribbean spatial imaginations and the intimate/political work that it does to connect Micaela and Miriam to a painful past. Lara imbues La Mar with traits traditionally associated with Erzulie in Vodou cosmology. While Erzulie's love connects both pairs of lovers (those ironclad lovers at the bottom of the sea and the pair floating above in the *yola*), this love is also used to comfort those floating above, alive in their movement toward a possibility of something better. Micaela and Miriam both claim to be followed by "Erzulie's skirt," another name for the wake that their *yola* leaves behind in the sea.

By occupying not only the wake of the *yola* but also the historical "wake" of history, these images and spiritual strivings in the text take on a decolonial project similar to the one discussed above in Danticat's *Breath, Eyes, Memory*. This concept is developed by Christina Elizabeth Sharpe and alludes to the extending and ever-present imprint that slavery has left upon the Atlantic. When Miriam and Micaela cross the sea, they are accompanied by the wake, or memory, of those enslaved personas and others who carry the history of enslavement on their backs.

Micaela ponders the sea and the ways in which she feels connected to the waters. She is described as a being that is at once "whole and broken" (159). Micaela, as well as Miriam, is pushed from her home in which she has lost all whom she loves; she is pushed to those spaces of in-betweenness and pain that bring violent histories to the present: first, as we have seen, the space where the Atlantic meets the Caribbean; second, to Puerto Rico, itself a type of border space between the Caribbean and the US; and finally to the bateyes of the Haitian-Dominican national frontier. In each of these zones, the spirits speak to both women and their love for one another is invoked as a type of healing. Moreover, as we saw in the passage above, the "other side of the water" provides a window into the spiritual realms that still haunt the waters of the Atlantic/Caribbean, as the voices and memories of those whose lives and experiences of violence cannot be fully put to rest. Thus it serves as another border, between the world of the dead and that one of the living. Erzulie resides over all beings—dead or alive—who long to reach out to each other, recognize the agony in the other, and feel their embrace.

At the end of Lara's novel, Miriam and Micaela once again find themselves in a border space between the Dominican Republic and Haiti. They have taken up a home in the Dominican bateyes among the sugar laborers and opened a *colmado*. As the construction process begins and both women watch as their building is erected, the batey community starts to whisper about these new female figures who have begun to live among them: " 'Those two brujas will place curses on us if we go in there.' [Micaela] got further and further away from the talking, bit it seemed to get louder and louder as she left" (204). When they see that the women have also planted a small *canuco*, the people are equally as angry: "Are they trying to insult us? We have no food and here they are growing it right in front of us? Who told them they are welcome here?" (205). The women are harassed because they do not live with their children or their families and ridiculed for wanting to start a business for themselves. The tense atmosphere is broken by the dreams of Micaela and Miriam: "Oya [deity of death and rebirth] danced on the tips of the trees across the road. She swings her red skirts through the air. Changó burst forth with lightning. From the other end of the earth, Ogun [deity of iron and war] gave his war cry. The darkness of the road gave way to the sound of thundering feet and voices. The storm had broken" (206). The people of the batey had begun a revolt against the *colmado* and the intrusion of the two women. The flowers and *canuco* are destroyed by the mob. In this moment, the spirits abandon the women and they are left alone.

The next day, Miriam and Micaela meet Yealidad, a young girl who lives on the batey with her parents. Yealidad is teased by the boys of the town and goes to Miriam and Micaela for help. She believes that the two women are in possession of love potions that would fix her problems with the patriarchal structure of the batey; however, Micaela responds: "I don't have love potions. I do, however, have other things that help people. You know Yealidad, true love requires that you know yourself. It is hard work, and not all women can do it. Some women prefer to believe in cheap powders and perfumes, and the trickery of sorcerers. I am not a sorcerer. I am a healer" (212). Micaela invokes the figure of the *curandera* or healer not only as one that has the power and knowledge to heal an ailing body but as a figure that has the ability to collectively heal the community through a love that recognizes and legitimizes the personal history of the other.

The body of Yealidad, like the bodies found at the bottom of the sea, is both whole and broken. Both Miriam and Micaela work to bring back a narrative of self-love that Yealidad lacks as well as the confidence to accept herself fully as a woman living between two worlds in the masculine atmosphere of the batey. Just like that, Lara transforms Miriam and Micaela from *brujas*—in the eyes of the community—to powerful *curanderas* that wield the ancient knowledge of the spirits. Thus, spiritual healing offers an important and necessary political vision that disturbs the boundaries of nation, belonging, and gender. Moreover, Yealidad can be read as a reference to Yelidá, the daughter of a white sailor and a Haitian woman, born in the Dominican Republic, representing the Dominican people in the poem "Yelidá" by Tomás Hernández Franco. The novel thus argues, along with Franco, that Yealidad embodies the fraught relationship between both nations and the transformative power that the *curanderas* wield to bring them together.

It is at this point that a reflection guided by Glissant's ideas becomes necessary. For Glissant, the belly of the slave ship that "dissolves you" and "precipitates you into a nonworld" becomes a space of gestation in which his concept of *relation* is born. He understands relation as a type of practiced knowledge, one created in communion with the land and with others: "Relation is not made of things that are foreign but of *shared knowledge*" (8, my emphasis). This knowledge is made by those who have been "dissolved" in the painful Middle Passage journey and have created themselves anew, destabilizing any fixed notion of belonging or national rootedness. This makes Glissant's conceptualization of relation an epistemology that enables freedom through an intimate and traumatic collective experience that is not closed off to a history of difference but assumes it as the foundation of reality. If we accept Glissant's invitation to conceive the space of relation as a radical site of contestation, we can redraw the map of the border as one of intimate, albeit violent, contact and assume it as a parallel poetic, a structure of thought and knowledge that talks back to fixed categories of nation.

In doing this, we can accept both Miriam and Micaela's challenge to transcend nation in the space of the spirit, to think all of the ways that both Haiti and the Dominican Republic are imbricated in a system and history that provides the possibility to define the island beyond racial, ethnic, and national limits. This painful in-betweenness echoes the desire of the women to invoke a spiritual memory and love that may bring recognition of humanity to those left out of or invisible to nationalist claims to citizenship. These projects seek to go farther than a facile struggle against exclusionary practices and racial/ethnic othering; they move to a new (imaginary) terrain in which questions such as Who are "we"? And where do "we" belong? can be politically reimagined and put into practice. Genuine spiritual connection—not an imposed national love—requires a different way of thinking and the risk of putting ourselves in intimate contact with the other in order to change the terms upon which nation is constructed.

Erzulie's Wake

The futures of social reconciliation throughout the three texts discussed in this chapter depend on addressing the painful histories incited in the legacies of colonial and imperial violence. Each author points to a knowledge that is communicated in the expression of an Afro-diasporic spirituality caught up in the modern experience, which suggests that the modern nation-state is complicit with a paradigm of racial violence. Thus, Hernández and Lara propose reparations that extend beyond the material to embrace a more intimate-spiritual decolonial worldview. If, as Nelson Maldonado-Torres argues, "slavery, death, and even torture form part of the structure of power and horizon of meaning sustained by coloniality," (225) then it follows the reparations deeply embedded in intimate-spiritual connections with the past demand that we look beyond the paradigm of violence and material gains. Indeed, the coloniality of power and patriarchy here refers not to a system that once existed but to the continued salience of racial tensions, systematic poverty, and dependency of an existing system of power. In this way, any attempt at decolonization and reparation must come to terms with coloniality.

As Hernández and Lara demonstrate, decolonial spirituality and love invite a remembering of erased histories through the spiritual practices of the African diaspora. This economy that straddles the often painful border spaces of past and present calls for renewed ideas about citizenship, belonging, and national identity. This intimate-spiritual connection between women and ancestors also answers Ahluwalia's call for a process of decolonization that would seek to break down cycles of revenge for a more intimate politics of spiritual liberation and mutual recognition.

Clearly these women express this radical move toward spiritual decolonization by embracing an Africanist vision of life, death, past, present, and love. Through an intimate connection with Erzulie, we come to see how each author rescues the memories of the past and inserts them as active participants in the temporal world of the living. Sophie comments on this intrusion of the spirits into her own world: "Our dead relatives who we had such a kinship to, as though they were our restless spirits, shadows wandering in the darkness" (205). Through these bonds of ancestral/divine kinship, what I refer to as spiritual intimacy, each woman works to destabilize the power dynamics embedded in the modern-colonial world. Similarly, Micaela and Miriam are granted power, knowledge, and respect through their use of witchcraft and spiritual healing recipes as well as the love that each share for one another.

Spirits, shadows, exiles, and outsides then remind us of the pain and violence embedded in the power structures of the modern African Caribbean. Their spiritual discourse ensures that history is not forgotten and underscores the lines of continuity between colonial systems of enslavement and contemporary experiences of displacement. Dyan comments on this particular vision of the importance of a return of colonial Haiti in the Vodou *lwa*: "In this regenerative, reinterpreted, and vengeful history, dissociated bodies return to find their place. What whites called 'superstition' and 'fetishism' turned out to be something more akin to the journeys of bodies that relocalize themselves as spirits" (258). As these authors continue to uncover and rescue spirits in their writing through African diasporic spiritual practices, the knowledge that their characters invoke continues to haunt their texts, passing on stories of daring Black women and violent, forced displacements.

Chapter 3

Afro-Latina Feminisms

Nuyorican, Domincanyork, and Afro-Latinx Political Resistance

In this third chapter, I turn to the Puerto Rican and Dominican communities in New York partly because they represent an extension of chapters 1 and 2—shifting focus away from the islands and toward the center of the empire—and partly because the racial politics that cut through these communities are deeply connected. I am interested in asking about the ways in which the emotional and spiritual practices in diaspora leverage religious ritual, ancestral oral traditions, and love to push against historical processes that seek to separate. I ask what alliances are forged between these two communities that have fought to stake claim and recognition through intellectual and cultural efforts such as the Schomburg Center for Black Studies, the CUNY Dominican Studies Center, and the Hunter Center for Puerto Rican Studies. What are narratives and rhetorical strategies that bring these three communities together while also recognizing the complexities of their differences?

Throughout the 1960s and 1970s, Puerto Rican poets were at the forefront of (counter)cultural movements in New York City and—as captured by Pedro Pietri's performances with the Young Lords—they were central to the Puerto Rican Movement: "[The work of Puerto Rican poets] would help shape emerging third world, decolonial, feminist, and other political horizons" (Noel 1). These poets were engaged in a variety of artistic and activist initiatives, including poetic and musical performances, community theater, and collaborations with nationalist, antiwar, and student organizations (Rivera; Opie; Wanzer-Serrano; Muzio).

Yet even as Puerto Ricans were visible participants in the artistic and literary countercultures, the strong presence of Dominicans and Afro–Puerto Ricans mostly remained invisible.[1] Thus, this chapter focuses on shared movements among Black Puerto Ricans and Dominicans in New York in the forging of a larger African diasporic consciousness, not necessarily tethered to a "Hispanic Caribbean" identity. I will look at contemporary slam poetry artists and singers to trace the struggle of Black Dominicans and Puerto Ricans against racism and colonial structures through their engagement with a longer archive of spiritual presences and shared emotions. The heart of this chapter rests in the collective experiences of the two communities and the questions provoked by moments of mutual recognition amid violent anti-Black and nativist politics. The spiritual connection each slam artist builds intends to construct a sense of belonging to a history of struggle, of being the descendants of those who survived the horrors of genocide and slavery, of recognizing the strength in community building after the ritual and music has paused. What we are left with are narratives and cultural acts that, emerging out of the margins of US histories and silences reproduced on the islands, offer an alternative view of Black Puerto Rican and Dominican identity, one that belongs to racexiled[2] others.

Many contemporary Afro–Puerto Rican slam poets, artists, and hip-hop producers have claimed the category of Afro-Latinx in order to take on these urgent concerns. For example, in her new album *Creature!*, hip-hop singer Nitty Scott reflects on her Afro-Boricua roots and embraces her African ancestry and spirituality in order to claim a space for herself in the US. In her single "La Diáspora," Scott proclaims in this song that "this is the story of the diaspora, a tribute to the daughters of the marooned societies, yo soy negra, Latina." Scott inscribes her music into a pedagogical line of thought that speaks to the discursive imaginary of the African diaspora and as a countercultural foundational trope for Black cultural and identitarian politics and political action. A key component of her album is the linkage with slave ship resistance culture and the liberatory impulses of maroonage. Claiming her position as direct descent of "marooned societies," Scott rescues the ghosts of her ancestors from the annihilation of the Middle Passage to resurrect a call for affirmation of her existence as Afro-Latina and a sturdy symbol of survivalism.

Throughout the remainder of this chapter, my goal is to study this type of spiritual connection among communities through the intimate sharing of experiences, emotions, beliefs, and religiosity in New York Afro–Puerto Rican and Dominican poets and musical producers. I continue my focus on Puerto Rico and the Dominican Republic. I also reflect on the emergence of Afro-Latinidad and the political urgency that the women analyzed in this chapter demonstrate to push against anti-Black sentiment in the US Latinx community. I ask how Afro-Latinx women poet-activists force us to move toward more other definitions of "Blackness," "social movements," and "power" in more dynamic ways.

These ideas elicit further examination into the racial politics and imaginations of the Latinx community, particularly the category of Afro-Latinx and the complex experience of Latinx Blackness in a diasporic context. García-Peña refers to this navigation between various systems of racial identification, disidentification, and oppression as "translating Blackness" (190). For the cultural and literary artists in question throughout this chapter, Blackness is always a transnational, transitory, and translinguistic experience that brings those who identify with it closer to understanding the trajectory of colonial projects in the present. Furthermore, it gives each woman a language to confront the colonial legacy of white supremacy and slavery that oftentimes silences their bodies and experiences from the historical and group imaginations of their host nation.

The complexity of Latinx racialization in the US is linked precisely to the fact that "Black" is a much more complicated and politically charged term in the host nations of the groups in question, that is, the Dominican Republic and Puerto Rico (García-Peña *The Borders*; Torres-Saillant *The Tribulations*). García-Peña writes that in the US "it is not just class, but also skin tone, hair texture, accent, education, level of cultural assimilation that define one's race" in a system that has traditionally wielded a Black-white binary function: "Confronted with a US racialization that is very much linked to the open wound of slavery and Jim Crow as foundational experiences of the [US] American Nation, diasporic [Caribbeans] find that Blackness provides a language for confronting their new place in the host nation while interpellating historical oppression from back home" (191). Therefore, following García-Peña, Dominicans and Puerto Ricans do not necessarily "find out they are Black"; as I discussed in the previous two chapters, racism in both nations stresses hierarchies based on skin color. Nevertheless, these Afro-Latinx communities find in the US "a political language" that allows them to communicate their pain and silence—something that will also allow them to create political coalitions with "other oppressed communities around the world" (García-Peña 192). This is not to say that Black and Afro-descendent populations in the Caribbean lack a political language but that Afro-Latinxs in the US feel the necessity to choose between being Black and being Latinx because for many in the US those two identities cannot coexist.

Occupying the Border, Inhabiting Pain

The protagonists and poetic voices in the works of Nitty Scott, Elizabeth Acevedo, and María Teresa Fernández inhabit and grapple with the multiplicity of violences and painful experiences sustained by the dominant narratives of the nation as white and English-speaking. To do this work of comparative Blackness in diaspora, I look to musical productions by Nitty Scott, three poems by Acevedo ("Salt," "Afro-Latina," and "Hair"), and two poems by Fernández ("Ode to the Diasporican" and "My Grifa-Rican Sistah"). In each of these poetic and musical projects, the literary voice engages with Afro-Caribbean spiritual practices to address racialized notions of belonging and to work through these painful experiences. My reading argues that, by drawing on Afro-Caribbean religiosity, these texts construct a diasporic Afro–Puerto Rican and Dominican identity that draws upon a history of the African diaspora to intervene in a racialized construction of diasporic Puerto Rican and Dominican identity.

While these slam artists have received relatively little critical and academic examination, generally, when critics (Somers-Willett; Flores; Noel) cover their poetry, they do so in a way that places each of these women within the evolving canon of Nuyorican literary production. Specifically, Noel insists on an "embodied counterpolitics" of Nuyorican slam poetry that complicates traditional literary modes of representation (xxii). He proposes slam poetry in the Nuyorican tradition as revisionism: "Operating across page and stage, Nuyorican poets question conventional ways of reading and relating to the institutional forces through which these are normalized" (xxiii). I agree with Noel's contention that Nuyorican poetry as embodied counterpolitic counters both mainstream and alternative politics "in which the poet nuances and repudiates the pious, marketable multiculturalism of the slam poetry he has helped to create," and I find his focus on locality and rupture relevant to what I am attempting in this chapter. At the same time, my own investment in an understanding of Afro-Nuyorican poetry also refers to its preservation of an African diasporic consciousness regardless of national affiliation. To this end, I study how these women engage with a literary tradition that emerged in the US and also consider the ways they look beyond Western traditions and knowledge and use African-derived beliefs and folklore to reconstruct a diasporic cultural, historical, and political memory.

Therefore—just like Nitty Scott—to reclaim their place in history, Acevedo and La Mariposa (Fernández) do not attempt to recover history but to inscribe upon it their own subjectivity denied to them by traditional historical discourses. This revision is at once a personal and collective experience, as the audience participates in the performance and embodiment of these stories and feelings of exclusion/rejection from both the official national imaginary and a US Latinx imaginary. In doing this, these women conjure up silenced experiences that are placed at the center of the emerging discourses surrounding Afro-Latinidad. In the US, and through interactions with Black feminist and political thought, María Teresa Fernández, Elizabeth Acevedo, and Caridad de la Luz find a locus from which to communicate their personal painful experiences to a larger transnational community, firmly rooted in movements of Black political incorporation and struggles against injustices that have helped shape the Afro-Latinx community in New York since the 1960s. Through their spiritual discourses and shared emotional experiences linked with larger structures of racial and class oppression, these artists wield their magic to forge new political communities and solidarities with each performance.

I will first trace a historical and critical examination of slam poetry in connection with my theoretical proposal. I then analyze Acevedo's poetic production to study how this slam poet smooths over painful experiences in the present by invoking a spiritual connection to a line of enslaved African women. She invokes the memories not only of the slave trade but also of armed rebellion and resistance of her ancestors in the Dominican Republic. I argue that this serves to mark her place in the second diaspora, that is, a Black Dominican woman born on the US mainland. Second, I examine the poetic and musical production of La Mariposa to look at those moments of spiritual connection that unite Afro-descendant women in New York. I note how the Espiritismo traditions of Puerto Rico are oftentimes resignified in the diaspora as *brujería* (witchcraft) and represent a powerful space for Afro–Puerto Rican women. This framework, along with the spiritual trajectory of the chapter, helps me link how the authors produce spaces through intimate-spiritual connections to the Middle Passage and those souls that have been lost to the waters of the Atlantic. It will also integrate concepts of decolonial love as it relates to racial belonging in the US.

An Alliance of Love and Survival

Throughout the late nineteenth and early twentieth centuries, scholars anchored in New York such as José Martí (Cuban), Arturo Alfonso Schomburg (Puerto Rican), and Pedro Henríquez-Ureña (Dominican) published and organized against Spanish and US imperial intervention in the colonies. Later on, with "economies structured to benefit US corporations and sectors of Puerto Rican and Dominican elite, large portions of the islands were overworked and underpaid" (Rivera 22). According Raquel Rivera, this "was the case in the early decades of the twentieth century, when US sugar companies" took control of the course of both island economies, "as well as during the 1940s with the launching of Operation Bootstrap when the shift from a largely agricultural to an industrialized economy once again displaced large numbers of workers" (Rivera 23). It was throughout this period, from 1940–1950, that New York became the primary space of migration for the Puerto Rican community. During the 1950s large settlements of Puerto Ricans and Dominicans developed. Many of these settlements included "the Lower East Side and Chelsea in Manhattan, and the areas close to Brooklyn Navy Yard, particularly Red Hook" (23). As already stated, large populations of Dominicans started to settle after the assassination of Trujillo in 1961 and lived close to African American neighborhoods: "Predominantly African American areas such as Harlem (Manhattan) and Bedford-Stuyvesant (Brooklyn) flow into largely Puerto Rican neighborhoods like East Harlem and Bushwick" (24).

This close proximity between these communities led to various shared grassroots movements among Black and Latinx workers, students, tenants, and political operatives in New York. While an exhaustive overview of Black and Brown labor coalitions and cultural/political projects is beyond the scope of this section,[3] I will briefly analyze a few of the artistic expressions that emerged from this time period, particularly those of Puerto Rican poets, in order to trace the ways in which Blackness, formerly restricted in the US by the bounds of African American-ness, began expanding to include certain Latinx groups.

In the *Anthology of Nuyorican Poetry*, editors Miguel Algarín and Miguel Piñero frame Puerto Rican poets on the streets of New York as organic intellectuals who wield a critical consciousness to produce new knowledges that emerge from the body and everyday shared experiences. Algarín writes:

> The poet sees his function as a troubadour. He tells the tale of the streets to the streets. The people listen. They cry, they laugh, they dance as the troubadour opens up and tunes his voice and moves his pitch and rhythm to the high tension of *"bomba"* truth. Proclamations of hurt, of anger and hatred. . . . The voice of the street poet must amplify itself. The poet pierces the crowd with cataracts of clear, clean, precise, concrete words about the liquid, shifting latino reality around him. (11)

This quote is important to my analysis because it describes the particular importance of early Nuyorican poets in the construction of a new identity in diaspora. There is also a clear reference to Afro-Caribbean heritage and culture with the rhythm of bomba. In bomba performances, community and the intimate connection that the audience share with the drummer are of utmost importance. The drummer surveys the audience and tries to match the beat to the movement. So too does the poet try to imitate those around her. The poet as organic intellectual emerges from the streets to tell the stories of her everyday existence, with which the audience intimately identifies. The poet's voice is laden with raw emotion as she narrates the "hustle" of everyday life. The contrapuntal response of the audience echoes the voice of the poet, identifying with the emotions that she sings, which transforms the shared space into an intimate, ephemeral archive[4] of historical and cultural identity formation as experiences come together and a new identity is born.

Together in an alchemical emotional magic, the poet and audience create together a new space for themselves as displaced "Latino" subjects, inventing new names for their particular experiences: "Poetry is the full act of naming. Naming states of mind . . . poetry is on the street burning it up with its visions of the times to be" (10–11). Not only does the audience see themselves in the poet's words, but in this echo new visions are produced. Through the poetic performance, the community resists the call for homogenization into a normative US American national identity by reaching out in a call of friendship and love to their neighbors in the city who have experienced similar processes of othering. What is more, this poetic action also represents a call to organize together as a community and take the community's resources into their own hands through active and creative collaboration. The role of the poet is to come up with a new language that may be able to account for these new community experiences and coalitions in everyday life. This reaching out to include a community of friends or "allies" is seen as the way in which a new future may be enacted and a new language of self-affirmation may be forged. Thus Nuyorican is the language of this experience and it is the poet (the philosopher) who can play with it and mold it into new forms. This language as emotional and affective identity frees the community from any imposed colonial structure, as if without an official grammar, and permits the community to explore the creative limits of its rebellious syntax: "Around existing, formally recognized languages whole empires of rules grow. . . . The Nuyorican will have to continue to express himself without 'legitimate rules' to govern his speech. We have to admit that speech comes first. We first verbalize the stresses of street experience and then later, in the aftermath of our street survival, we will sit and talk of our newness and how to shape it" (Algarín 19). This loving call from the poet to enter into a new order according to the emotional experiences of everyday life in the barrio works to disarticulate any official national identification or patriotism in order to reach out and embrace the other in an act of mutual recognition and love. The community that emerges from this collective act may then be enacted as a form of resistance in the sense that there is a rejection of the colonial identification (legitimate language) and a recognition that takes place between the other and the other's others that "undoes" colonial/imperial discourses.

An example of this new discourse of love and collective identification in action emerges in the poetry by Nuyorican poet Pedro Pietri. Specifically, the performance of Pietri's "Puerto Rican Obituary" calls upon audience members to view their own lives through a political lens, examining the extent to which they are able to identify with the liturgical story he weaves. The obituary is at once about the stories of dislocation, survival, and death contained within the poem but also echoed in the audience as witnesses to the narratives and protagonists of the ritual itself. This poem, then, represents a decolonial pedagogy as it awakens the members of the audience to their own politicized existence and potential interventions they may make with their embodied presence: "Pietri the performer also asks his audience to resist instrumentalization, to tap into the political resonances encoded in their own bodies, to work through their (and his) own complex (in)visibility" (Noel xix).

While I agree with Noel that Nuyorican poetry such as Pietri's encodes an "embodied counterpolitics," which "mines the body as a site of political articulation while simultaneously testing its limits," I would like to extend this meditation on embodiment to incorporate the emotional, loving call that Algarín describes in his definition of the "poet" and that Pietri himself will explore in "Puerto Rican Obituary," published in Algarín and Piñero's anthology. At the end of this poem, Pietri writes: "Aquí the men and women admire desire / and never get tired of each other / Aquí Que Pasa Power is what's happening / Aquí to be called negrito / means to be called *LOVE*" (my emphasis). The last lines of this poem offer new social visions and spaces for racialized Puerto Ricans and other people of color in New York. These visions are at once pragmatic and at times also profoundly utopian, that is, through love, Pietri makes an explicit gesture toward relations that negates the poverty that is often linked to the Caribbean island colonies. In this way, "Aquí" becomes an emotional locus of enunciation that stands as a space from which to articulate a new future, one marked by coalitional bonds between Puerto Ricans, Latinxs, and African Americans (among other oppressed communities in New York). More specifically, the last two lines of the poem ("Aquí to be called negrito / means to be called LOVE") take up Blackness as a way to communicate a shared history and social condition. In a talk given at Penn State University (2016), Martínez-San Miguel analyzed this connection between love and Blackness as a marker of historically shared experiences of Afro-Latinxs through an analysis of Fanon's *Black Skin White Masks* and the novel *Down These Mean Streets* by Piri Thomas. I propose that "negrito" is not merely a racial marker but a collective lived experience that works to bring the community together in harmonious recognition of painful othering and shared future goals.

This type of emotional and spiritual work that love and religiosity does throughout writings by early Puerto Rican poets continues into the contemporary period. Similar constructions of Latinx spaces of coalitions in New York appear, for example, in the musical productions of Caridad de la Luz (La Bruja) when she theorizes Nuyorico as the "space between the Empire State Building and El Morro" (in San Juan, Puerto Rico) in the song "Nuyorico." However, rather than focusing solely on the Puerto Rican community, La Bruja describes New York as a space of intimate and loving/spiritual connection. She sings, for example: "Love is in the air / and nothing compares to Nuyorico / It'll make you fall in love, bésame mucho and all the above, / You'll be greeted with kisses and hugs" ("Nuyorico"). Mirroring Pietri, contemporary songwriters create an open space of relation in New York to define their community as one that is brought together through the shared collaborative, community-based work in order to make a comfortable space for themselves and their loved ones.

Nitty Scott and Ancestral Remembrance

Like many other dark-skinned Puerto Ricans and Dominicans, Nitty Scott is often forced to confront questions of political and cultural belonging and to choose ethnic alliances in order to garner success in the streets of New York. In a recent interview, she tells us: "I speak like a Puerto Rican, and I do my hair like an African American girl. . . . I'm owning and discussing the experience of being Afro-Boricua, woman, bisexual, then bruja." Defying the norm, Scott embodies the multiplicity of the New York City underground while searching for a place of belonging. But as sociologists Ginetta Calendario and Isar P. Godreau demonstrate throughout their scholarly production, these alliances require that one navigate a set of contradictions that are often intersected by a long history of colonialism and oppression.

Amid this racial, sexual, and spiritual contradiction, Scott argues that embracing her Blackness while maintaining her identity as Boricua constitutes a way of survival and strategy for confronting the painful binary Black-white history that is often imposed on her: "And you ain't gotta stand there like you ain't feel the pain / You ain't gotta pretend that you don't feel the change / And your silence much louder than the violence / So don't wait until I die to give me violets." Scott's pedagogical soundtrack, which speaks to a silenced and painful history of Latinx Blackness in the US, summons an *other* history of political struggle.

Her music gives her a language to confront the colonial legacy of white supremacy that has worked to silence her "racexiled" body from the historical and social publics of her host nation (Martínez-San Miguel 34). In her singles "Negrita" and "For Sarah Baartman," Scott proudly asserts her relationship with Blackness and colonial violence. In the first song, the artist imagines a space in Puerto Rico where she can come into close contact with her Indigenous ancestors. There is a mutual recognition between her Black body and the imagined Indigenous inhabitants of the island that forms a type of alliance against subsequent waves of colonial experiences (Spanish and US American). The song opens with images of a graveyard and references to Africanized religious practices: "It's very necessary / but I'm in a cemetery / niggas swear they're scary / but they're really temporary / Santería heavy have 'em seeing little fairies." The vision of a "temporary cemetery" recalls previous references to the historical haunting of diaspora and the residual pain that the artist occupies to exorcise the song from her body as locus of historical and spiritual knowledge. This space of memory is also occupied by the "heavy" presence of Santería and later mentions of Espiritismo. Both of these creolized practices are often implemented by authors and artists on the Island to recall the ways in which Afro–Puerto Ricans have reclaimed a space for themselves and the memory of their ancestors. However, the experience of the second diaspora in the US imbues the spiritual practices with a more political marker of Blackness and otherness, transforming Scott into her self-proclaimed identity of "bruja." It is from this magical space infused with Africanized spirituality and the ghosts of the past that Scott makes room for her complex negotiation of identity.

In the second song, "For Sarah Baartman," Scott reflects on the experience of Sarah "Saartjie" Baartman, who was captured in Africa, transferred to Paris, exposed in a human zoo exhibit with various animals, and ultimately dissected after her death.[5] Scott sings: "You strip the pride that is rising in my follicles / but these curves are not a caricature for your capitalizing / decolonize me as a western a metropolis / yes down to Mississippi all the way down to the west / I feel my back is breaking and yanking my chest / the fruit is getting stranger and the streets never rest / but this is for you Sarah Baartman / you're an art to this marksmen." Here Scott draws a direct connection between her body as it is consumed and marketed in the US and Baartman's experience of consumption under the colonial/patriarchal desires of Western Europe. Recalling the name of her album *Creature!* and the ways in which her body is often interpreted as "caricature," Scott astutely frames her life as Afro-Boricua residing in the Metropolis as one that is weighted down under coloniality of power and gender,[6] reminding us that colonized peoples were often judged as beasts and were thus constructed as nongendered and grotesque (Lugones 22). While the colonial "civilizing mission" was the front for exploitation and violent sexual violation, we can see this through the story of Sarah Baartman. As María Lugones writes in "Toward a Decolonial Feminism," this civilizing transformation "justified the colonization of memory, and thus of people's sense of self, of intersubjective relation, of their relation to the spirit world, to land, to the very fabric of their conception of reality, identity, and social, ecological, and cosmological organization" (745). Therefore, in this reference to Baartman, Scott brings to the fore the residue of the "colonial gender system" and the dehumanization that accompanies it.[7]

As Scott's voice yearns for change in her call to "decolonize me," she proposes a type of decolonial feminist border thinking as a space of memory and spiritual connection. She embraces the wounded locus of her colonial difference to see the world anew, claiming her title *Bruja*. This wounded locus, where she inhabits the pain of her position in the US empire, becomes coalitional in calls to the US Black community (echoes of "Strange Fruit" and Africa through Baartman) and other Afro-Latinx communities by her use of Spanish. In this way, Scott proposes that the way out of the coloniality of power and gender in the US diasporic communities is through mutual recognition, a resistance that is understood as shared emotionally and spiritually, not individualist isolation—the passing back and forth of lived experiences, values, beliefs, and cosmologies that consolidate the multiplicity of identities that she inhabits. This is to say that Scott is animated by anger at the past but also propelled forward toward a decolonized future by the spiritual love so often explored in the works of Lorde and Sandoval.

Elizabeth Acevedo: Beauty, Religiosity, and Liberation

Throughout her spoken-word poetry, Acevedo charts her personal journey as a Dominican and member of the Afro-Latinx community. Her migratory history and racial experiences are portrayed through metaphors of her body that conjure the voices of her ancestors both in the Dominican Republic and in the trans-Atlantic slave trade. In her recently published collection of poetry *Beastgirl & Other Origin Myths*, Acevedo writes about the witchy connection she experiences with the Caribbean and a line of ancestral knowledges that emerge from African religious practices. In the poem "Salt"—one of the first to appear in this particular collection—the poetic voice narrates the mystic experience of finding a carton of salt on the ledge of a wall separating her and the Hudson River, a body of water that imaginatively transports the poetic voice back to the Caribbean. In the poem, the mother scolds the poetic voice for pouring a small amount in her hand: "Mami upends the back of my hand. Says, *Deja eso, eso lo dejó una bruja*" (7). This experience of coming into close contact with the salt by the Hudson imbues on the poetic voice the power of memory and uncovers the deep spiritual impressions that her ancestors have left on her own body:

> Mami sensed the salt inside, knew the blue dog you are
>   painted to be.
> Close-lipped witch, I've felt your cowrie shells of teeth along
>   my wrists.
> I've learned to chew magic like it was cassava.

As the salt enters her body, the speaker recovers the central role that the mineral plays in the lives of Caribbean women and the spiritual power with which salt is often imbued in the African tradition.

Many Afro-Caribbean women writers including Dione Brand, Michelle Cliff, and Edwidge Danticat, for example, have reclaimed phrases such as "sucking salt" as a metaphor for the creation of radical spaces for Black women who have left the Islands, connoting adaptation, improvisation, and creativity (Gadsby 17). For the poetic voice in Acevedo's poem, salt acts as a forceful reminder of her position in diaspora and the spiritual and political power that this particular locus provides. For many Afro-descendant people in the Caribbean, salt conjures memories of the "flying Africans" tale, linking it to political movements in the nineteenth century. According to legend, the flying slaves visit their descendants on the day of their liberation to celebrate annually. However, some children did not want to lose their fathers so they would feed them salt, thereby preventing them from taking flight,[8] representing enslavement or a hindrance to the transcendence of enslavement.[9]

The salt that enters her body when she pours a small mound on her hand angers the mother of the poetic voice but also imbues her with a new power. Whereas the mother recognizes the salt to be a type of curse, making her spirit heavy and immobilizing the girl's body and soul, Acevedo writes that it has taught her how to "sharpen [her] nails into stone" and "sharpen [her] daggers." The image of sharpened nails and daggers raises questions of armed resistances to slavery and the conditions of a second diaspora. Although she is unable to return to the Dominican Republic or find a sense of comfortable belonging in the US, the salt that she has ingested—signifying separation and an attempt to break her spirit through feelings of isolation—creates a new feeling of rebellion. Thus, while physical return to "home" is theoretically impossible, her constant acts of resistance against both her displaced condition and the violence inflicted on her body by anti-Black sentiment in the US connects her to a fierce history of resistance.

Acevedo astutely relates these particular visions of slave uprisings and rebellious Black women in the Caribbean to Black and Latinx movements in the US through the dedication that accompanies the same poem, which reads: "After *Pariah* by Marcos Dimas, c 1972" (Acevedo 7). The rebellious attitude that the salt conjures throughout her poem and the visions of active resistance to the structures of slavery in the Caribbean are extended to New York by this particular dedication. *Pariah* is a canvas painting by Nuyorican artist Marcos Dimas finished in 1972. The painting depicts a defiant figure painted in red and various shades of black. On the bottom left corner of the painting, the figure wears an indigenous amulet accompanied by wavy black hair that suggests African ancestry. The collar of seashells, reminiscent of the cowry shells that the poetic voice of "Salt" wears on her wrists, reflects African religious beliefs in their symbolic reference to the strength of the ocean, the power of destiny, and female empowerment. Dimas painted this particular piece shortly after cofounding Taller Boricua, an artists' collective that participated in the Puerto Rican civil rights movement in New York. This workshop, along with groups such as the Young Lords,[10] created works that affirmed their Black identity and deeply rooted African cultural inheritance. This was done as a political stance to create strong coalitional bonds with the African American Civil Rights movement and more radical groups such as the Black Panthers and the Brown Berets.

In making a reference to both a history of slave rebellions and resistance to anti-Blackness/coalitions between the Black communities and Latinx communities in the US, Acevedo inscribes her poetry into a radical tradition of political and cultural activism. She embraces the borders of Blackness and the wake of violence that has historically affected both of these communities to communicate her position as Afro-Latina, a racial category that is oftentimes silenced in the traditional conceptualizations of Latinidad in the US.

This same intermixing of African and Latinx political imaginations and resistances inspires Acevedo's slam poetry production. In the tradition of the Black and Latinx arts movements, Acevedo utilizes her slam productions to weave together and produce her identity as an Afro-Latina woman actively working against political, economic, and cultural oppression. Acevedo's poems develop a relationship between her own anger and frustration at the current political climate in the US in an attempt to make a connection with her imagined audience that has experienced similar moments of painful racial anxiety, discrimination, and violence. In "Afro-Latina," one of Acevedo's most well-known poems, histories of both Latinx and Puerto Rican ancestors blend into one painful memory, which recurs to code switches as an attempt to negotiate identities: "Afro-Latina / camina conmigo / salsa swagger anywhere she go / como la negra tiene tumbao / ¡azúcar! / Dance to the rhythm / beat the drums of my skin / afro-descendent / the rhythms within." In an unflinching self-diagnosis, Acevedo dramatically recounts the story of her racialized Dominican identity as she grew up in New York. It is important to note that this identity is not one that is created in isolation but circulates and gains power in the echo of the audience. As she emphatically shouts "Azúcar," her audience erupts in cheers and echoes the same word as they recognize themselves in her words. Here, Acevedo alludes to Celia Cruz's hit single "La negra tiene tumbao," in which a strong Black woman walks the streets of Miami.[11]

It is this coalitional alliance through the sharing of the same cultural memory that Acevedo highlights in "Afro-Latina." The poem also underscores the complexities of Afro-Latinx self-identification, while simultaneously situating Afro-Latinidad as a function of overlapping painful cultural articulations. However, unlike other celebrated enunciations of Afro-Latinidad on the slam stage,[12] Acevedo mends the colonial wound that drives both apart with an appeal to spiritual remembrances of her ancestors and a decolonial vision of the future.

She begins the poem by invoking the pain of her childhood, where her body inhabited the uncomfortable border space of identities that seemed to contradict themselves: "The first language I spoke was Spanish / Learned from lullabies whispered in my ear. / My parents' tongue was a gift which I quickly forgot / After realizing my peers did not understand it. / They did not understand me. / So I rejected habichuela and mangu / Much preferring Happy Meals and Big Macs / Straightening my hair in imitation of Barbie." We can read the beginning of this poem as a recognition of the wounded locus from which Acevedo's body speaks, highlighting the painfully racialized diasporic body. In a moment the audience begins to feel the process of colonization that befalls the raced body of the Black Dominican subject. We begin to see how language, cultural practices, and food, as well as beauty, become sites of contestation and otherness in the US empire.

Acevedo continues to review the ways in which she felt betrayed by her culture and othered by the colonizing discourses of her adolescence: "I was embarrassed by my grandmother's colorful skirts / And my mother's broki ingli / Which cracked my pride when she spoke. / So, shit, I would poke fun of her myself / Hoping to lessen the humiliation." In these lines, Acevedo alludes to the poem "¿Y tu agüela aonde ejtá?" (And your grandmother, where is she?)[13] by Puerto Rican writer Fortunato Vizcarrondo. In this particular piece, the poetic voice confronts racist attitudes about Blackness in Puerto Rico by pointing out the hidden African inheritance that many on the Island share, embodied by the grandmother. However, in Acevedo's piece, this shameful history is located not only in the grandmother but also in the mother when the poetic voice herself adopts the anti-Black sentiment of the dominant culture and begins to turn against her mother's accent and language. Shame turns into anger as Acevedo continues her piece: "I hated caramel colored skin / Cursed God I'd be born the color of cinnamon, / How quickly we forget where we come from." Acevedo's performance employs pain and discomfort as a means of underscoring the difficult readability of her Black Dominican body in the US, as when she adopts the discourse of the dominant national culture and begins to hate her "caramel colored skin." Her body and language seem to become unavoidably, painfully visible, and through this hypervisualization a new space is created upon which she—along with her audience—can inscribe a new future onto their bodies through a spiritual remembrance of the past. As Acevedo begins to verbally transport the audience back in time, and the members come alive at the mention of the Yoruba: "So remind me. / Remind me that I come from the Taínos of the Río, / The Aztec, the Mayan, los Inca / Los Españoles con sus fincas buscando oro, / And the Yoruba africano que con sus manos built a mundo nunca imaginado." The mythical stories of the ancestors in the poem quickly become corpo-realized, imbued upon the body and the everyday experiences the poetic voice collects as she moves through her life: "We are every ocean crossed, / The North Star navigates our waters. / Our bodies have been bridges, / We are the sons and daughters. / El destino de mi gente: / Black, Brown, beautiful, / Viviremos para siempre, / Afro-Latinos hasta la muerte." In this section of her poem, Acevedo begins to use a "we" or "us" that draws in her audience, connecting them intimately to her experiences as a self-identified Afro-Latina woman, while at the same time creating a poetic coalition between Afro-Latinidad and Latinidad in claiming that their destiny is intertwined ("Black, Brown, [and] beautiful"). She is successful in equating the forced, violent displacement of the Middle Passage to other experiences of migration, recognizing that systemic pain is what brings their bodies together in beauty and love. It is for this reason that in the next poem, the poetic speaker emphasizes the love that she has for her community, a love that seeks out those others who have been broken by long and painful colonial/imperial histories.

Acevedo extends this spiritual locus of enunciation from which she reclaims and Afro-Latina identity to her own body in her poem "Hair." In this poem, Acevedo questions Western standards of beauty and implies that her hair is also a spiritual site of decolonial politics. The poem links the pathological representation of "wild," curly hair as "bad" to racial prejudice and to the exclusion of Black women from the political and cultural sphere of the Dominican Republic as well as the US. Her words in this poem not only defy dominant discourses of racial harmony and democracy, but they also bring to light the prominence that hair acquires in this Dominican racial and racist discourse.[14]

Acevedo intervenes in these racialized constructions of difference that stem directly from a long history of colonial violence and enslavement. As a Dominican woman who identifies as Afro-Latina, Acevedo critiques this history not only as it relates to Dominican women on the Island but also as the process changes in the US diaspora. She begins the poem: "My mother tells me to fix my hair, / And by fix, she means straighten, / She means whiten." In New York, the mother in the poem identifies the poetic voice as one who does not belong or one who occupies an uncomfortable position within society and therefore must be "fixed." These models are also imposed on the islands.[15] In this way, hair symbolizes a complex matrix of power and colonial histories that are kept alive through enforced beauty standards.

As Acevedo continues with her poem, she places the locus of spiritual power and memory seen in her "Afro-Latina" in her own curls that adorn her head: "But how do you fix this shipwrecked history of hair? / The true meaning of stranded." While hair-straightening has traditionally functioned in the creation and maintenance of Dominican group identity in the diaspora by occupying the liminal space between whiteness and Blackness keeping with the hegemonic ideological codes of what is considered Dominican, Acevedo abruptly destabilizes this construct by invoking again a marooned community linked intimately with the Middle Passage.

Acevedo resurrects the image of marooned women and a linkage with slave ship resistance culture. This becomes a political project suggestive not only in terms of the collective generated by the slave ship as a colonial instrument but also as a community that has been created in the fires of coloniality and projected forward by love. The spiritual connection and intimate community that the lines "hugged tight" consider, then, stand as a counter to the divide of colonialism and enslavement. Hair becomes a tool of recognition and resistance and a counter-ideology to the social death of slavery, that is, an affirmation of life and a monument to those spirits who have passed.

The interlocking tresses that Acevedo narrates and her gesture toward larger histories make it clear that her references are metonymical to the larger historical phenomenon of dislocation and to revisit painful sites of history in a didactic attempt to (re)claim her space in the second diaspora as a Black Latina woman. There is also a noteworthy intimacy expressed in the above lines that emerges from a shared suffering among fellow "shipmates," whose eventual outcome charts a trajectory of solidarity struggles and rebellion. This sense of identification expressed in references to "African cousins hugged tight," and the intimate-spiritual connection to the ancestors that inhabit these memories, inform the rest of her piece: "Our bodies curl into one another like an eco, / And I let my curtain of curls blanket us from the world. / How our children will be beautiful, / Of dark skin and diamond eyes, / Hair, a reclamation, / I will braid pride down their backs, / So from the moment they leave the womb, / They will be born in love with themselves." The love articulated at the end of this passage is one that stems from the embrace and recognition of those who were lost in the slave ships. Acevedo traces a line between love and her hair and uses this as a force to connect women in the diaspora. It is a promise, symbolized in her hair, to love the body of other Afro-Latinx women while recognizing the historical pain and annihilation that their bodies have endured, caught between Blackness and Latinidad. This love would imply an understanding of the responsibility that accepting it would entail and the potentially liberating politics that it may perhaps enact in the future. This "undefined" love would then work to disarticulate national love or patriotism in order to reach out and embrace the other. This community may then be a type of collective resistance in the sense that there is a rejection of the colonial identification and a recognition that takes place between the other and the other's others that "undoes" painful, colonial/imperial discourses.

María Teresa Fernández (La Mariposa): Happiness and the Embodied Borders of Latinidad

The poetic and musical production of Fernández (La Mariposa) builds on the historical archives of Afro-Latinidad in New York City. Both Noel and Flores have studied the rise of this younger generation of poets and activists working in the tradition of the Nuyorican poets. Flores, in his essay "Nueva York, Diaspora City," writes that these particular poets document the city's evolution into a "Latino/a hub," as the population of Dominicans, Mexicans, Colombians, Ecuadorians, and other Latinx groups began to grow. To illustrate this point, Flores analyzes La Mariposa's "Ode to the Diasporican," quoting the lines: "Yo no nací en Puerto Rico / Puerto Rico nació en mí." He concludes that this particular poem traces a "defiance of a territorially and socially confined understanding of cultural belonging" (73). In Noel's response to Flores's reading, Noel extends La Mariposa's conceptualization of diaspora by comparing the same poem to the works of Pietri: "Fernández situates her art in a diaspora city that is partly her native Bronx—a space distinct not only from the island of Puerto Rico but also from the islands that make up the rest of New York City ('cause I was born on the mainland / north of Spanish Harlem')—but also in the embodied territory of the Diasporican: 'Mi pelo vivo / mis manos morenas'" (145). Noel concludes by stating that, not unlike the works of Pietri and the Nuyorican poets of the 1960s and 1970s, La Mariposa employs the same "visibility politics" of utopian fantasies, underscored in her statement that "being Boricua is a state of mind and a state of heart and a state of soul and as far as I'm concerned that's the only kind of state it's ever gonna be" (145). That is, while stating that it does, indeed, make sense to read her performances as a statement of Afro-Latinx pride, Noel considers that La Mariposa speaks particularly about an embodied poetics of utopian geographies of puertorriqueñidad.

In this section, I would like to take seriously the emphasis on her Blackness that La Mariposa takes in her poetry in order to trace the ways in which she engages with a diasporic consciousness that speaks to the multiple levels of displacement that her body and her ancestors have lived. In doing so, I will demonstrate that it represents an urgent intervention into the construction of Latinidad in the US mainland, which often limits the voices that fall outside of its normative limits.

While claiming that "Ode to the Diasporican" underscores the spiritual state of being Boricua, La Mariposa also, not unlike the lyrics of

Scott's latest album, highlights the centrality of her own body. The speaker demands that we see her "cara Puertorriqueña," her "nappy hair," while close-up shots of her face and hands populate the official video of the poem. What is more, her Afro-Latina diasporic sensibilities are strengthened in her "Poem for My Grifa-Rican Sistah or Broken Ends Broken Promises." This poem is in dialogue with Acevedo's "Hair," as it traces a long history of hair as it has contributed to the ongoing colonization of Black bodies. However, unlike Acevedo, La Mariposa's rendition of this theme does not represent a hopeful future of decolonial love, instead it takes up painful memories and inhabits them to rescue a common, but often silenced, experience of shame.

The poem begins with images that stifle the reader and physically bind the body of the poetic voice: "Pinches y ribbons / to hold back and tie / oppressing baby naps / never to be free." Through the metonymic act of recurring to the speaker's hair, La Mariposa describes the painful lived experience of Black womanhood and the restricted space that the Black body is allowed to freely occupy. The poetic voice continues to state that these tactics to hold back her hair impede her from ever "hav[ing] the dignity to be" (Noel 280), hinting at the complex relations of power that are hidden behind the process of hair straightening.

This pain then involves a certain attribution of historical meaning through experience, as well as associations between negative feelings and larger histories of colonial domination. As the poetic voice experiences the pain of chemical burns, she becomes acutely aware of the limits to what is considered "proper" for her as a Black Latinx woman in the US. In this way, we can say that through the pain of the poetic voice, she occupies the borders of her Puerto Rican identity as well as her racialization as Latinx in the US. Going back to Ahmed's words on pain (discussed in chapter 2), by inhabiting this painful border space, La Mariposa intends to explore the ways in which her contact with her own culture (Puerto Rican in the US) impresses her with various feelings—not always loving—and how these feelings involve different intensities of painful interactions with not only her family but the larger Latinx community.

The speaker in the poem recalls the scene as if it were a religious ceremony, invoking a deliberate set of practices that must be carefully executed if the subject is to be properly sacrificed:

> The ritual of combing / parting /sectioning
> the greasing of the scalp / the neck

the forehead / the ears
the process / and then the burning / the burning
"It hurts to be beautiful, 'ta te quieta."
My mother tells me.

This repetition of the "ritual" year after year in the life of the speaker echoes the repetition of historical violence imposed on the body of Black women in Puerto Rico and in the US. The past lives of her ancestors live in the pain that remains in the present, perpetrated by the girl's own family and their desire to force her body to conform to their definition of beautiful, a term that also implies not only "Puerto Rican," but also "Latina." This pain is not just an effect of historical beauty standards but the "bodily life" of a narrative that seeks to silence African features ("'tate quieta") so that the body may comfortably "fit" into the Latinx community, an anxiety that the mother imposes on her daughter.

This parental intervention into the poetic voice's construction of identity in this particular poem brings to mind narratives of *mestizaje* propagated in the "*madre*-patria."[16] The speaker (as a child) holds the Afro-Latinx subject captive in space of pain that suffers under the mother's (intentional) failure to recognize her daughter's full self. The *mestiza* or light-skinned mother intervenes in the scene almost apologetically in an attempt to make sure her daughter produces a Puerto Rican/Latinx identity by altering the speaker's physical appearance and deforming the natural shape of her body. The mother's enunciation and imposition on her daughter produces a racial/cultural sensation of disconnect. The maternal intervention, and that of the larger Latinx community that this intervention represents, makes impossible the integration of the daughter into the fantasy of Latinidad, which affirms that racialized subjects are not always welcome within this particular sphere, thus solidifying an identity that, consciously or not, creates a physical and mental boundary between itself and Blackness.

As the poetic voice closes the poem, she reflects on the "broken promises" that result from this process, represented by various boxes of hair straightening chemicals ("Carefree Curl," "Kitty curl," "Revlon," and "Fabulaxer"): "Chemical relaxers to melt away the shame / until new growth reminds us / that it is time once again / for the ritual and the fear of / scalp burns and hair loss / and the welcoming / of broken ends / and broken / promises." As I discussed in chapter 2, the promise of happiness (Ahmed *The Promise*) determines the flow of bodies in social space. In this poem, La Mariposa offers her audience an *other* view of Latinidad and Puerto Rican identity in the US by considering her own body that cannot comfortably exist within its limits. That is, by centralizing her own body, which has been banished from both puertorriqueñidad and Latinidad, the speaker offers an alternative view of the happy promises made by products used to deform the body so it "fits" more easily into the social fabric of the US. However, the poetic voice considers the ways in which happiness and comfort within larger communities may never come in the empty promises of these communities. In this way, she reorients her body, and by extension the collective bodies of Afro-Latinidad, so that happiness is not necessarily the end goal of their movements. La Mariposa then creates an "unhappy archive," which "emerge[s] from feminist queer, and antiracist histories, as well as in socialist and revolutionary modes of political engagement. . . . [That is,] the negativity of a political figure as their organizing trope" (Ahmed 17). In focusing her energies on killing the promises of happiness, the poem provides another vision of Latinidad, one that restricts and polices the frontiers of its territory to discipline the body of the other into a sovereign subject. This is particularly the vision of Latinidad that an emphasis on Afro-Latinx stories seeks to disrupt, and one that Fernández links intimately to long histories of colonial occupation and to the omnipresence of Hispanism.

Afro-Latinx Expressions

In both Acevedo's and La Mariposa's encounters with themselves through discourses on hair, they explore the ways in which their identities have been rendered unintelligible within the realm of normative Dominican, Puerto Rican, and Latinx identifications. In the case of Acevedo's and La Mariposa's poetry, racialization marks them as "foreign" within their communities of Latinx and Caribbean women in the US.

For the contemporary reader, Scott, Acevedo, and Fernández question the ways in which colonialism exists as a pervasive logic of belonging, even within supposed racially blind societies. These poets bring to the foreground and complicate even more our conceptions of Latinidad in the metropole by rescuing those voices who remain marginalized in the borders of New York.

In these three cases, racialization of Blackness locates the poetic voices as outsiders within Latinidad; that is, they remain outside of hegemonic identity discourses—both in the US and Caribbean—even though these subjects form an integral part to both of these societies. Scott, through her musical productions, embraces her identity as Afro-Boricua to disrupt normative identifications of Puerto Rican-ness in the US. Her references to African diaspora spiritual practices and beliefs as well as to the indigenous past of Puerto Rico create a musical coalition that reverberates in the imaginations of her presumed Afro-Latinx listeners. In Acevedo's case, her "out of placeness" takes her on a poetic journey of remembrance to the liberation struggles of women slaves, tales of African flight, and the sense of family and kinship forged in the bellies of slave ships in the Middle Passage. On the other hand, Fernández brings painful colonial metaphors alive in her narration of hair straightening, an indoctrination of youth described as a violent and painful repetition of colonial/imperial historical cycles.

For all of these women, the narratives of pain and the spiritual archives/connections forged through these narratives make use of oral and poetic traditions forged in the coalitions between Black and Latinx groups residing in New York. For these reasons, restrictive and restricting ethnic nationalisms that extend into the metropolitan US from the Dominican Republic and Puerto Rico still barred them from full access.

Chapter 4

The Raw Ones

Ibeyi, Las Krudas CUBENSI, and Pedagogies of Resistance

> Ni amo, ni estado, ni partido, ni marido (Neither master, nor state, nor party, nor husband).
>
> —Las Krudas CUBENSI, "Mi cuerpo es mío"

In an article published on March 24, 2016, hours after President Barack Obama visited Havana, racist epithets donned Elias Argudín's title in the *Tribuna de La Habana* "Negro, ¿tú eres sueco?" The impact of this particular comment that adorns the article is twofold; on the one hand, it puts into question the legitimacy of one's racial heritage, and on the other, it builds upon and reinforces historically-rooted racial stereotypes in Cuba. The meaning of this phrase puts Blackness into question, when someone who identifies as Afro-descendent behaves or expresses themselves in a way that would otherwise be considered "logical" and "civilized." Among those who reacted to this article is Cuba's Afro-feminist blogger Sandra Álvarez Ramírez, who considers: " 'Negro, ¿tú eres sueco?' es un refrán que forma parte del patrimonio oral racista de Cuba y quizás también de otros países del área. Es una frase, diría yo, lapidaria, que pone en entredicho lo expresado por una persona negra a partir de su identidad y cuya conclusión es: tu color de la piel te condena y habla por ti y no muy bien" ("Negro, are you Swedish?" is a saying that is part of the racist oral heritage of Cuba and perhaps also of other countries in the area. It is a phrase, I would say, lapidary, that questions what is expressed by a Black person based on their identity, and whose conclusion is: your skin color condemns you and speaks for you, and not very well). The article received fierce criticism on the island, throughout the Hispanic Caribbean, and in the US. On March 30, six days after publication, the *Tribuna de La Habana* removed the article from its website, only to republish it hours later. That same day, the *Tribuna* published Argudín's apology, "Paradojas de la racialidad," in which he defends his choice of words by claiming that his title must ultimately win the attention of his readers. Argudín also seems to misunderstand the offense taken to his article, as he specifically laments the use of the word "negro" without considering the cultural politics of the phrase that appears in the title and again several times in the body of the text: "La palabra negro se menciona dos veces, en el título y la frase que lo justifica, la cual ni siquiera es mía. Guarda relación con una obra humorística. El periodismo tiene sus reglas. También permite algunas licencias. Entre los mandamientos del oficio, hay uno muy importante: captar la atención desde el título mismo" (1; (The word black is mentioned twice, in the title and in the sentence that justifies it, which is not even mine. It is related to a humorous work. Journalism has its rules. It also allows some licenses. Among the commandments of the trade, there is one very important one: to capture the attention from the title itself). First, Argudín seems to believe that the criticism of the article was aimed at his free use of the term "negro," claiming that it was only used two times and is descriptive so it should not offend so easily. He then tries to deflect his complicity in moving forward a racist cultural trope in Cuba by retorting that (1) the phrase is not *his* so obviously *he* cannot be held accountable for any negative connotations it may have and (2) the phrase itself is considered "humorous," and as a journalist it is his responsibility to attract readers. After all, this type of dialogue demonstrates the urgent need for a more radical anti-racist movement and broader understanding of the racial complexities in Cuba.

Many who responded to this article—including Álvarez Ramírez, Julio Moracen Naranjo, and Andy Petit—were called insecure and told that they had an inferiority complex for taking offense to the language. Naranjo recalls his first encounter with the phrase, which took place in a movie theater and made him physically uncomfortable: "Continuaba el sketch cinematográfico, con la imagen del hombre negro sin dientes, riendo y diciendo palabras incoherente onomatopéyicas. Al final vi como todos los que salían del cine, reían a carcajadas por el chiste, estoy seguro que en ese momento ya nadie recordaba el filme que había visto, sino ese mal chiste abiertamente racista, aceptado en aquel momento, por todos, como algo normal" (1). The joke, as I have argued in chapter 1, works to pry open the often-hidden intra-national borders of the nation. These anecdotes of pain in everyday life as experienced by Afro-descendent people in Cuba thus tells a radically different story from those official voices of the nation, who engage in a rhetoric of a revolution that has eradicated racial difference for all.

Revolution and Race in Cuba

For Devyn Spence Benson, the Cuban Revolution (1959) served as an early platform to openly discuss racism in Cuba and the long history of slavery on the island. During a televised interview on March 25, 1959, only three days after his speech in which he announced the Revolution's aim to eliminate racial discrimination, "Fidel Castro felt the need to defend this particular project in the face of strong opposition from certain sectors of Cuban society" (Benson 30). Castro spoke of moments in which crowds who cheered for his plans for the country fell silent when he talked of "helping the negro." Benson writes that the then-youthful revolutionary decided that this discrepancy emerged from "people who call themselves Christian and who are racist . . . people who call themselves revolutionaries but are racist . . . [and] people who call themselves good but are racist" (Castro qtd. in Benson 32). In doing this, Castro seemed to have opened a public space to address the issues faced by people of color, specifically those of African descent.

According to Benson's archival research, headlines of newspapers would reprint the speech made by Castro in March of 1959, and Afro-Cuban groups would pressure the new government to include in its plans a call for the termination of racial discrimination in work centers and schools and the importance of mobilizing nineteenth-century Afro-Cuban heroes of Independence as a way to unify the population. However, specific plans to implement these ideas were never included in the Revolution's M 26-7 *Program Manifesto*. Much of Castro's post-racial program seemed to mirror Martí's call for racial unity. In his "Nuestra América," he would even implement Martí's own words as a way to promote his policies. But similar to Marti, Castro had not actually mentioned any specific ways that these plans would be carried out and much was lost in long lists of other intolerances (Benson 32).[1]

Black intellectuals like Roberto Zurbano tell a similar story today, reporting and writing about the same nefarious representations:

> If the 1960s, the first decade after the revolution, signified a move toward opportunity for all, the decades that followed demonstrated that not everyone was able to have access to and benefit from those opportunities. It's true that the 1980s produced a generation of Black professionals, like doctors and teachers, but these gains were diminished in the 1990s as Blacks were excluded from lucrative sectors like hospitality. Now in the 21st century, it has become all too apparent that the Black population is underrepresented at universities and in spheres of economic and political power, and overrepresented in the underground economy, in the criminal sphere and in marginal neighborhoods.

The above text was published in the *New York Times* after talk of lifting the travel and trade restrictions on Cuba took the US by storm. Cuba was painted as a country beyond race issues, which had supposedly been resolved with state-sponsored inclusion projects and official discourses that recognized Afro-descendent individuals. However, anti-racist thought on the island shows the ways in which structural changes since the Revolution have carried racist and colonial undertones.

This is even more evident if we consider the July 11 movement in Havana in 2020, which drew fierce responses from Cubans both on and off of the island. One of these responses was the Declaración del Colectivo Cuba Liberación Negra, signed by Sandra Ramirez and Odaymara Pasa Kruda (a member of Las Krudas CUBENSI), among many others. Within this statement, they declare, "Somos personas Negras cuir cubanas que, desde una perspectiva abolicionista y antiimperialista, militamos dentro y fuera de Cuba, algunas afiliadas a grupos de liberación Negra y al movimiento Black Lives Matter en las ciudades y países donde residen." In grounding themselves in their Blackness as well as their queerness, they force the reader to recognize the many pitfalls of resistance movements that leave them and their histories out of the equation. They denounce the erasure of the realities that Black Cubans inhabit in their everyday lives, including police brutality, economic disparity that has been expanded due to the COVID-19 pandemic, and the persecution of their speech and even religious practices. This group of Black Cubans also asks that whatever path toward "human rights" on the island be grounded in the experience of Blackness and not the imagined utopia of a colorblind Revolution:

> Frases como "la revolución hizo a los Negros personas," por ejemplo, refuerzan el mito de que el proceso revolucionario acabó con la desigualdad y la discriminación raciales y pretenden colocar a las personas Negras en un lugar de subordinación e indefensión y eterno y acrítico agradecimiento. Además, desconoce los logros y luchas de las poblaciones Negras en Cuba anteriores a 1959 y les deshumaniza. Antes de 1959 ya eran personas. Tanto las personas esclavizadas en Cuba como sus descendientes participaron de manera destacada de las gestas libertarias y en el desarrollo económico, cultural, político, científico y social de la nación. Fueron protagonistas de la historia y no simples espectadoras que esperaron a que los poderes blancos reivindicaran sus derechos. La revolución no fue solo ni fundamentalmente blanca. (Cuesta et al. 2)

Here they declare that their objective is to create a new vision of Cuba, one that would perhaps not discursively work to dehumanize their bodies, voices, and cultural practices. For Cubans who are Black *cuir*, nonbinary, androgenous, trans, and so on, criminalization is closely related to the control and policing of their bodies (*sus cuerpas*), their mode of dress, and their gender/sexual expression: "El hecho de no respetar el nombre según la identidad de género, tan común en las detenciones por parte de la policía, representa una conducta represiva que responde al 'cis-tema' sexo-género por el cual vela la hegemonía blanca." In this way, they envision their fight as one that would build radical networks of solidarity between Black and *cuir* women, nonbinary Cubans, and those most vulnerable who refuse to engage with a system that has for centuries rejected their bodies, desires, and freedom. They ground their own revolution in sovereign practices that center Blackness and a spirit to overthrow colonial and carceral mindsets that limit Black life, love, and joy.

It is significant that two members of the Cuban Underground Hip-Hop Movement (CUHHM) played a part in constructing the document and call for solidarity in the most recent resistance movements on the island. It is not only indicative of the power that this music has to bring people together, but it also moves Las Krudas's radical pedagogy, built in their songs, toward the realm of praxis. For a "community of the heart" to be connected as one, a politics and practice of radical love and visionary joy is necessary.

Anti-Racist Spiritual Politics in Contemporary Music and Hip-Hop

It is from these debates that revolve around questions of race, gender expression, and sexuality in Cuba that the Cuban Underground Hip-Hop Movement (CUHHM) has surfaced and branched out to include many iterations and musical genres that span the diaspora. While a full history of the CUHHM is beyond the scope of this chapter, I do engage studies of its political trajectory in order to demonstrate how this music-based political activism hopes to act as a propeller of social change. I then go on to consider the musical productions of Ibeyi, a group who formed in the US diaspora, and Las Krudas CUBENSI, members of the CUHHM. For the members of the CUHHM, as we have seen, "revolution" is disconnected from the revolutionary and exclusionary discourse of the nation and is directed at raising consciousness through the pedagogical impulse of their lyrics (Saunders *Cuban Underground*). For Ibeyi, this revolutionary consciousness is taken into diaspora to forge cross-cultural connections between Black Latinx communities. For me specifically, both of these groups engage with a form of cultural politics that uses the memory of African history and spirituality to create a path forward and reimagine Black life.

Throughout the remainder of this chapter, I argue that Las Krudas and Ibeyi participate in this search for other ways of knowing beyond Western concerns through an intimate interaction with the orisha and spiritual beliefs of Cuban Santería. Through their music and their engagement with these practices, they help their imagined audience develop a critical consciousness of social reality, a necessary component to the envisioning of alternative future societies. Furthermore, as Casas-Cortés et al. demonstrated, "the participants of the CUHHM's critique of coloniality challenges the key hegemonic ideology in the region: the notion that racism is an individual concern, ended with Spanish and Portuguese colonialism, exists in the racially divided system of the US and ended in Cuba with the Revolution of 1959" (18). In this regard, Las Krudas's and

Ibeyi's music rearticulates marginality, and they use their unique position as historical outsiders as one of power and unity. In this manner, both of these groups have reclaimed their marginal space as the site in which to produce an oppositional view of society and engage/challenge national discourses from an Afro-feminist perspective. They each take on the spiritual locus of the *uno múltiple* to imagine new ways of being for Black Cuban and queer women. Here, we must ask ourselves, what kind of "new worlds" and "alternatives" are created by embracing the margin as a site of radical (re)articulation? How does "discomfort" and the failure to "fit" in the normative landscape of the nation push bodies to desire differently? How does this oppositional desire find a home within systems of Africanized spiritualities?

The goal of this chapter is to engage in a scholarly and popular investigation into the transnational connections between Afro-Cuban religious practices, music, and cultural activism in interdisciplinary and diasporic ways. I trace the ways in which the orisha of the Santería tradition are employed as sites of creative and political subjectivity production that span the Cuban and US geographies. This chapter and the musical productions analyzed within it illustrate the ways in which ritual, narrative, and music about certain orisha (such as Yemayá and Ochun) transform these contexts into urgent sites of complex negotiation and open a locus from which a contestatory knowledge of Black women's liberation may be spoken.

Yemayá's Many Paths

While an overview of the pantheon of entities within Cuban Santería is beyond the scope and focus of this chapter, it is important comment specifically on Yemayá, as this presence marks the productions of both musical groups. She is an orisha of the Santería religion in Cuba and was forged in the voices of those slaves who were lost in the Middle Passage.[2] She represents a syncretic spiritual being that incorporates the Cuban Virgen de la Cobre and beliefs of the Fon cultures in Western Africa. Yemayá was often conceived as a "goddess of the sea" during the genocide of the Middle Passage. Micaela Díaz-Sánchez writes that "when African slaves threw themselves overboard in the Atlantic Ocean, their lives became offerings to this underwater force as they leapt into the arms of Yemayá rather than live as captives in the Americas" (154). Contemporary practitioners of Santería continue to honor Yemayá as the mother of the Yoruba pantheon and she is consistently (not unlike the Vodou *lwa* Erzulie) refigured by feminist artists, authors, activists, and other cultural producers to imagine a new life beyond the colonial confines of geography, national identity, gender, and sexual orientation.

Lydia Cabrera in *Yemayá y Ochún: Kariocha, iyalorichas y olorichas* preserves the many iterations or paths of this particular orisha. Often claimed as a sacred ancestor herself (Otero 21), Cabrera underscores how Yemayá is rooted in the spaces between closed, definitive categories and geographies. She inscribes the presence within a line of spiritual thought that seeks to upend easy classifications of gender and sexuality in order to rethink what it means to inhabit a space of crossing. For example, Yemayá exhibits both masculine and feminine paths that bend to meet her needs—always culminating in a powerful act of creation: "En el más profundo nació Olokún, el océano. Olokún, la Yemayá más vieja—Yemayá masculino—raíz" (21). Cabrera also tells, through quotations of her many interlocutors, how before the emergence of Yemayá, the planet was inhabited by fires and burning rocks, but "al extenderse el mar y salir las estrellas y la Luna de su vientre, éste fue el primer paso de la creación del mundo" (21). In this light, Yemayá is born of an androgenous being, one that is referred to as "root" and "foundation" of the planet, Olokún, and manifests herself in various forms—at once a fount of life and powerful seeker of vengeance when her children are crossed. One of the most invoked forms of this being, specifically by the women whose work is the focus of this chapter, is Yemayá Awoyó. Cabrera describes this path of Yemayá as "la Mayor de las Yemayá, la de los más ricos vestidos, la que se ciñe siete faldas para guerrear y defender a sus hijos" (28). She also tells us that when Yemayá Awoyó leaves her waters to tread on land, she adorns herself with the markings of Olokún and crowns herself with the rainbow, Ochumaré, an entity that represents both sexes. In all of her forms, she is represented as a being of power, donning her starry mantle to lay claim to creation itself. In the sea, Yemayá presents as a siren: "La Yemayá más vieja tiene escamas nacaradas de la cintura para abajo, cola de pez, los ojos blancos, saltones, redondos, muy abiertos, las pupilas negras, pestañas como pinchos y los pechos muy grandes" (32). On land, "es una negra lindísima y muy vistosa" (32). Her undulating beauty and sensual nature while on land eradicates any easy narratives of the pure virgin that gave birth to salvation—as is the Virgin of Regla, with whom she is syncretized in Cuban Santería. Instead, from the impure depths of the sea, she brings knowledge and life—two things that purity, in any form, inherently squanders.

Yemayá's children, referred to as omo-Yemayá, are made through the rites of initiation, where—much like Haitian Vodou—Yemayá mounts her host. Specifically, Las Krudas will invoke initiation rituals in their musical productions and act as santeras who call out to their children, asking for them to gather and look to Yemayá for knowledge and strength. Her children take on the attributes of the sea-mother and make up both men and women. Yemayá is often claimed as the orisha of many members of the LGBTQIA+ communities on the island because of her positionality that disrupts colonial, Judeo-Christian understandings of gender and even sexual orientation. Yemayá's knowledge as border being is claimed by these initiates—particularly by the women of this chapter who engage with Yemayá's history and tales in order to forge a pedagogy of liberation rooted deeply within the spiritual systems of their island.

Yemayá's deep historical rootedness in religious and political crossings also extends to the borders between Cuba and the US, further establishing her as a goddess of borderland (id)entities. In particular, Regla, the town in Western Cuba where the shrine of Yemayá is located on the island, has historically functioned as a border zone. Devotees of Yemayá cross several waterways on their journey to Regla, which are at once sites of encounter, painful sites of memory, and sites of diaspora. In addition to this, the water between Florida and Regla, and that connects Regla with the rest of the Atlantic, holds the memory of forced exiles, violent colonial arrivals and drowned voices of the enslaved, and a liquid borderland that separates those Cubans on the Island from Cubans who have left (Viarnés 1). Apart from these internal crossings and the role that it plays as launching point to the US, Regla also functions as a transatlantic wound, as it was also the first port of entry for enslaved Africans to the island. The port holds at once a traumatic history of dispossession and also a space of future potential in the hopes of Cubans who come to pay homage before taking up their own crossings. In contemporary times, Yemayá is often seen as the ambassador to Cubans leaving the island without documentation, as many Afro-Cubans also make the pilgrimage to Regla in order to make an offering to the goddess of the sea before leaving (Viarnés 3). This makes Yemayá a concrete symbol of crossings and borders, at once bridging Cuba, Africa, and the displaced communities living in the US while carrying a fraught history of creation, destruction, and gender/sexual fluidity.

Taking these ideas into account, I first analyze Ibeyi's lyrics concerning Afro-Cuban spiritual deities and their interventions into conceptualizations of Latinidad in the US. I will argue that they engage with this particular type of spirituality to make room for Blackness and the shared cultural inheritance of the African diaspora. Second, I continue the chapter with a close reading of Las Krudas CUBENSI's poetic production in the realm of hip-hop. I argue that through a close relationship with Yemayá, Las Krudas takes on the identity of the goddess to create a pedagogical music that might perhaps work to teach a silenced history of pain and open paths for moving forward.

The following section analyzes Las Krudas's musical production as the group moves from Cuba to the US Southwest, particularly Austin, Texas. Using Anzaldúa's passage as a point of entry, this section also interrogates a set of musical productions by las Krudas CUBENSI, who not only incorporate African and African American diasporic spiritual reference into their work but also contextualize their work as deeply rooted in multiple racial and ethnic communities, mostly (Afro-)Latinx and African American. In particular, I focus on Las Krudas's portrayal of Yemayá and other entities of the Yoruba pantheon in several of their songs. Specifically, I am interested in how Las Krudas's representations of an African diasporic consciousness work to disrupt traditional representations of "border discourse" or "border theory" that manifest mainly in scholarship about Chicanx aesthetic and cultural and artistic practices. While Anzaldúa constructs her theory and border methodology from very intimate experiences situated on the Mexico/US frontier and expressions of mestizaje, I am interested in the ways that she gestures toward spiritual deities of African cosmologies that are often overlooked when engaging her work. The passages in which she references other spiritual systems complicate what Yarbro-Bejerano calls Anzaldúa's "conceptual communities" and expand the reach to encompass those racialized subjects who carry the experience of diaspora (Díaz-Sánchez 155–56). Therefore, Yemayá and other orisha take us beyond conversations of the border by centering a history of the transatlantic slave trade and disrupting an overreliance on mixture and betweenness.

In sum, I will extend these thoughts to engage with decolonial love and the integral part that bearing witness together plays in shaping the future. If, as Yomaira Figueroa-Vásquez has claimed, "bearing witness" entails "the recognition of the violence of dehumanization as necessary for forging ethical relationships based on love and affinity . . . [and] bearing witness to violence, to the past, and even to the present, is central to achieving decolonial reparations," then "the musical projects analyzed here do indeed bear witness to an ever unfolding past in order to imagine a future otherwise, free from the colonial violence that manifests itself today" (44). After all, within Santería cosmology, the concept of "belonging" becomes a matter of participation in a spiritual community beyond any national or regional allegiance. This process follows a path based on intricate ritual knowledge and sacred memories of ancestors and the spiritual realm—a conjuring that leads to thinking beyond and otherwise.

Ibeyi: Transnational Orishas

Ibeyi—the musical duo consisting of twin sisters Naomi and Lisa-Kaindé—has incorporated Yoruba religious and cultural expression into their music. Their name, *Ibeyi*, draws from the spiritual twin orishas who give power to each other. The duo appeared alongside Beyoncé in the utopian farm scenes of her album *Lemonade*, in which they return to Cuba and establish a healing space for Black women. The twins watched over the album and other women present to imbue the space with their ancestral powers of hope, redemption, and love. Their music demonstrates that remastered spiritual practices become a political move toward a practice of love and ethical relationships that bears witness to the past while looking toward a reparative future by questioning the way power is imbued in our conceptualizations of gender and bodies.

An article published by *Remezcla* in 2018 comments on the very specific histories of pain and bliss that these religious undertones imbue on the sisters' work: "To hear the music of Ibeyi is to hear the spirits of enslaved people stolen from Africa and brought to the Caribbean over the middle passage, filtered through the lens of Spanish colonialism and French Enlightenment. They lie at the intersection of the African diaspora, elegantly weaving West African rhythms with modern jazz, soul, and hip-hop in minimalistic arrangements imbued with a rich history. And rarely has that history sounded so beautiful" (Ruiz). Through a remixing of spiritual incantations and musical traditions, Ibeyi has successfully brought the religious culture of Africa to the US as Afro-Cuban women living in the second diaspora.

It is this recovery of Yoruba heritage and religious traditions that has so powerfully made a deep connection with Latinx fans across the African diaspora. According to the two sisters, the music serves to highlight Latinxs' long inheritance of African roots, which in their music, function as a type of healing for the wound of erasure that many Afro-Latinx people still experience today: "Yoruba exists in Cuba because of slaves who continued to sing their songs. . . . [For] everybody who incorporates it in their music, it will be important for them, it will be truthful. It would make a writing on the wall, and the more writings on the wall, the more people from that culture will connect with it" (quoted in Ruiz). This description, as told by Lisa-Kaindé, imagines a type of public tethered to a past that still lingers in the present but that, through an intimate communion with an archive of ancestral knowledge and shared experience, can forge the path for a new future of liberation. In another interview, Lisa-Kiandé reinforces this type of connection, *el uno múltiple*, that tethers her intimately to a community of Black bodies and spirits that comfort her and give strength:

> We sing in Yoruba because those songs talk to us. When we were sixteen our mother took us to a Yoruba choir, and actually the funny part is we didn't want to go, but when we arrived there we heard the songs for the first time we fell in love with them and it just speaks so deeply to us. And every night we get to sing those chants, every night we get to hear the thousands of people that sang those chants before us, and it's really special. (Edes)

Further, Lisa claims herself as a "daughter" of Yemayá, stating, "I was chosen by Yemayá, who is orisha of the sea. And it's, like, in our DNA. When we were little, I used to sing in front of the sea a Yoruba song, and it was the only one I knew at that time. And so when my Babalawo [a priest], told me, 'You're daughter of Yemayá,' it all made so much sense" (Edes). Naomi, who is the "daughter" of Changó, and Lisa move within this spiritual space to share the gifts that their saints have bestowed upon them. It is through the power of the sea-mother and the god of war that they come together and share their chants in hopes of forging a community of Black Cuban women who see themselves and their people in a new way—a love that connects beyond time and space to move each participant together and to demand equity.

This type of call-and-response chanting that connects people on an intimate-spiritual level to a long history of shared struggle makes Ibeyi's music a revolutionary type of contemporary pop cultural production.

Just as Yoruba spirituals became part of their own lives, these religious echoes started to naturally appear in their music. Their first LP opens with the song "Elegguá," which they claim emerged directly from their daily prayers at home. The song repeats an invocation to the Yoruba entity Elegguá: "Bara suayo / Omonia lawana mama kenirawo e / Bara suayo / Omonia lawana mama kenirawo e / Obbara suayo eke eshu oddara / Omonia lawana mama kenirawo e" (Vital force that through length and breadth appears, child who separates fissures and divides our pathway, do not cut the flow of spirit from me). Here, the sisters symbolically begin their musical journey with a purification ritual in order to open a new realm of dignity, love, and voice for Afro-Latinx women that centers their histories. This ritual takes the form of an offering to Elegguá and the sacred union of both voices in the sisters' trance-inducing chants. Elegguá represents the deity of the crossroads in Santería religious beliefs and represents beginnings and endings. According to Julia Cuervo-Hewitt, Elegguá opens new spaces of poetic creation and must be greeted at the beginning of ceremonial acts (302). Vanessa Kimberly Valdés also writes that Elegguá must always be "the first entity acknowledged in religious ceremony . . . the guardian of the crossroads . . . a reference to destiny itself" (8). In this way, through invoking Elegguá, Ibeyi begins to peel back the veil that separates the spiritual realm from the physical in order to glean knowledge to lead them into the future.

In keeping with such ceremonial requirement, the next song on their first album, titled "Oyá," features the sisters offering themselves to both Elegguá and Oya, the orisha of fresh water and women's revenge, in a mesmerizing mixture of repetitive vocal harmonies and remastered ritual chanting. In *Electric Santería*, Aisha M. Beliso-De Jesús analyzes these Santería spiritual practices as they manifest themselves in emerging technologies and the differing waves of knowledge and power they transmit to a wide audience. She argues that through the use of new media and technologies, recorded chants can imbue certain social spaces with the haunting marks of the orisha (78). This is to say that as Ibeyi incorporates the ritual music into their music, they make a critical mark on their audience, reminding the imagined intended listener of her African roots and the violence of her past that still lives on in contemporary experiences and political/social life. This spiritual imprint carried by the music can potentially connect the wider Afro-Latinx community to a line of ancestral voices that speak, bringing them together as a community that shares common experiences and histories. The voices incorporate the audience into their painful memories and create a ritualistic "we" that will perhaps push back against harmful and uncomfortable structures.

On their 2017 album, *Ash*, the title song moves the use of Afro-Cuban spiritual practices to the next level by filtering traditional chants through an auto-tune device. This particular move mirrors the transference of spiritual energy between she who chants and the audience, as traditional prayers are often contrapuntal; as one chants, the audience responds and, in the back-and-forth, all are brought together into one powerful community. The ritual words are elongated by the filter, which reflects the long history of multiple generations that are imbued into each syllable, as if drawing out and extending the chant recalls the vast history of African and Afro-descendent peoples in the Caribbean. After the ritualistic invocation to Elegguá, similar to the chants analyzed above, the sisters reflect on the deep imprint of colonial pain and the futures that recognition of this pain may open: "We can feel something's wrong / Can we keep going on? / We are ashes / Moving around / No more heart, no more home / Can't keep walking alone / We are achés / Moving around." In the first lines of the song, this radical intimation of love guided by the ashes of the ancestors frames the work of Ibeyi as a political and pedagogical project. This is to say that their music represents a space in which the imagining of decolonial futurities is constructed upon genuine intimate-spiritual relationships.

Beyond ashes, Ibeyi invokes another ethereal substance that coexists within the reality that is conjured in this song. Both of the women pronounce "ashes" in a way that recalls "aché," or a personal vital force that guides life in Santería. Aché is also used to recognize the spiritual attributes of an individual or group and functions as an ontological category that signifies the conditions of being in Yoruban cosmology (Laó-Montes 614). In a space where women are fragmented and separated like ashes in the wind, their subjectivities also become separated and scattered as they mourn a lack of "heart" and "home"—conditions that mirror the fragmentation of diaspora.

Following the pataki, or fable, the Ibeyi are healers that protect their kin. They are often described as "children of Changó and Ochún, although they were raised by Yemayá" (Cabrera, *El Monte* 57). In this way, the Ibeyi often act as guides and protectors and even help their devotees to avoid sickness and general danger. In being daughters of Yemayá, they also take on healing properties. In the passage cited above, the group Ibeyi invokes their spiritual namesake in order to suture a fragmented whole—and to change the kind of aché they emit into the world. With the loss of "heart," they claim they must become aché, moving through space. This particular move is imbued with the energies of crossings, and they draw their strength from Yemayá, who "allows [them] to mix up the logics of patriarchal forms of Santería in terms of how aché is distributed and wielded—allowing for a metaphysical reordering of energies and possibilities" (Otero 134). The song builds on the altar that they constructed in "Elegguá" to move toward a new space of imagined power, where reality is reorganized through their protective and healing aché to begin creating the future anew.

The final song on their 2017 album represents the culmination of each step we have followed throughout their discography—initiation, ritual, and the reorganization of energies. This final song is named "Deathless," and it is conjuring throughout their EP. In an interview with Steffanee Wang of NPR, Lisa-Kiandé speaks about this particular track:

> "Deathless" was inspired by me meeting a racist policeman when I was sixteen. I got arrested by this policeman and he said, "Do you smoke?" And I said, "No." And he said, "Do you drink?" And he would come closer after every question, and I said, "No." And he said, "Do you use drugs?" And I said, "No." And he said, "Are you fucking kidding me?" And then he took my bag and he threw it, and all my things were on the floor. And he froze for a second because he saw that I had a book. I think I was reading *War and Peace*, and I had Chopin. And I think he thought, "Oh, she might be intelligent and have something in her head." So he just gave me my empty bag and left.
>
> To be "Deathless" means that there's no end. Someone wrote, "They buried us, but they didn't know we were seeds." It means there's no end to love, there's no end to joy, there's no end to music.

Joy is precisely what this song seeks to invoke after the healing rituals of the previous tracks. As their aché moves toward love, the poetic voice defies the imposition of racist and racialized categories that violently mark their bodies as Black Cuban women residing in the US to claim a space of endless joy and potential.

The song begins with a second person singular "you" being addressed by a voice that speaks with definitive authority. This authoritative voice makes assumptions about the "you" of the song and recalls a type of Fanonian moment where the subject is violently and rhetorically put into her place and formed in the racist iteration of white authority. Instead of "Look, a Negro!," the voice seems to proclaim "Look, a Black woman!": "You're not clean / You might deal / All the same with that skin / (She was, she was) / Final looks / With her books / Left for dead in the streets / Whatever happens, whatever happened (oh hey) / We are deathless." In speaking back to the voice that calls her "addict" and "dealer," the song is defying an imposed logic of being to generate the conditions for a new narrative to take place within a space of spirituality and love. Lisa-Kiandé calls this particular action "joy," and here this type of joy functions as a politics that is closely tied to love, seeking to make the world in a different way. Frances Negrón-Muntaner writes in her essay "Decolonial Joy: Theorizing through the Art of *Valor y cambio*" that the joyful subject possesses the ability "to *share* his or her specific form of joy, which recalls Sandoval's notion of decolonial love and Lorde's Black feminist joy. In both cases joy and love are capable of bridging difference" (191). In "Deathless," joy is found in the defiance of order and in the knowledge that this feeling has "no end." In conjuring the spirits and proclaiming that they, as Black Cuban women, are without end, the imagery of being "deathless," they reach out to an imaginary of Black Caribbean women living in diaspora by invoking a "we." This "we" binds the listeners together as they identify with the lyrics of the song and invites them to share their own experiences of being pushed aside, being made "other," and feeling their own joy without end or limit.

This joy in the demand for Black life amid conditions that would see it snuffed out critically addresses the same matrices of power within colonial/capitalist modernity that their use of Santería also seeks to disrupt. The group's reliance on joy bestows freedom and autonomy upon the decolonial imaginations of the audience. As Negrón-Muntaner also points out, decolonial joy seeks eternity but can manifest itself in very different ways within different contexts and for different individuals. She asks us to consider: "What do we do with the various temporalities and locations of decolonial joy? That is, if there is no decolonial joy but, rather, multiple forms of radical joys, how does one sustain the other?" ("Decolonial Joy" 190). Negrón-Muntaner seems to be concerned with what comes through as a fragmented emotion, which lends itself to distinct imaginaries of future worlds that may even be at odds with one another. However, I do not believe that Ibeyi and their call for a joyful approach to Black and feminist liberation would share these same concerns. In declaring that the feeling of joy is without death, they celebrate not a fragmented movement but a fractal yearning for another way of life in which each member of their community creates their own feeling of wholeness and boundlessness.

This fractal joy conjured within a space of Yoruba spiritual power extends the politics of radical joy. For Bergman and Montgomery in *Joyful Militancy*, joy is a messy emotion—that is, they tell how joy is indicative of a process, a space of becoming, not a concrete position. For this reason, within joy there is experimentation, struggle, and a realm of creativity that has not yet solidified into something new—joy is the feeling that is experienced when one is in the process of breaking tradition, moving against, and building. They write, "Rather than the desire to . . . direct others, it is resonant with emergent and collective capacities to do things, make things, undo painful habits, and nurture enabling ways of being together" (29). It is precisely this kind of radical joy that the lyrics of Ibeyi intend to bring about. Being deathless is a challenge for them and their imagined audience to *feel* more and embrace an identity in difference—one that is emergent. Thus, when this joyful space is embraced, and Black women come into contact with the power to imagine on their own terms their own liberation, freed from imposed suppositions from the white authoritative voice, they reclaim their capacity to participate in the creation of radical futurities. When they recognize that they are being told their bodies and lives matter and are loved, and see their power in the shared aché of the sacred space, the joy that emanates from their bodies connects them in a spiritual-affective bond that leaves them more willing and able to confront the violence that they have had to face.

In this way, the musical work of Ibeyi conjures visions of the orisha, claims Yemayá as spiritual mother, and opens a space of joy from which it invites Afro-descendent women to connect and defend what they are building. The bonds of love, care, and trust that a newly found "heart" bestow upon this community, then, make them a people more powerful together. As empire is forced out of their lives, and with it the social death to which they had been condemned ("you're not clean"), more space is opened for love and solidarity. This diasporic call for joy, love, and life is also reflected in the lyrics and artwork of Las Krudas CUBENSI, who follow in the paths of Yemayá toward emergent forms of life.

Raw Pedagogies:
Cuban Hip-Hop and Challenges to Coloniality

Las Krudas CUBENSI began their career as performance artists working in Old Havana. They eventually began to explore musical production in the mid-1990s as hip-hop began to work its way into Cuban culture via signals that the Island would receive from Miami, Florida. The group consists of Olivia and Odaymara Prendes, a couple that proudly declares themselves Black first, then lesbian, and finally Cuban. Their name "Krudas," which in English means "raw," is representative of the type of music they produce. The knowledge and history that they communicate can be unfiltered and often makes others uncomfortable, but it is their philosophy that topics such as heteropatriarchal violence and systemic white supremacy must be fought in the public sphere, and if the space does not exist, they will make new spaces with their concerts, performances, and poetry readings. Their "raw" knowledge is also coming from a specific place and historical context: Cuba. This is why they adopted the second name for their group "CUBENSI" or "CUBAN-SÍ," a play on words that shouts (in all capital letters) that "YES, WE ARE CUBAN," despite what others may say because of our skin color, sexual orientation, and/or gender expression.

Las Krudas has been the study of several contemporary scholars from such diverse disciplines as cultural and ethnic studies, sociology, African diaspora studies, anthropology, and gender and sexuality studies (Armstead "Growing the Size"; Saunders *Grupo OREMI, La lucha, Black Lesbians, Black Thoughts, Cuban Underground*; Rivera-Velázquez; Zurbano "For Blacks in Cuba"). In particular, Saunders argues that Las Krudas's musical production represents a radical feminist political standpoint because of the way they incorporate political and historical commentary into their hip-hop art. Furthermore, Ronni Armstead argues that in La Habana, they "borrow from shared diasporic resources (hip-hop culture/rap music, African drum rhythms and chants) when fashioning a musical aesthetic that allows for the articulation of the local as well as the global" ("Las Krudas" 1). In addition to Saunders's and Armstead's thorough analysis of Las Krudas's social impact in Havana, Rivera-Velázquez studies the ways in which Las Krudas used their artwork and hip-hop production to secure a space for themselves in Cuba and the US. She notes how even within their artistic production, Las Krudas relies on symbols of Afro-diasporic spiritual and epistemological systems to communicate their radical call for social change.

This analysis can be complicated by engaging the resistance practices produced in Las Krudas's dialogue with Santería. This particular aspect of their musical production has remained underrepresented in the studies of the CUHHM, despite the large quantity of emerging literature produced in the past decade. By giving voice to spiritual presences such as Yemayá, Las Krudas takes on an activist role to highlight the systematic silencing and misrepresentation of Afro-Cuban women and religious practices in the island and the diaspora. This group employs these specific spiritual and religious practices in moments of crisis and pain (e.g., exile or patriarchal violence) as sites of recovery for the silenced and lived histories of violence, rupture, and displacement that official histories and ideologies hide away.

This intimate interaction with spiritual presences, particularly that of Yemayá, can be seen in the many collaborations that Las Krudas has recorded and enacted both in Cuba and in the US. In their single "Mundo azul," whose music video was recorded on the Malecón of Havana, Las Krudas invokes Yemayá as a spiritual guide and as antidote to their feelings of pain within the ongoing projects of empire. As the official video (2013) opens, images of the blue sea and waves crashing into the rocks that adorn the side of the Malecón appear on the screen, reminding the reader of the ever-present role that water and the sea play in Havana. The first woman to appear on camera is Luz de Cuba, another popular singer on the Island who also engages African-rooted spiritual systems, adorned in traditional santera priestess garb, a white robe with white headdress. As her body fades onto the screen in front of the water, she begins to chant:

> Colosal majestuosa ante mí, savia dulce, maternal con una incesante danza,
> Siempre luciendo su traje multicolor, de claroscuros e intensos profundos.
> La luna y las estrellas te adornan y fascinas a todos con tu belleza.
> Naces en la confluencia abrazando horizontes, dueña de misterios indescifrables y tesoros invaluables.
> Mis pies desnudos bailando en ti y yo con mi dialecto de tierra negra inclinada al sol lleno de palabras,
> Y escucho el rumor de caracolas. Lloro por adentro, lloro por adentro mis penas te cuento.
> Sé que me escuchas porque lo siento.
> Habrá una mañana, paciente lo espero.

(Colossal majestic before me, sweet, maternal sap with an
    incessant dance,
Always wearing your multicolored costume, of chiaroscuro
    and intense depths.
The moon and the stars adorn you and you fascinate all with
    your beauty.
You are born at the confluence embracing horizons, owner of
    indecipherable mysteries and priceless treasures.
My bare feet dancing in you and I with my dialect of black
    earth bent to the sun full of words,
And I hear the rumor of conches. I cry inside, I cry inside
    my sorrows I tell you.
I know you hear me because I feel it.
There will be a morning, I patiently wait for it.)

These first few lines invoke Yemayá as spirit of the sea and protector of Afro-descendent women on the island. The maternal and protective presence of Yemayá adorned in her traditional mantel of stars is called upon as a fierce force ready to lead her children into a new future removed from pain and discomfort. As Luz de Cuba sings to Yemayá, she slowly places on her head a white headdress. This symbolic gesture connects the singer to a line of powerful women of the Santería religion.

As Luz finishes her line promising a new tomorrow through the presence of Yemayá, Odaymara and Olivia offer their own adulations to the orisha:

Odaymara: Afrekete Awoyo. I rhyme you, in your name and
    with my voice,
your belly gave the world, blue varieties and white foam.
I call my warrior, touch, firm value crash, mysterious pride.
Black queen, regal Black, the oldest one, candela off water,
    smoke snuff, hull and sail.
Come on in Kruda worships you, oceanic amazon, Yemoya,
    Afreketona, Afrekete, Aboyo.
Olivia: Everything I tell you, is little. You are the origin of
    everything, past, now, future.
You are responsible of all this people Aché. Greetings and
    Blessings Yemayá til the end.

> By surrounding land with supervital mantle, to purify it all,
>   to refresh,
> with your salt you give the point to our sensual culinary.
> You possess us, you contain us, Your great power without equal.

Odaymara begins the ritual by performing a type of spiritual mounting, claiming that her voice carries with it the power of maternal creation held by the Afro-Cuban entity. Odaymara labels Yemayá as her spiritual "warrior," calling upon the ocean to wield its power in order to aid the construction of alternative knowledge projects. Las Krudas invites the deity "in" to their spiritual space of future possibilities by declaring that they "worship [her]," marking their lyrics and imagined audience as fierce spiritual warriors ready to birth a new reality.

As Olivia begins her own call to Yemayá, she subtly gestures toward the spiritual entity's origins in the violence of the Middle Passage and the haunting mark/imprint that this traumatic journey has left on Yemayá's children. By claiming to be possessed by Yemayá and taking her on as their spiritual "warrior" and "Black queen," Las Krudas symbolically undergoes initiation as *iyawos*, or "brides" of the female orisha. The presence of water and the white garb throughout the official video can be visually read as the washing or "nourishing" of the women's bodies in the aché of the orisha and subsequent mounting, in Cuba, of the women's heads. The process is closed in the song by the chanting of "kariocha" at the end of the video by all of the women involved in the creative piece. The word *kariocha* refers specifically to the initiation ceremony as a whole in the Lucumi[3] ritual language, meaning to place *ocha*, spiritual knowledge, in the head (see Cabrera *Yemaya y Ochun*). In this way, Las Krudas converts Yemayá into their own *cabecera*—referred to as the initiate's "crown," the spiritual presence of the orisha that has been internalized and "rules" the head. This makes Las Krudas potential rulers of other initiates consecrated under the name of Yemayá, and they take up the throne as Afro-feminist warrior queens and bearers of knowledge for those queer, Black, and women-identified individuals on the island. Here, I would like to refer back to my analysis of Rita Indiana Hernández's video "Da' pa' lo' do'" and the ways in which similar Vodou symbols (of the crown and sovereignty) were used to pave a way into the future following the *lwa* Erzulie. While Erzulie's love in Hernández's video was shared evenly by her children, in the case of Las Krudas, Yemayá imbues her queenship upon Odaymara and Olivia, placing two queer, Black Cuban women in a position of power. This distinction is important because it uncovers an inner power in the women and makes them the central agents in the recovery and dissemination of their historical legacy. For now, they move forward under the sign of the rainbow, wearing the garb of the Olokún, in order to call out to potential children and bring them in under the protective veil of knowledge and history.

By the end of the video, all three women chant Yemayá's name in a musical ode to the spirit, two adorned with blue and all wearing cowrie shells. Odaymara wears a gown depicting the four cardinal colors of Ocha (another name for Santería), representing the four orishas received by *iyawos* in modern initiations: Obatala, warrior spirit (white/silver); Ochun, spirit of freshwater (yellow/gold); Yemayá (blue and white/silver); and Changó, spirit of fire and war (red) (D. Brown 170). Not only does this display reflect the orishas received in the initiation ceremonies, but it also distorts the formal hierarchy of the orisha by wearing the blue at the top, closest to each woman's head. This elevation of the blue and white reiterates Yemayá's role as the "owner" of the Las Krudas heads, displacing the "father" or "king" of the Ocha pantheon, Obatala, as the principal orisha.

In this regard, Yemayá "purifies" and "refreshes" the hip-hop group and offers a space for a critical reimagination of Cuba's racial history and decolonial future. While symbolically claiming Yemayá as the mother of all Black, queer, and/or women-identified individuals in Cuba, Las Krudas creates a radical genealogy of Black women as descendants of the Afro-Cuban goddess. Under the presence of Yemayá, the women are resignified in the video through the power of the divine Yoruba ritual. They symbolically enter into a new divine order removed from the inherited and ongoing racialized colonial oppressions and enter into a new intimate community that is forged on loving connections between women—the proposed sovereign move that establishes their own bodies and spirits as the foundation of new life.

The dance, the embrace, and the love shared at the end of the video are not done solely on a personal level but also for the benefit of the community. In embracing Yemayá's love and recognizing the shared humanity and historical trajectory in each other, a new future is made possible at the end of the video—one that centers the voices of the Afro-descendent, women, and queer.

"Yemayá Blew That Wire Fence Down": Transatlantic Crossings

Working in genres such as contemporary hip-hop production, highly influenced by the CUHHM on the island, as well as visual artistic production, Las Krudas positions their work in the US as a vociferous assertion of those stories of migration/displacement that are often systemically silenced or forgotten. This is to say that in their representations of traditionally subaltern communities, Africanized spiritual practices function as an epistemic framework in which these subjects employ—as M. Jacqui Alexander writes—"spirit knowing/knowledge as the medium" to shed light on the agency and legacy of Afro-descendent women (4). Therefore, Las Krudas positions the sacred as a praxis of resistance and methodology rather than as a mythology of transcendence. The spiritual stories are deeply rooted in a long and painful history of forced migration and colonization experiences that continue to inform contemporary politics. Their musical and cultural production, through references to Yoruba spiritual deities, also opens a space in which they negotiate racialized, gendered, sexualized, and classed subjectivities.

As quoted in the title of this section, Anzaldúa invokes the Yoruba entity to actively resist the imposed border between Mexico and the US. Therefore, she makes space for an analysis of Yemayá in the context of the US Southwest precisely by placing this deity in a position of power that enables her subsequent inhabitance of the border, that third space from which the *mestiza* consciousness is communicated: "dividing a *pueblo*, a culture, / running down the length of my body, / staking fence rods in my flesh, / splits me splits me / *me raja me raja* . . . / But the skin of the earth is seamless. / The sea cannot be fenced, / *el mar* does not stop at borders. / To show the white man what she thought of his / arrogance, / *Yemayá* blew that wire fence down" (Anzaldúa 4). However, even if Anzaldúa does not fully acknowledge the cultural importance of Yemayá in the subversion of geopolitical borders, as explained earlier, by implicitly gesturing toward these painful Atlantic crossings, she carves a space for Yoruban religious cosmologies in the US Southwest as spaces connecting geographies and temporalities.

Las Krudas dynamically engages with these ideas, interrupting traditionally held notions of border theory and inserting at its core a deeply intimate connection to the violence of the Middle Passage and a genealogy of enslaved African women, which are often left outside of traditionally conceptualized "mestiza" and border narratives. This communion with the spiritual realm enters into their music production in the US mainland through their song "Wemilere": "Ven para esta fiesta / Welcome everybody, wemilere, este es el modo / Te invito a presenciar la fiesta, / Sienta la gozadera de mi gente, / Viva, presente, coronada, feliz, gozada, / Sienta la reunión de mis luases haciendo los pases, / Haciendo el bien, puntas inclusivas todas a mí incluida, / Huela a tabaco, aguardiente, / Huela a tambores agentes, / Huela a libertad, / A cicatrices curadas con flores" (Come for this party / Welcome everybody, wemilere, this is the way / I invite you to witness the party, / Feel the joyfulness of my people, / Alive, present, crowned, happy, enjoyed, / Feel the gathering of my luases making the passes, / Doing good, inclusive tips all to me included, / Smell tobacco, brandy, / Smell drums my people, / Smell freedom, / scars healed with flowers). Wemilere (also *güemilere*) is the name given to traditional celebrations in honor of an orisha. Elements of these celebrations include tobacco (many times to please Changó), libations such as rum to drink after the orisha has left the ritual, and consecrated batá drums usually in the service of Elegguá to close the ceremony.

In the section of the song cited above, Las Krudas incorporates this Santería ceremony into their larger project of forging transnational connections between Black women and queer-identified individuals—Anzaldúa's border subjects. The duo also mentions the "luases," or spirits (of Vodou), as necessary components of this "gozadera." As those individuals who have been historically left outside of nation-building projects in the US celebrate themselves in a ritual of self-care, the spirits accompany them and guide them toward a future of "libertad." At the end of this particular section of the song, "liberty" or "freedom" is equated with "scars cured by flowers." Spiritual baths in Santería are often seen as a way of cleansing or healing the body, oftentimes employing herbs and particularly flowers in the abolition of bad energy. Las Krudas borrows the images of this cleansing ritual as an antidote to years of colonial and imperial violence. Those scars become powerful spaces of liberation when the Black body comes into intimate contact with the knowledge passed down from the spiritual realm and in the company of other bodies adversely affected by the coloniality of power and gender. Therefore, it is metaphorically through the care given to the Black body within a spiritual space of love and connection that we might locate a type of radical politics. Las Krudas is demanding that the Black body be loved and privileged to heal the scars of the past and to demand that their lives matter.

After this celebration and invocation of the orisha in "Wemilere," Las Krudas directly addresses their Afro-descendent pride and the anti-racist fight that they see as necessary in the production of a decolonized future world. This song complements the coalitional desires—mediated by the spirits—we saw in "Wemilere" and the urgency to recognize radical acts of love between Black women. The song begins:

> En este mundo hetero-patriarcal,
> Donde el abuso blanco es el peor animal,
> . . .
> Hemos sobrevivido.
> Hemos creado.
> Hemos construido.
> Hemos perdonado.
> Hemos sufrido todo lo que manda los sistemas.
> . . .
> Pero ni vayan a soñar que les daremos lo que piden.
>
> In this hetero-patriarchal world,
> Where white abuse is the worst animal,
> . . .
> We have survived.
> We have created.
> We have built.
> We have forgiven.
> We have suffered all that the systems command.
> . . .
> But don't even dream that we will give you what you ask
>   for.

The song at once draws from the past (invoking the process of colonization) and from a future space where they envision liberation. By evoking residual discourses and structures of white, European colonial histories and hegemonic sexual systems that these histories entail, Las Krudas attempts to develop an emergent discourse rooted in self-love, coalitional lines of affinity, and shared feelings of pain and exclusion. This discourse is intended to produce a consciousness and vocabulary to discuss and understand the present predicament of (queer) Black women and women of color. The goal of this musical project is to anchor their listeners in an understanding of how the factors of race, gender, and sexuality, as well as the shared material inequality, become oppressive ideologies rooted in the colonial history of the Americas. The song continues:

> Hoy yo desaprendo todo lo que me impusieron.
> Hoy yo me sacudo de aquello que me obligaron.
> Hoy yo dejo atrás todo el odio que me dieron.
> Hoy yo doy entrada al amor que me entregaron.
> . . .
> Y si no hay na, nosotras lo buscamos
> Les deseo que se amen, como nos amamos.

> Today I unlearn everything that was imposed on me.
> Today I shake off that which was forced upon me.
> Today I leave behind all the hatred they gave me.
> Today I give entrance to the love that was given to me.
> . . .
> And if there is nothing, we look for it.

> I wish for you to love each other, as we love each other

By reflecting on the ongoing effects (and negative effects such as pain, anger, and discomfort) of the coloniality of power and gender and framing the present (toxicity of institutionalized and structural whiteness), they ask Black women and women of color to remember to love their own bodies, to envision a process of liberation that leaves the false colonial consciousness behind.

The loving bonds mentioned at the end of the song express the desire for a connection between women that articulates the enactment of a future community by embracing the very Blackness that the metropolis fears. In this way, love becomes another way of "knowing" the other that transforms the colonial subject into a visible agent of history, while at the same time unlearning the self-hate and prejudice that colonialism has taught. This type of love contends with past evils and traumas and the current social and political injustices that stem from those traumas. The racial/temporal borders throughout the songs are refigured through love as a reparation of the self and the community beyond the cycles of violence and erasure in a new decolonial pedagogy that emerges from their music.

Santeras Beyond Cuba

This chapter has focused specifically on the spiritual and loving discourses of Ibeyi's and Las Krudas CUBENSI's work in Cuba and the US Southwest. Their critical intervention is an important part of the Afro-feminist movement and needs to be critically engaged and documented. Their engagement with Afro-Cuban spiritual practices and rituals in their artwork and musical activism has crossed international borders in order to conjure a spiritual-loving community of women.

As we have seen throughout the songs analyzed above, Las Krudas and Ibeyi employ visions of powerful archetypal spiritual figures to be reincorporated into the politics of their hip-hop movement. The images of women, seashells, and the ocean suggest a connection in diaspora to the Santería orisha Yemayá even after the group leaves Cuba. Specifically, the translation of the goddess into an embodiment of border subjects gets to the heart of Las Krudas's and Ibeyi's musical production, which articulates Black queer women's experiences of transformation, underscoring the urgent need to address historical, cultural, and psychological legacies of trauma and pain. By giving a voice to Afro-descendent women's silenced histories, Las Krudas creates a radical space of liberation that challenges Cuban hegemonic discourses that have failed to substantially address Black women.

In their attempt to capture the history of Black queer women and imagine an alternative future free of the coloniality of power and gender, Las Krudas CUBENSI and Ibeyi construct a rich musical narrative that reappropriates folk stories, Santería symbols, and queer love to produce a space for the celebration of a diasporic culture of Black queer women long ignored by official discourses on the island and beyond.

Conclusion

Conjuring Paths, Points of Departure

Through stories of pain, spiritual healing, love, and joy, the women in *Feminist Spiritualities* not only share their experiences of being worn down but also provide resources for moving forward in difference. As these women embrace their own histories, emotions, and spiritual visions, they each highlight the political necessity of emphasizing lived experiences to forge new theories. They also shape themselves as spiritual healers, promoting a type of love found in diasporic *uno múltiple*; that is, each woman of this text seeks out intimate ways to bridge the past, present, and future. Their projects push against division and domination in order to bring women of the Afro-Caribbean together and honor traditions that have been criminalized and demonized for centuries. They push against Western-Cartesian logics that are fundamentally about dividing the mind from the body and the heart from the spirit to inhabit the intersections of time and space as multiplicity through love.

The four cases I have studied represent critical approximations to Blackness within Caribbean and Latinx worlds by granting it a transcorporal dimension, disrupting the spatiotemporal flow of Western time. The protagonists, self-reflections, and intimate-spiritual meditations represent a defiant, rebellious spirit that works on the emotional relationship between bodies, space, and time—making room for *other* types of existence and movement-in-relation. This rebellious spirit not only conjures visions of liberated future worlds but also wields history to levy its power against those who have left them out. While these creative endeavors do not necessarily offer immediate solutions to deeply embedded inequities, the spirit of connection, love, and community offer urgent political points of departure, especially for the current moment (as I write after the global Black Lives Matter protests in 2020 and 2021). The radical spirit of the *uno múltiple* as well as the site of collective knowledge conjured in loving communion signals the potentiality to imagine otherwise, to dare to rip open space and time to walk together in a "dance" imbued with ashé—to glean knowledge together that may perhaps lead toward a new path.

This methodology of preserving, documenting, and enacting diasporic spirituality as a force of community building and alternative knowledge creation necessarily spills beyond the confines of the literary and cultural works within the pages of this book. Others continue to tap into this ceremony of spirit manifestation and cocreation. For example, in April of 2020, Alaí Reyes-Santos and Ana-Maurine Lara launched the digital humanities project titled Caribbean Women Healers Project. This project honors native and Africanized spiritual traditions and practices through what both women refer to as "deep listening." In conversations with elders, both Reyes-Santos and Lara listen to and learn from everything they are told, without interruption or question—this is a spiritual code that is rooted in respect and the knowledge that everything around them is alive and is imbued with lifeforce, a clear example of becoming multiple in practice (see figure C.1).

Reyes-Santos and Lara speak about their conceptualization of "deep listening" on their website (https://healers.uoregon.edu), seen in Figure C.1 below:

Figure C.1. Caribbean Women Healer's Project Welcome Portal. Source: Caribbean Women Healers Project.

The first thing we were taught was deep listening. Over the last decade, we have learned to understand deep listening as a practice that is central to the pedagogical methods of Caribbean religious traditions. It involves listening with the whole body, to what is both articulated and unarticulated, and paying attention to what is seen and not seen. Deep listening is about observing collective ritual behaviors and the utterances that take place between people. To listen deeply is to be a part of, extending beyond ethnographic participant observation and into the realm of being in loving community. To listen deeply is to also listen to dreams, to listen to "the counsel of spirits and ancestors" (Abebbe Oshun 2016), to dance to music, and to be present to the ups and downs of our elders' (and their families') lives. Deep listening changed us, as researchers, because it changed our orientations to "being," to space-time, and to our relations.

This underscores what Lara lays out as the foundation of the project: *convivir*, *compartir*, and *cara-a-cara*. Each of these ideas invokes an intimacy that is not bound by historical logic. They conjure an intimacy that transcends time and space, generated through stories, emotion, being-in-community, and finding knowledge in "each other's faces." This runs counter to the academic project of the institutionalized university, where, as Lara claims, "knowledge has to be objective, disinterested; it has to be from our minds and not our hearts or spirits." Thus, love and spirit come to the fore, guiding an alternative methodology for cocreating knowledge rooted in Black and Indigenous communities that can be put to use for these same communities.

This practice of walking together, deep listening, intimate sharing, and engagement with a line of ancestors runs counter to the values of the academic project that says that knowledge has to be objective, that it has to be rigorously hierarchical and removed from personal relationships. In the Healers project, we see that holding space for each other and the relationships we establish in a space of spiritual and loving intimacy is central to the epistemology that emerges within its digital pages. It is within this space that ancestral knowledge, moments of joy, and rebellious spirits are conjured as we open a fractal portal to touch an epistemological mode of consciousness that ardently pushes against the destructive wake of Western modernity.

In the presentation of this project in 2022, Las Brujas de Brooklyn, Afro-Dominican twins Dr. Miguelina Rodriguez and Dr. Griselda Rodriguez-Solomon, joined Reyes-Santos and Lara in conversation at the CUNY Graduate Center. Las Brujas works primarily to dispel fear and misinformation surrounding Afro-diasporic religious practices, particularly those that emerged historically in relation to the Caribbean geography. In their conversation about the Healers project, they invite the viewer and audience into their sacred space by engaging in an Adi mantra in order to tune into a higher consciousness—that is, to connect to a creative wisdom, to shed light into the dark and, conversely, to bring darkness into the light. In this way, they grounded the project in a loving and spiritual connection that weaves its radical presence through each participant.

Griselda elaborates on the urgency of the knowledge made possible through rebellious spiritual work: "This is revolutionary . . . what we know is that the people being archived in this project were not supposed to be here. Via the Crusades, the Inquisition, starting around the 12th century in Europe, the Trans-Atlantic Slave Trade, through so many attempts at ostracizing and even obliterating the so-called other . . . the healer was often the first to be targeted because they were often the most powerful in the community. And they still are." She goes on to claim that this work becomes much more important within "the dehumanizing space of Academia." She claims that the "masculine-patriarchal" cult of objectivity within the academy "needs to continue to die out" because it does not serve those populations, specifically Black and Brown, who understand their world through ritualistic and emotional/embodied experience—and when they are pushed to remove themselves, their voices, and their experiences from work that is first and foremost about their own communities, the urgent need to connect with and change their circumstances is lost—leading both twins to ask: "How can we be the objective anthropologist *and* work on a project where we need to be at the center?"

This question drives the writers and cultural producers of this book. Each of these women looks to place agency and ownership of historical processes and cycles back into the hands of Black women and African diasporic forms of knowledge in a loving move to heal themselves and their communities. Each does this through an engagement with Afro-diasporic spiritual systems. Because it has been Black women who have historically carried spiritual traditions, the women here all speak from a space of subjectivity. Thus, each of them forces us to question the bifurcations of knowledge and existence often imposed by systems grounded in a violent logic that has historically worked to dehumanize and discredit—body, spirit, and intellect come together to forge connections and to archive experiences, which lead us to radically question what can be understood as theory. What becomes central are stories passed down by abuelitas, tías, babalawos, santeras, and brujas that guide down different paths and give permission to carve space for alternative forms of connection, rooted in a deep love for Black bodies, stories, families, and histories.

The voices throughout this project all partake in this particular type of spiritual identity politics to validate themselves as Afro-Latinx/Caribbean women while demonstrating solidarity through discourses of decolonial love and ancestral affinity with others throughout the islands and the US diaspora. In this way, the literary and cultural works studied in this book beg us to question populations across the Caribbean and US diaspora that are steeped in colonial histories of white supremacy, thinly veiled as mestizo and Hispanic nationalisms. They aim to actively resist the myriad policies of forgetting in the name of national harmony as we have seen in each of the chapters. At the heart this book lies a spirit of reciprocal cultural exchange among Black women from all over the Afro-Caribbean, firmly rooted in deeper struggles of state-sanctioned terror against Black bodies and spiritual traditions. And the valorization and dissemination of Black, African, and Afro-diasporic epistemologies and customs that occur in their work thus constitute a "reeducational" endeavor, fostering spiritual restoration and empowerment beyond national categories. In this way, the logic of a Western spirit of linear progression, a culture of individuality, and Judeo-Christian coloniality are renegotiated and reframed—thus locating the space of uno múltiple as one of radical pedagogical importance; when lovingly embraced, the many-in-one is a space of knowledge production that has much to teach about how conceptualizations of nation, community, and Hispanidad are undergirded by a xenophobic and anti-Black modernity.

This is, for example, the project of Arroyo Pizarro, as she works to mine the stories of enslaved Black women from the archives of Puerto Rico and bring recognition through her literary production to the ongoing effects of both European and US colonialism on the island to a wider audience; it is the project of Hernández as she engages the tiresome rhetoric of Dominican citizenship, which seeks to exclude the (dark) Haitian migrant; it is what Acevedo searches for as she struggles to express herself caught between the hegemonic categories of white, Black, and Latinx in the US, as well as the fraught relationship that she shares with old racial assemblages carried over from the Dominican Republic; and it is the project of Odaymara and Olivia Prendes to create a new pedagogy through their lyrics that mightpave the way toward understanding a collective history to move forward in the struggle for liberation. Together, these women are (dis)connected parts of a whole diasporic body, held together and pushed forward by a shared spirit of liberation, not only to "make room" but to take control of the imaginary and open paths toward alternative futures of loving and joyful resistance.

Notes

Introduction

1. This "ritmo" of connection also physically binds the pages of this book together. The cover image, expertly chosen by Aimee Harrison, depicts two women enraptured in ceremony in Cartagena, Colombia. Although a direct analysis of this context falls outside of the scope of this study, the image is powerful in that it gestures toward other geographies and bodies that must be brought into this conversation and that spill beyond and disrupt the confines of my book.

2. Later in this interview, she underscores the importance of reclaiming her body, spirit, and emotions as a radical act of defiance: "A mí me recuerda muchísimo a los conquistadores españoles que decían que no tenemos alma. Y como no tenemos alma, en el cuerpo este de nuestra comunidad no hay nada en el corazón. Y no podemos sentir ni el dolor ni el placer . . . ¡anjá coño! Entonces nos jodimos. Y por eso yo trabajo desde el placer y la alegría" (I am reminded of the Spanish conquistadors [and European explorers] who used to say we do not have a soul in order to exclude us from the human. And, since we lacked a soul, in this collective body there can be nothing in our hearts. Thus, we cannot truly feel pleasure or pain . . . well fuck! Then we are all fucked! It is for this very reason that I choose to work from a position of pleasure and joy).

3. My use of the first-person plural in this book will be accompanied by quotation marks in those moments when I, writing as a white scholar, will not include myself in the imagined collective. This boundary is important to delineate because the futures and presents being imagined in many of these works do not necessarily represent "universal" visions of change. They each come from a very specific context and are uttered for a certain group of historically dispossessed peoples that forge spaces for themselves and on their own terms. I am also careful with my citations, as these represent the foundation upon which I cocreate this argument. I will not rely, as Báez hints, on what many would term "traditional cultural and literary theorists." Instead, I follow the paths laid out by Black, Latine,

and Caribbean queer- and women-identified intellectuals. These voices guide my conclusions but are also given the space and opportunity to speak for themselves. My hope is that this text will not be read in isolation but in tandem with the authors cited. This is only one piece of a larger conversation in which the voices of Black academics must be amplified, celebrated, and engaged.

4. Unless otherwise noted, all translations are mine.

5. Here I use the term "ghost" following Dixa Ramírez's theorization in her book *Colonial Phantoms: Belonging and Refusal in the Dominican Americas, from the 19th Century to the Present*. In this text, Ramírez invokes the "gap" or silences of racial and historical archives in the Dominican Republic as an act of ghosting—that is, the misrecognition and absence of Black bodies in the national imagination.

6. Mignolo engages with decolonial feminists such as Gloria Anzaldúa, Cherríe Moraga, Chela Sandoval, and Chandra Mohanty to theorize this knowledge at the borders of modernity/coloniality. Mignolo's project theorizes ways in which we might rethink the legacies of colonialism and the various forms in which they live on in our contemporary time.

7. Judith Sierra-Rivera defines the emotional locus of enunciation as a space from which connectivity to the other through emotion underscores the limits of reality in order to offer a third option—carving a new (oppositional) space in social fabric. See Sierra-Rivera.

8. In an essay of the same name, "On the Edges of Belonging," Xhercis Méndez asks: "What forms of radical love and vulnerabilities must I embrace in order to activate new modes of belonging, safety and support? How do we cultivate intentional rhizomes of belonging that include care for survivors of systemic and intergenerational harm, care for those of us on the edges, that include freedom from assault, mobility unrestricted by militarised police, the abolition of prisons, and the cultivation of joy, healing and support even in times of crisis?"

Chapter 1

1. Throughout this chapter I refer to Puerto Rico as a "nation." Following Jorge Duany, in *The Puerto Rican Nation*, I use the term nation to underscore a history and culture shared by the island: "The vast majority of Puerto Ricans—on and off the island—imagine themselves as part of a broader community that meets all the standard criteria of nationality, such as territory, language, or culture, except sovereignty" (4). This conceptualization emerges from Duany's distinction between political nationalism and cultural nationalism, which is based on "the assertion of the moral and spiritual autonomy of each people" (5). In this sense, diasporic communities play an essential part in the Puerto Rican national imagination

and will be considered as an extension of the archipelago, a type of mainland Caribbean, particularly in chapter 3 of this book.

2. As writer and scholar Hilda Lloréns comments in her blog post titled "Una breve reflexión sobre la práctica blanca de pintarse el rostro de negro/negra (o "rostro-negro"/Blackface) en Puerto Rico," "Este importante y fructífero debate sobre la práctica de 'rostro negro' en Puerto Rico, ha traído a la superficie la 'fragilidad blanca', que es otra de las características en culturas donde se ha naturalizado la supremacía blanca" (2). She further demands that the island recognize that racism in Puerto Rico is not a colonized way of thinking imported from the US, but it is very much alive in Puerto Rican culture and a very intimate part of Puerto Rican history.

3. The article became the immediate target of condemnation and opened a space for a more nuanced and inclusive analysis of race in Puerto Rico, engaging the voices of Afro-Puerto Ricans who spoke against the colonial and racist histories implicit in Montero's reading. Besides Santos-Febres and Arroyo Pizarro, other authors and intellectuals responded to the publication including Lloréns, Isar Godreau, and Maria García-Quijano.

4. This event represents a worldwide gathering of writers and literature enthusiasts organized by the Salón Literario Libroamérica de Puerto Rico. The idea behind this event is to pay homage to "the word" as a fundamental form of social and cultural expression. Arroyo Pizarro and Santos-Febres are consistently involved in this event and deliver talks and readings about Blackness, feminism, and anti-imperial political imaginations. In this way, the authors participate in an effort to intervene in the sociocultural imagination on the Island through their literary work.

5. This particular project is done in conjunction with the Decade for the People of African Descent launched by the United Nations in 2015. The initiative acknowledges the history of the African diaspora and encourages a dialogue on identity and political issues. Arroyo Pizarro has worked in tandem with a team of researchers to rescue information from sites such the Archivo General Historico de San German and the Archivo General de Viejo San Juan. From these investigations have emerged fictionalized stories of characters that actively opposed the power of their oppressors.

6. Both Yolanda Martínez-San Miguel (*Caribe Two Ways* 150–65) and Alaí Reyes-Santos (40–45) underscore the ways in which ethnic humor, jokes, and comical representations construct a border between those who are able to comfortably live out their Puerto Rican-ness and those who fall short because of the perception that they are poorer, less educated, and less developed. Martínez-San Miguel uses ethnic humor in Puerto Rico to demonstrate what she terms the island's "interethnic borders." In her *Caribe Two Ways*, she writes: "El chiste étnico funciona como otro de los discursos represivos contra las identidades

minoritarias" (163). Martínez-San Miguel goes on to refer to the "repulsión" that the national subject feels toward the racialized "other" (the Dominican immigrant or the dark-skinned Afro–Puerto Rican) and the hostile border that the joke produces (155). These jokes reinforce a discourse on *mestizaje*, that is, a cultural and historical process to whiten the nation by invisibilizing/hypervisibilizing those that are viewed as "too Black" and therefore as elements of backwardness, uncleanliness, criminality, and a lack of intelligence (Godreau "La semántica"; Zenón Cruz *Narciso*).

7. By coining the phrase "border of *puertorriqueñidad*," I am following García-Peña's analysis when she talks of "borders of dominicanidad." García-Peña defines this proposition as those borders and cultural histories that are carried upon the backs of dark-skinned Dominicans, made visible through everyday experiences and interactions with others.

8. As Godreau (*Scripts*) demonstrates, Afro–Puerto Rican practices are often limited to very specific zones of the Island, such as the town of Loíza and the coast, as the visibility of these bodies, and of spiritual and cultural practices, might disrupt the mestizo (read: whitened) spatial representation of the island.

9. One need only to consider writers such as Antonio Pedreira, who argued that in order to be "capable of the grandest and most heroic feats" Puerto Ricans must embrace their European "blood." Pedreira also derides the fact that Puerto Ricans remain "drenched under waves of African blood," which in turn leads to being "indecisive, almost stupefied by the colors and threatened by the cinematic vision of witches and ghosts" (29). Pedreira was the Puerto Rican essayist that produced the founding identitarian text that established ethno-cultural definitions for the nation (*Insularismo*, 1934).

10. Godreau also warns of the pitfalls that plague these efforts to rescue Blackness in Puerto Rico, particularly those that have been institutionalized by Island government. In "Folkloric Others," she warns that when these celebratory renderings of African inheritance are taken on by the state apparatus, they often become something that exists in a distant past, or they are represented as a facet of Puerto Rican culture that is gradually effacing from the general population. This state-sponsored recognition of Blackness, then, renders the African presence to a space of folklorization and myth, often at odds with ongoing modernization projects. In this way, state-sponsored inclusionary projects targeting communities of Afro-descendants oftentimes simultaneously invoke ideologies of *blanqueamiento* because they perpetuate distance between puertorriqueñidad and Blackness (172–73).

11. Here I use the idea of creolization following Édouard Glissant (as opposed to the post-structural imagination and Cuban-centric discourse of Benitez-Rojo) as a system that can never be neutral and is always in confrontation with relations of power, race, and history. Furthermore, I use the term here to describe a cultural and literary phenomenon characteristic of the African Americas as a whole, and

not just in the Caribbean. Thus, creolization will be understood as a diasporic concept that encapsulates the process or the processes of cultural, spiritual, and linguistic fusion (smooth and violent) that characterize African diaspora histories. In *The Black Atlantic*, Paul Gilroy addresses the difficulty in theorizing creolization against a discourse of cultural nationalism and ethnic purity: "From the viewpoint of ethnic absolutism, this [theorizing of creolization] would be a litany of pollution and impurity" (2). Thus, the theory of creolization carries with it the power to subvert cultural codes. It is in this way that I am utilizing the term, that is, to address the ways in which Arroyo Pizarro challenges the cultural hegemony of whiteness in Puerto Rico through creolized belief systems.

12. Haunting as political intervention into a painful history of slavery and colonization can be seen in various sociological, literary, and theoretical works (see Morrison 1987, 2008; Gordon *Ghostly Matters*; and Arroyo). Haunting also functions to highlight what cannot be seen: "[It] occupies the space between what we cannot see and what we know. It wrestles with elusive non-transparent power, and not least, with attunement to the unexpected site and lineaments that such knowledge requires" (Stoler xii).

13. References to religious creolization as a type of resistance becomes a powerful stance against the colonizer or slave holder because these African diasporic spiritual practices not only "posed a challenge to official Christian practices and were believed to be associated with magic and sorcery, but they also allowed the most vulnerable sectors of Caribbean societies to manifest their spirituality and express cultural and political practices suppressed by colonial forces" (Olmos and Paravisini-Gebert 24).

14. Olmos and Paravisini-Gebert write that "Aché is a current or flow, a 'groove' that initiates can channel so that it carries them along their road in life. The prayers, rhythms, offerings, taboos of Santería tune initiates into their flow. They are lifted out of the . . . frustration of ordinary life into the world of power where everything is easy because all is aché, all is destiny" (41). Likewise, Robert Farris Thompson understands *aché* as the "power-to-make-things-happen," whose goal is the fundamental restructuring of society and reinstate a sense of balance. The ancestors and the orisha work aché to effect change in the lives of humans. Their presence is intimately linked with a type of knowledge whose objective is to create a balanced, healthy, and harmonious world. The divine lessons of the spirits guide the ailing and provide further insight into actions that should be taken to better life on the mortal plane.

15. Among the codes in the document is the code that slaves should be indoctrinated in the Catholic faith, that slaves should be prohibited from owning property, and that slaves should abide by strict public decency laws or be subject to punishment (Moitt). The Code Noir also summarized those conditions that must be met for a slave to earn their freedom. Both the enslaved and the recently freed continually came up against these policies, and the movement of their bodies,

spiritual practices, and herbal knowledges were subject to state intervention in the name of public order and reputation (Suárez Findlay 21–22).

16. Bondage and race play have been previously linked to a history of slavery and historical haunting of slavery's ongoing trajectory in the present. In "Beyond Black and Blue," Ariane Cruz specifically demonstrates that the history of slavery acts as a type of "slime." This is to say that slavery remains an active "marketplace" for the production of Black female sexuality and its cultural representations (409). Cruz maps the ways in which the impact of slavery and the pervasive rape of Black female slaves on modern constructions of Black women has been theorized, but more importantly, she considers the ways in which Black women *deliberately* employ the phantom of slavery in the deliverance and/or receiving of sexual pleasure (also "Playing with the Politics" and *The Color of Kink*). Her analysis argues that this "slime" becomes a type of "lubricant" to stimulate sexual fantasies, access sexual pleasure, and power in performances in the realm of BDSM. Cruz specifically addresses the productive possibilities in considering intimate connections in the space of BDSM: "[It is] a critical site from which to reimagine the formative links between Black female sexuality and violence . . . race play is a BDSM practice that explicitly uses race to script power exchange and the dynamics of domination and submission" ("Beyond Black and Blue" 410). Christina Elizabeth Sharpe, along with Cruz, argues in *Monstrous Intimacies* that sadomasochist "desire might be a place from which to perhaps exercise power and to exorcise it through the repetition of particular power relations" (32).

17. In the Catholic tradition, this day is set aside to remember those who have passed on to heaven, as it celebrates the crossing-over from one world to the next. This day is often associated with Halloween in the US, but it is also tied to rituals that have mixed with Santería practices. Moreover, Sam Hain is closely associated with the orisha Oya and the Vodou *lwa* Papa Legba. Both of these figures represent a type of bridge or pathway opened between the world of the living and the world of the dead. They are also those deities charged with carrying messages into the spiritual realm.

18. Júnia Ferreira Furtado explores this history in his *Chica da Silva: A Brazilian Slave of the Eighteenth Century*, where he maintains "that she used miscegenation and her connections as a tool to achieve a higher social status, as did other African Brazilians at the time."

19. See for example the film *Angélica* (2017) by Marisol Gómez Mouakad, which critiques Eurocentric notions of beauty and love on the Island. The protagonist must return to Puerto Rico from her home in New York and makes an intimate-spiritual connection with her ancestors. This intimate spirituality underscores the importance of loving her body and of putting back together the fragmented pieces of herself that have been dismantled by years of violence that carry colonial/imperial discourses on beauty and womanhood.

Chapter 2

1. For more details see, "SENTENCIA TC/0168/13," Tribunal Constitucional Republica Dominicana, 23 Sept. 2013, https://www.refworld.org.es/pdfid/5d7fcd99a.pdf.

2. Not unlike the rhetoric of Haiti in Paris where Louis Napoleon had declared in 1848, "Haïti, Haïti, pays de barbares!" (Dayan, *Haiti* 10).

3. Following Reyes-Santos's study on the Caribbean, by "kinship" I refer to the ways in which family narratives in Antillean political and cultural thought are mobilized to establish transcolonial, national, and colonial/imperial connections based on feelings of unification (11). In other words, Reyes-Santos studies how certain bodies are imagined as moving toward a (trans)national family unit.

4. The dance performed around this tree in Vodou ceremonies is done in remembrance of the ancestors who came and who did not come to the island of Hispaniola. The tree is believed to serve as a bridge and antidote to those ripped apart in the Middle Passage.

5. The articulation of these particular cities in both Haiti and the Dominican Republic traces a geography that crosses the border from Haiti to the Dominican Republic and back again. It is worth noting that each of these cities is intimately related to a history of enslavement but also liberation on the island. Juana Méndez, Haiti, is named after the name of the Haitian ex-slave who birthed Buenaventura Báez Méndez, the first mulatto president of the Dominican Republic (1849–1853). Maimón, Dominican Republic, was a major indigenous settlement before the arrival of the European colonizers and is named after an indigenous man of the same name. Dajabón, Dominican Republic, brings us back to the border between the two nations and was a site of Trujillo's 1931 Haitian Massacre, a genocide that cemented the dictator's racial politics of Hispanophilia and whiteness, resting them on the Haitian (Black) body. It is considered the sister city of Juana Méndez and exists as a major crossing site for Haitians who temporarily enter the Dominican Republic as vendors and day laborers.

6. Erzulie Freda is the goddess of luxury and excess in Haiti. She is often invoked by women when decorating their rooms with lavish items in an attempt to create a space to escape from their everyday reality: "Ezili moves in an atmosphere of infinite luxury, a perfume of refinement, which, from the first moment of her arrival, pervades the very air of the *peristil* and becomes a general expansiveness in which all anxieties, all urgencies, vanish" (Deren 6). It is worth noting that Ezili is another name for Erzulie.

7. Frances Negrón-Muntaner has commented on this particular phenomenon of "crowning" as it appears in the works of Haitian–Puerto Rican artist Jean-Michel Basquiat: "[The crown is] offsetting the shame of racialization and the pain of incommensurable definitions of value by affirming the self in alternative

terms ... the power of the crown [also acts] as amulet, transfiguring socially low subjectivities into royalty" ("Contested Sovereignties" 140).

8. Negrón-Muntaner has also analyzed the symbol of the crown in Basquiat as a symbol of sovereignty (122). If sovereignty is achieved through spiritual knowledge, then "nation" does not refer to an ethnic or geographical concept but rather becomes a means of organizing communities by the spirits that they serve and the rites that these communities perform to connect with these spirits. Therefore, "Vodou is, foremost, a system in which people are bound together as a spiritual community and become sovereign in this way. This community works together to serve the *lwa* in a search for knowledge and growth" (Murphy 16–17).

9. "Stickiness" is a concept developed by Sara Ahmed, used to describe how objects become sites of contact between the personal and the social. Ahmed defines emotions as feelings that involve not only movement but also attachments—about what connects us to our world: "What moves us, what makes us feel, is also that which holds us in place, or gives us a dwelling place. ... Attachment takes place through movement, through being moved by the proximity of others" (*The Cultural Politics* 11). In this way, I suggest how Erzulie's spirit in this video functions as a "stickiness," driven by past histories, to produce an alternative sovereignty of bodies that have been rejected from national imaginations. Working with spirit as stickiness, I suggest that Erzulie's spirit shapes the bodies of a decolonial community through how it sticks certain bodies together and not others.

10. The Parsley Massacre took place in 1937 and represented a culmination in the racial and geopolitical project of the Trujillo regime to consolidate a Dominican identity and define the borders of the nation. The massacre is named after the word *perejil*, "parsley" in Spanish, as the Spanish language became the defining factor in delimiting Dominican from Haitian. Those who were able to pronounce the word in Spanish, without a Creole accent, were seen as legitimate citizens in the eyes of the state.

11. For more on the concept of both women as figurative "shipmates" and the queer undertones that stem from the word "mati" (shipmate), see Tinsley's "Black Atlantic, Queer Atlantic: Queer Imaginings of the Middle Passage" (2008).

Chapter 3

1. See Ramón Grosfoguel and Chloe S. Georas's "Coloniality of Power and Racial Dynamics: Notes Toward a Reinterpretation of Latino Caribbeans in New York City," in which the authors demonstrate not only the ways in which Puerto Ricans are constructed as colonial racialized subjects but also the subsequent "Puerto Ricanization" of light-skinned Dominican and Cuban immigrants.

2. Following Lorgia García-Peña and Yolanda Martínez-San Miguel, the body of the "racexile" is doubly marginalized, as she has been cast from her coun-

try of origin because of racial (and other) paradigms but cannot fully assimilate into the "multicultural" fabric of the US racial system (here: Latinidad) for the same reasons.

3. For example, in New York from 1965 to 1969, Black and Puerto Rican youth collaborated throughout the city to demand greater working class access to higher education, more Black and Puerto Rican faculty at all levels of education, and curricula that included Black and Puerto Rican studies. They joined other activists to oppose the Vietnam War and successfully thwarted Columbia University's development initiatives that would have accelerated gentrification in Harlem. Under pressure from Black lawmakers, New York State established the SEEK program in 1967, which significantly increased Black and Puerto Rican college enrollments by 1969.

4. Ann Cvetkovich argues that the ephemeral archive is one that values the embodied (shared) experience as valuable historical resource, that is, ephemeral (feelings, desires, memories, etc.) and offers a new archive of experiences.

5. bell hooks comments on Baartman in *Black Looks: Race and Representation*, saying, "Her naked body was displayed on numerous occasions for five years. When she died, the mutilated parts were still subject to scrutiny. The audience which had paid to see her buttocks and had fantasized about the uniqueness of her genetalia when she was alive could, after her death and dissection, examine both" (62).

6. In "Toward a Decolonial Feminism," María Lugones complicates Quijano's understanding of the capitalist global system of power and critiques his "understanding of gender as only in terms of sexual access to women." In using the term *coloniality*, Lugones means to "name not just a classification of people in terms of the coloniality of power and gender, but also the process of active reduction of people, the dehumanization that fits them for the classification, the process of subjectification, and the attempt to turn the colonized into less than human beings" (3).

7. The concept of coloniality and the process of dehumanization is attributed to Nelson Maldonado Torres and defined as the historical processes of colonization that continue to impress upon certain bodies in the present (*Against War*).

8. This belief is also held in many Rastafari teachings and rituals, Vodou, and Santería, in which the spirits are not offered food containing salt. In Nalo Hopkinsons *The Salt Roads* (2003), salt is literally the way that Ezili moves through the lives of the women in Saint Domingue, who try to transcend their entrapment on the Island.

9. One tale from Suriname narrates:

> It was a long time ago, many years before Emancipation, that word had gone round that those of us who could stop eating salt would be able to fly back to Africa. So we all went on a salt-free diet. But

our wives and children were forced to eat food in the houses where they worked. So it became clear that it would be mostly us men who would fly back. (Traylor et al. 110)

The flying slaves would then return year after year to warn their wives and children not to attempt flight into the sea, for they had been contaminated by their consumption of salt. Instead, their duty was to stay behind and live their lives in constant resistance to slavery and racial persecution: "Forever bound to the land to which they were now held hostage, the enslaved, in body and spirit, could not physically return home" (Gadsby 26). This constructs Black women in the Caribbean as both marooned hostages to a violent new world and radical political subjects with the ability to forge new possibilities of radical and transformative community building while maintaining the spiritual connection between the living and the ancestors.

10. The Young Lords Organization was an organized movement of Puerto Ricans inspired by the Black Panther Party and the Young Lords of Chicago. The main goal of the organization was to fight for equal rights for those residing in Spanish Harlem.

11. The woman removes her clothes piece by piece throughout the video and exerts her power and agency as a Black woman through the movement of her body. Celia Cruz became a Latinx cultural icon in 1950s and 1960s New York and sang regularly in places such as the Palladium, which brought together the Afro-Cuban, Afro-Puerto Rican, and Afro-Dominican communities through her music and references to the orisha of the Santería religion.

12. For example, Willie Perdomo's "Nigger-Reecan Blues" has been analyzed as a racial performance founded on unresolvable difference and tension (Noel 128).

13. My translation.

14. A study by Ginetta Candelario about Dominican beauty indicates, for example, that "for Dominicans hair is the principal bodily signifier of race, followed by facial features, skin color, and last, ancestry. . . . The role of race as a signifier of race dates back to at least the late eighteenth century" (140). She also underscores how "allusiones to hair are also frequent in the negrista poetry of Puerto Rico, like that of Fortunato Vizarrondo (1942), and the poem by Juan de Matta "Oda a mi cabello" (1991)." Likewise, in Cuba, hair has been a contemporary topic of underground hip-hop by women, such as "Mi belleza" and "Los pelos" by Obsesión (2011). Furthermore, slave censuses from the nineteenth century indicate, for example, the texture, color, and type of hair of the slaves as categories of racial classification (Candelario 141). One of the most prominent words utilized to describe the hair of the slaves was "grifo" (Candelario 142). She tells us that "today the word is still used in Puerto Rico and the Dominican Republic, whether to describe curly hair or a person who is thought of as Black. This construction of hair as marker of racial difference continues despite long

processes of mestizaje that continue to propagate the fantasy of racial harmony" (Candelario 142).

15. Candelario studies this phenomenon of Dominicans in the US, stating that Dominican staff at various beauty salons prefer a whiteness that indicates mixture: "The identity category labeled 'Hispanic' is deployed as the signifier of somatic, linguistic and cultural alterity in relation to both Anglo whiteness and African American Blackness" (130). The sociologist argues that this alternative intermediary space also operates as a site of whitening that distances Dominicans from Blackness, a classification that they traditionally reserve for Haitians and African Americans. Thus, the label "Hispanic" and hair straightening are used as representative of their valorization of mestizaje and an extension of cultural/historical anti-Blackness. Candelario continues to state that far too often "hands are being laid on Black hair to change it from its natural form to a style that marks the body as 'Indian' rather than Black" (181–82).

16. This follows Yolanda Martínez-San Miguel's analysis of Piri Thomas's novel *Down These Mean Streets*, in which she refers to the "aporia" created between the Black diasporic subject and the lens through which family/community attempts to "read" their body. In the case of Thomas, Martínez-San Miguel writes that "his father constantly reminds him of his Antillean—and even Taíno—condition in an effort to remove him from his black identification, but Piri cannot deny the visibility of his own blackness and how this racial condition dislocates his incorporation into his familiar (familial) context" (*Coloniality of Diasporas* 122).

Chapter 4

1. Meanwhile, articles, advertisements, and political cartoons across Cuba actively engaged with Blackness and whiteness in a variety of ways on a daily basis. These media would depict Black and mulatto Cubans as either "negative" or "positive," invoking colonial representations of Blackness and the politics of respectability that went into constructing Cuban revolutionary subjects (Benson 37). In the late 1950s and early 1960s, Cuban racial representations in everyday print sources continued to promote racial hierarchies, with representations of Black Cubans as service workers and domestic servants in white homes. In an analysis of Cuban beauty and homegoods advertisements, Marc D. Perry writes that many shops and company advertisers would associate dark skin with manual labor, casting Afro-descendent Cubans in roles such as domestic and service workers. Fair skin, *metizo* identity, and "good hair" quickly became the images associated with financial success and Cuban beauty (45).

2. According to Vanessa Kimberly Valdés in *Oshun's Daughters*, "The orishas serve as intercessors between Olodumare, who is God, the Creator, and

humanity. The orishas are the spiritual entities endowed to be recipients of *ase*, defined by Robert Farris Thompson as 'spiritual command, the power-to-make-things-happen" (15). In this way, the orisha are expressions of the divine infused with elements of nature.

3. Spoken in Africa and brought to Cuba during the slave trade.

Works Cited

Abdallah-Álvarez Remírez, Sandra. "Complejo De Inferioridad." *Negra Cubana Tenía Que Ser*, 30 Mar. 2016, https://negracubanateniaqueser.com/2016/03/30/complejo-de-inferioridad/.
Acevedo, Elizabeth. *Beastgirl & Other Origin Myths*. YesYes Books, 2016.
Ahluwalia, Pal. "Towards (Re)Conciliation: The Postcolonial Economy of Giving." *Relocating Postcolonialism*, edited by David Theo Goldberg, Blackwell, 2002, pp. 197–98.
Ahmed, Sarah. *The Cultural Politics of Emotion*. Routledge, 2004.
———. "Happy Objects." *The Affect Theory Reader*, edited by Melissa Gregg and Gregory J. Seigworth, Duke UP, 2010, pp. 29–51.
———. *The Promise of Happiness*. Duke UP, 2010.
———. *Strange Encounters: Embodied Others in Post-Coloniality*. Taylor and Francis, 2013.
Alamo-Pastrana, Carlos. *Seams of Empire: Race and Radicalism in Puerto Rico and the United States*. UP of Florida, 2016.
Alexander, M. Jacqui. *Pedagogies of Crossing: Meditations on Feminism, Sexual Politics, Memory, and the Sacred*. Duke U, 2005.
Algarín, Miguel, et al. *Nuyorican Poetry: An Anthology of Puerto Rican Words and Feelings*. William Morrow, 1975.
Andre, Richard. "The Dominican Republic and Haiti: A Shared View from the Diaspora." *Americas Quarterly*, Summer 2014.
Anzaldúa, Gloria. *Borderlands/La Frontera*. Aunt Lute Books, 2007.
Anzaldúa, Gloria, and Analouise Keating. *Light in the Dark / Luz En Lo Oscuro: Rewriting Identity, Spirituality, Reality*. Duke UP, 2015.
Argudin, Elias. "Negro, ¿Tú Eres Sueco?" *Tribuna De La Habana*, 24 Mar. 2016.
Armstead, Ronni. "'Growing the Size of the Black Woman': Feminist Activism in Havana Hip Hop." *NWSA Journal: National Women's Studies Association Journal*, vol. 19.1, 2007, pp. 106–17.
———. "Las Krudas, Spatial Practice, and the Performance of Diaspora." *Meridians: Feminism, Race, Transnationalism*, vol. 8.1, 2008, pp. 130–43.

Arroyo, Jossianna. *Writing Secrecy in Caribbean Freemasonry*. Palgrave Macmillan, 2013.
Arroyo Pizarro, Yolanda. *Los Documentados*. Editorial Situm, 2010.
———. "Mayra Montero es muy inteligente . . ." Facebook. 6 November 2016, 6:54 p.m.
———. "Oye, Se Busca Una Negra Como Esta!" *Afrofeminas*, 10 September 2017.
———. *Saeta: The Poems*. Boreales, 2011.
Beliso-De Jesús, Aisha M. *Electric Santería: Racial and Sexual Assemblages of Transnational Religion*. Columbia UP, 2015.
———. "Santería Copresence and the Making of African Diaspora Bodies." *Cultural Anthropology*, vol. 29.3, 2014, pp. 503–26.
Benson, Devyn Spence. *Antiracism in Cuba: The Unfinished Revolution*. U of North Carolina P, 2016.
Bergman, Carla, and Nick Montgomery. *Joyful Militancy: Building Thriving Resistance in Toxic Times*. AK Press, 2018.
Bernard-Carreño, Regina. *Nuyorganics Organic Intellectualism, the Search for Racial Identity, and Nuyorican Thought*. Lang, 2010.
Brodber, Erna. *Myal*. Waveland Press, 2014.
Brown, David H. *Santería Enthroned: Art, Ritual, and Innovation in an Afro-Cuban Religion*. U of Chicago P, 2003.
Brown, Tammy L. *City of Islands: Caribbean Intellectuals in New York*. UP of Mississippi, 2017.
Buscaglia-Salgado José F. *Undoing Empire: Race and Nation in the Mulatto Caribbean*. U of Minnesota P, 2003.
Cabrera, Lydia. *El Monte: Igbo, Finda, Ewe Orisha, Vititi Nfinda Notas Sobre Las Religiones, La Magia, Las Supersticiones y El Folklore De Los Negros Criollos y El Pueblo De Cuba*. n.p, 1983.
———. *Yemayá y Ochun*. C.R., 1980.
Candelario, Ginetta. *Black Behind the Ears: Dominican Racial Identity from Museums to Beauty Shops*. Duke UP, 2007.
Casas-Cortés, María Isabel, et al. "Blurring Boundaries: Recognizing Knowledge-Practices in the Study of Social Movements." *Anthropological Quarterly*, vol. 81.1, 2008, pp. 17–58.
Castillo, Debra. "She Sings Boleros: Santos-Febres' Sirena Selena." *Latin American Literary Review*, vol. 29, 2001, pp. 13–25.
Chancy, Myriam J. A. *From Sugar to Revolution: Women's Visions of Haiti, Cuba, and the Dominican Republic*. Wilfrid Laurier UP, 2012.
Clarke, Kamari Maxine. *Mapping Yorùbá Networks: Power and Agency in the Making of Transnational Communities*. Duke UP, 2004.
Clifford, James, and George E. Marcus. *Writing Culture: The Poetics and Politics of Ethnography*. U of California P, 2011.

Conner, Randy P., and David Hatfield Sparks. *Queering Creole Spiritual Traditions: Lesbian, Gay, Bisexual, and Transgender Participation in African-inspired Traditions in the Americas*. Harrington Park, 2004.

Cruz, Ariane. "Beyond Black and Blue: BDSM, Internet Pornography, and Black Female Sexuality." *Feminist Studies*, vol. 41.2, 2015, pp. 409–36.

———. *The Color of Kink: Black Women, BDSM, and Pornography*. New York UP, 2016.

———. "Playing with the Politics of Perversion: Policing BDSM, Pornography, and Black Female Sexuality." *Souls*, vol. 18.2-4, 2016, pp. 379–407.

Cuervo-Hewitt, Julia. *Voices out of Africa in Twentieth-Century Spanish Caribbean Literature*. Bucknell UP, 2009.

Cuesta, Odaymar, et al. "Declaración Del Colectivo Cuba Liberación Negra." *Afroféminas*, 8 Aug. 2021, https://afrofeminas.com/2021/08/08/declaracion-del-colectivo-cuba-liberacion-negra/.

Cvetkovich, Ann. *An Archive of Feelings: Trauma, Sexuality, and Lesbian Public Cultures*. Duke UP, 2003.

Dayan, Joan. "Erzulie: A Women's History of Haiti." *Research in African Literatures*, vol. 25.2, 1994, pp. 5–31.

———. *Haiti, History, and the Gods*. U of California, 2010.

Dávila, Arlene. "'This Is Our Time': Mayra Santos-Febres on Changing Narratives about Race Across the Americas." *The Latinx Project at NYU*, 24 June 2021, https://www.latinxproject.nyu.edu/intervenxions/mayra-santos-febres-on-changing-narratives-about-race-and-social-equity-across-the-americas.

De Leon Monsalvo, Alfredo. "Serie De Estudios Sociales Para Escuela Elemental." *Sociales Huellas*, vol. 3, 2009.

De Maeseneer, Rita. "Cinco zambullidas en Boat People." *Confluencia: Revista Hispánica De Cultura y Literatura*, vol. 25.2, 2010, pp. 94–105.

Decena, Carlos Ulises. *Tacit Subjects: Belonging and Same-Sex Desire among Dominican Immigrant Men*. Duke UP, 2011.

Deckman, Joshua. "El Nï'e: Inhabiting Love, Bliss, and Joy." *El Nï'e: Inhabiting Love, Bliss, and Joy; Small Axe Project*, 2018, smallaxe.net/sxsalon/interviews/el-nie-inhabiting-love-bliss-and-joy.

Derby, Lauren. *The Dictator's Seduction: Politics and the Popular Imagination in the Era of Trujillo*. Duke UP, 2009.

Deren, Maya. *Divine Horsemen: The Living Gods of Haiti*. Foreword by Joseph Campbell, McPherson, 2004.

Desmangles, Leslie G. *The Faces of the Gods: Vodou and Roman Catholicism in Haiti*. U of North Carolina, 1997.

Díaz-Sánchez, Micaela. "'Yemayá Blew That Wire Fence Down': Invoking African Spiritualities in Gloria Anzaldúa's *Boderlands/La Frontera; The New Mestiza* and the Mural Art of Juana Alicia." *Yemoja: Gender, Sexuality, and Creativity in the Latina/o and Afro-Atlantic Diasporas*, edited by Solimar Otero, State U of New York P, 2013, pp. 153–86.

Dillard, Cynthia B. *Learning to (Re)member the Things We've Learned to Forget: Endarkened Feminisms, Spirituality, and the Sacred Nature of Research and Teaching*. Peter Lang, 2012.

———. *On Spiritual Strivings: Transforming an African American Women's Academic Life*. State U of New York P, 2006.

Duany, Jorge. "Caribbean Migration to Puerto Rico: A Comparison of Cubans and Dominicans." *International Migration Review*, vol. 26.1, 1992, pp. 46–66.

———. "The Dominican Diaspora to Puerto Rico: A Transnational Perspective." *Blurred Borders*, 2011, pp. 187–208.

———. "Ethnicity, Color, Class among Dominicans in the United States and Puerto Rico." *Latin American Perspectives*, vol. 25.3, 1998, pp. 147–72.

———. "Exiliados, indocumentados y diásporas: Las migraciones contemporáneas en Puerto Rico." *Del Caribe*, vol. 31, 2000, pp. 13–20.

———. *The Puerto Rican Nation on the Move: Identities on the Island and in the United States*. U of North Carolina, 2002.

Duany, Jorge, et al. *El barrio gandul: Economía subterránea y migración indocumentada en Puerto Rico*. Ed. Nueva Sociedad, 1995.

Dunham, Katherine. *Island Possessed*. U of Chicago P, 1994.

Edes, Alyssa. "Ibeyi on Spirituality and Joy in 'Ash.'" *NPR*, 4 Oct. 2017, https://www.npr.org/2017/10/04/555046429/ibeyi-on-spirituality-and-joy-in-ash.

Figueroa, Luis A. *Sugar, Slavery, and Freedom in Nineteenth-Century Puerto Rico*. U of North Carolina, 2005.

Figueroa-Vásquez, Yomaira C. *Decolonizing Diasporas: Radical Mappings of Afro-Atlantic Literatures*. Northwestern UP, 2021.

Findlay, Eileen. *Imposing Decency: The Politics of Sexuality and Race in Puerto Rico, 1870–1920*. Duke UP, 1999.

Flores, Juan. *From Bomba to Hip-Hop: Puerto Rican Culture and Latino Identity*. Columbia UP, 2000.

Fumagalli, Maria Cristina. *On the Edge: Writing the Border between Haiti and the Dominican Republic*. Liverpool UP, 2015.

Furtado Júnia Ferreira. *Chica Da Silva: A Brazilian Slave of the Eighteenth Century*. Cambridge UP, 2009.

Gadsby, Meredith M. *Sucking Salt: Caribbean Women Writers, Migrations, and Survival*. U of Missouri, 2006.

Gaffield, Julia. *Haitian Connections in the Atlantic World: Recognition after Revolution*. U of North Carolina, 2015.

García-Peña, Lorgia. *The Borders of Dominicanidad Race, Nation, and Archives of Contradiction*. Duke UP, 2016.

———. "One Hundred Years After the Occupation: A Century Later, the Legacies of the U.S. Military Intervention of the Dominican Republic Persist." *NACLA Report on the Americas*. Routledge, 25 May 2016.

Glissant, Édouard. *Poetics of Relation*. Translated by Betsy Wing, U of Michigan, 1997.
Godreau, Isar P. "Changing Space, Making Race: Distance, Nostalgia, and the Folklorization of Blackness in Puerto Rico." *Identities*, vol. 9.3, 2002, pp. 281–304.
———. "Folkloric Others: 'Blanqueamiento' and the Celebration of Blackness as Exception in Puerto Rico." *Globalization and Race: Transformations in the Cultural Production of Blackness*, edited by Kamari Maxine Clarke and Deborah A. Thomas. Duke UP, 2006, pp. 171–87.
———. "La semántica fugitiva, raza, color y vida cotidiana en Puerto Rico." *Revista De Ciencias Sociales, Nueva Época*, vol. 9, 2008, pp. 52–71.
———. "Peinando diferencias, bregas de pertenencia: El alisado y el llamado 'pelo malo.'" *Caribbean Studies*, vol. 30.1, 2002, pp. 82–134.
———. *Scripts of Blackness: Race, Cultural Nationalism, and U.S. Colonialism in Puerto Rico*. U of Illinois, 2015.
Gordon, Avery. *Ghostly Matters: Haunting and the Sociological Imagination*. U of Minnesota, 2008.
Grau-Lleveria, Elena. "Sirena Selena Vestida De Pena De Mayra Santos Febres: Economía, Identidad y Poder." *Hispanic Research Journal*, vol. 4.3, 2003, pp. 239–50.
Gregg, Melissa, and Gregory J. Seigworth. Introduction "An Inventory of Shimmers." *The Affect Theory Reader*. Duke UP, 2010, pp. 1–25.
Griffith, R. Marie, and Barbara Dianne Savage, editors. *Women and Religion in the African Diaspora: Knowledge, Power, and Performance*. Johns Hopkins UP, 2006.
Grosfoguel, Ramón. *Colonial Subjects: Puerto Ricans in a Global Perspective*. U of California, 2003.
Grosfoguel, Ramón, and Chloe S. Georas. "'Coloniality of Power' and Racial Dynamics: Notes toward a Reinterpretation of Latino Caribbeans in New York City." *Identities*, vol. 7.1, 2000, pp. 85–125.
Hall, Stuart. "Cultural Identity and Diaspora." *Identity: Community, Culture, Difference*, edited by Jonathan Rutherford. Lawrence and Wishart, 1990, pp. 222–37.
Hartman, Saidiya. "Venus in Two Acts." *Small Axe: A Caribbean Journal of Criticism*, vol. 12.2, 2008, pp. 1–14.
Hegel, Georg Wilhelm Friedrich. *Phenomenology of Spirit*. Clarendon Press, 1977.
Hernández Hiraldo, Samiri. *Black Puerto Rican Identity and Religious Experience*. U of Florida P, 2006.
Hidalgo de Jesús, Amarilis. "Images of Afro-Caribbean Female Slaves in the Works of Yolanda Arroyo Pizarro." *Twenty-First Century Latin American Narrative and Postmodern Feminism*, edited by León De Ponce Gina. Cambridge Scholars Publishing, 2014.

Hoffnung-Garskof, Jesse. "To Abolish the Law of Castes: Merit, Manhood and the Problem of Colour in the Puerto Rican Liberal Movement, 1873–92." *Social History*, vol. 36.3, 2011, pp. 312–42.

Hong, Grace. "'The Future of Our Worlds': Black Feminism and the Politics of Knowledge in the University under Globalization." *Meridians*, vol. 8.2, 2008, pp. 95–115.

hooks, bell. *Black Looks: Race and Representation*. Routledge, 2015.

Horn, Maja. *Masculinity After Trujillo*. U of Florida P, 2014.

Indiana, Rita, and Los Misterios. "Da pa' lo' do.'" *YouTube*, web.

Informe sobre la situación de los derechos humanos en la República Dominicana. Rep. no. 45/15: Inter-American Commission on Human Rights, Organization of American States, 2015.

Jaime, Karen. "'Da' Pa' Lo' Do': Rita Indiana's Queer, Racialized Dominicanness." *Small Axe*, vol. 19.2, 2015, pp. 85–93.

Johnson, Paul C. *Spirited Things: The Work of "Possession" in Afro-Atlantic Religions*. U of Chicago P, 2014.

Laó-Montes, Agustin. "Afro-Latin American Feminisms at the Cutting Edge of Emerging Political-Epistemic Movements." *Meridians: Feminism, Race, Transnationalism*, vol. 14, no. 2, 12 Feb. 2002, pp. 1–24.

Lara, Ana-Maurine. *Erzulie's Skirt*. RedBone Press, 2006.

———. "I Wanted to Be More of a Person: Conjuring [Afro] [Latinx] [Queer] Futures." *Bilingual Review*, vol. 33.4, 2017, pp. 1–14.

———. *Queer Freedom: Black Sovereignty*. State U of New York P, 2020.

Lipsitz, George. *Footsteps in the Dark: The Hidden Histories of Popular Music*. U of Minnesota P, 2007.

Lloréns, Hilda, and Rosa E. Carrasquillo. "Sculpting Blackness: Representations of Black-Puerto Ricans in Public Art." *Visual Anthropology Review*, vol. 24.2, 2008, pp. 103–16.

———. "Una Breve Reflexión Sobre La Práctica Blanca De Pintarse El Rostro De Negro/negra (o "rostro-negro"/Blackface) En Puerto Rico." Blog post. *CreateLIVEflourish*, 6 Nov. 2016, web.

Lorde, Audre. *Sister Outsider: Essays and Speeches*. Crossing Press, 2007.

Lugones, María. *Pilgrimages/Peregrinajes: Theorizing Coalition against Multiple Oppressions*. Rowman and Littlefield, 2003.

———. "Toward a Decolonial Feminism." *Hypatia*, vol. 25, no. 4, 2010, pp. 742–59.

Maldonado-Torres, Nelson. *Against War: Views from the Underside of Modernity*. Duke UP, 2008.

Marouan, Maha. *Witches, Goddesses, and Angry Spirits: The Politics of Spiritual Liberation in African Diaspora Women's Fiction*. Ohio State UP, 2013.

Martínez-San Miguel, Yolanda. *Caribe Two Ways: Cultura de la migración en el Caribe insular hispánico*. Ediciones Callejón, 2003.

---. *Coloniality of Diasporas: Rethinking Intra-colonial Migrations in a Pan-Caribbean Context.* Palgrave Macmillan, 2014.

---. "'Con mi música pa' otra parte': Desplazamientos simbólicos dominicanos." *Caribe Two Ways: Cultura de migración en el Caribe insular hispánico.* Ediciones Callejón, 2003, pp. 263–320.

---. *¿Confederación caribeña? Migraciones de cubanos y dominicanos a Puerto Rico y la formación de fronteras intranacionales en la representación cultural.* Proc. of XX Congress of the Latin American Studies Association, Mexico, Guadalajara.

Matory, James Lorand. *Black Atlantic Religion Tradition, Transnationalism, and Matriarchy in the Afro-Brazilian Candomble.* Princeton UP, 2009.

---. "The Many Who Dance in Me: Afro-Atlantic Ontology and the Problem with 'Transnationalism.'" *Transnational Transcendence: Essays on Religion and Globalization,* edited by Thomas J. Csordas. U of California P, 2009, pp. 231–62.

McCarthy Brown, Karen. *Mama Lola: A Vodou Priestess in Brooklyn.* U of California P, 2010.

McKittrick, Katherine. *Sylvia Wynter: On Being Human as Praxis.* Duke UP, 2015.

Méndez, Danny. *Narratives of Migration and Displacement in Dominican Literature.* Routledge, 2012.

Méndez, Xhercis. "On the Edges of Belonging." *Feminist Review,* vol. 121, no. 3, 1 July 2020.

Mignolo, Walter. "Epistemic Disobedience, Independent Thought and Decolonial Freedom." *Theory, Culture & Society,* vol. 26, no. 7, 2009, pp. 159–81.

---. *Local Histories/Global Designs: Coloniality, Subaltern Knowledges, and Border Thinking.* Princeton UP, 2012.

Moitt, Bernard. *Women and Slavery in the French Antilles, 1635–1848.* Indiana UP, 2001.

Montero, Mayra. "El Entierro De Chianita: Un Complot Chino." Editorial. *El Nuevo Dia* [San Juan] 5 Nov. 2016.

Moraña, Mabel, et al. "Jáuregui." *Coloniality at Large: Latin America and the Postcolonial Debate.* Duke UP, 2008.

Moreno, Marisol. "Bordes líquidos, fronteras y espejismos: El Dominicano y la migración intra-Caribeña en *Boat People* de Mayra Santos Febres." *Revista De Estudios Hispánicos,* vol. 34.2, 2007, pp. 17–32.

Mosby, Dorothy. "'The Erotic as Power': Sexual Agency and the Erotic in the Work of Luz Argentina Chiriboga and Mayra Santos Febres." *Cincinnati Romance Review,* vol. 30.1, 2007, pp. 83–98.

Moya Pons, Frank. "Dominican National Identity and Return Migration." *Migration and Caribbean Cultural Identity: Selected Papers from Conference Celebrating the 50th Anniversary of the Center,* pp. 25–33. Center for Latin American Studies, University of Florida, 1982.

Murphy, Joseph M. *Working the Spirit: Ceremonies of the African Diaspora*. Beacon Press, 2003.

Muzio, Rose. *Radical Imagination, Radical Humanity: Puerto Rican Political Activism in New York*. State U of New York P, 2017.

Naranjo, Julio Moracen. "Definitivamente Sueco, No Soy Tu Hermano y Pa' Tras Ni Pa Cojer Impulso." *Afro Cuba Web*, 30 Mar. 2016, https://www.afrocubaweb.com/negro-sueco.html.

Negrón-Muntaner, Frances. *Boricua Pop: Puerto Ricans and the Latinization of American Culture*. New York UP, 2004.

———. "Contested Sovereignties: Puerto Rico and American Samoa." *Sovereign Acts: Contesting Colonialism across Indigenous Nations and Latinx America*, edited by Frances Negrón-Muntaner, U of Arizona P, 2017, pp. 130–55.

———. *None of the Above: Puerto Ricans in the Global Era*. Palgrave Macmillan, 2007.

———, and Ramon Grosfoguel, eds. *Puerto Rican Jam: Rethinking Colonialism and Nationalism*. U of Minnesota P, 1997.

Nobles, Melissa. "The Myth of Latin American Multiracialism." *Daedalus*, vol. 134, no. 1, 2005, pp. 82–87.

Noel, Urayoán. *In Visible Movement: Nuyorican Poetry from the Sixties to Slam*. U of Iowa P, 2014.

Olmos, Margarite Fernández, and Lizabeth Paravisini-Gebert. *Creole Religions of the Caribbean: An Introduction from Vodou and Santería to Obeah and Espiritismo*. New York UP, 2003.

Opie, Frederick Douglass. *Upsetting the Apple Cart: Black-Latino Coalitions in New York City from Protest to Public Office*. Columbia UP, 2015.

Otero, Solimar. *Archives of Conjure: Stories of the Dead in Afro Latinx Cultures*. Columbia UP, 2020.

Otero, Solimar, and Toyin Falola. *Yemoja: Gender, Sexuality, and Creativity in the Latina/o and Afro-Atlantic Diasporas*. State U of New York P, 2013.

Palmié, Stephan. *Wizards and Scientists: Explorations in Afro-Cuban Modernity and Tradition*. Duke UP, 2002.

Paschel, Tianna S. *Becoming Black Political Subjects: Movements and Ethno-Racial Rights in Colombia and Brazil*. Princeton UP, 2016.

Pedreira, Antonio. *Insularismo*. Vosgos, 1979.

Perez, Emma. *The Decolonial Imaginary: Writing Chicanas into History*. Indiana UP, 2009.

Perry, Marc D. *Negro Soy Yo: Hip Hop and Raced Citizenship in Neoliberal Cuba*. Duke UP, 2016.

Quijano, Aníbal. *Colonialidad, modernidad/racialidad*. *Perú indígena*, vol. 13, no. 29, 1991, pp. 11–29.

Ramos, Juan G., et al. *Decolonial Approaches to Latin American Literatures and Cultures*. Palgrave Macmillan, 2016.

Renda, Mary A. *Taking Haiti: Military Occupation and the Culture of US Imperialism, 1915–1940*. U of North Carolina P, 2006.
Reyes-Santos, Alaí. *Our Caribbean Kin: Race and Nation in the Neoliberal Antilles*. Rutgers UP, 2015.
Richardson, Jill Toliver. *The Afro-Latin@ Experience in Contemporary American Literature and Culture: Engaging Blackness*. Palgrave Macmillan, 2016.
Rivera, Raquel Z. *New York Ricans from the Hip Hop Zone*. Palgrave Macmillan, 2003.
Rivera-Rideau, Petra R., et al., editors. *Afro-Latin@s in Movement: Critical Approaches to Blackness and Transnationalism in the Americas*. Palgrave Macmillan, 2016.
Rodríguez-Silva, Ileana M. *Silencing Race: Disentangling Blackness, Colonialism, and National Identities in Puerto Rico*. Palgrave Macmillan, 2012.
Rogoziński, Jan. *A Brief History of the Caribbean: From the Arawak and the Carib to the Present*. Facts on File, 1999.
Rosa Abreu, Aida Liz de la. "La identidad cultural de la mujer dominicana de clase trabajadora en Puerto Rico: Su articulación en la comedia televisiva." Master's thesis, Universidad de Puerto Rico, 2002.
Ruiz, Matthew. "Why the Yoruba Roots of Ibeyi's New Album 'Ash' Are a Necessary Force in Latinx Culture." *Remezcla*, 29 Sept. 2017.
Sandoval, Chela. *Methodology of the Oppressed*. Foreword by Angela Y. Davis, U of Minnesota P, 2008.
Santos-Febres, Mayra. "Afroepistemologías: Fractalidad vs Fragmentación En Las Identidades Afrolatinoamericanas y Caribeñas: Aproximaciones Teóricas." Biblioteca y Centro de Investigación Social Jesús T. Piñero. Diálogos de la biblioteca. 2020.
———. *Boat People*. Ediciones Callejón, 2005.
———. "Contestación a Mayra Montero. . ." Facebook. 6 November 2016, 5:34 p.m.
———. *Fe En Disfraz*. Alfaguara, 2009.
Sarduy, Pedro Perez. *Afrocuba: An Anthology of Cuban Writing on Race, Politics and Culture*. Ocean Press, 2005.
Saunders, Tanya L. "Black Lesbians and Racial Identity in Contemporary Cuba." *Black Women, Gender, and Families*, vol. 4, 2011.
———. "Black Thoughts, Black Activism: Cuban Underground Hip Hop and Afro-Latino Countercultures of Modernity." *Latin American Perspectives*, vol. 39, 2012.
———. *Cuban Underground Hip Hop: Black Thoughts, Black Revolution, Black Modernity*. University of Texas Press, 2015.
———. "Grupo OREMI: Black Lesbians and the Struggle for Safe Social Space in Havana." *Souls: A Critical Journal of Black Politics, Culture, and Society*, vol. 11, 2009.
———. "La Lucha Mujerista: Krudas CUBENSI and Black Feminist Sexual Politics in Cuba." *Caribbean Review of Gender Studies*, 2009.

Sharpe, Christina Elizabeth. *In the Wake: On Blackness and Being*. Duke UP, 2016.

———. *Monstrous Intimacies: Making Post-Slavery Subjects*. Duke UP, 2010.

Shemak, April Ann. *Asylum Speakers: Caribbean Refugees and Testimonial Discourse*. Fordham UP, 2011.

Sierra-Rivera, Judith. *Affective Intellectuals and the Space of Catastrophe in the Americas*. Ohio State UP, 2018.

Smallwood, Stephanie E. *Saltwater Slavery: A Middle Passage from Africa to American Diaspora*. Harvard UP, 2008.

Sommer, Doris. *Foundational Fictions: The National Romances of Latin America*. California UP, 1991.

Somers-Willett, Susan B. A. *The Cultural Politics of Slam Poetry: Race, Identity, and the Performance of Popular Verse in America*. U of Michigan P, 2009.

Strongman, Roberto. *Queering Black Atlantic Religions: Transcorporeality In Candomblé, Santería, and Vodou*. Duke UP, 2019.

Stoler, Ann Laura. *Duress: Imperial Durabilities in Our Times*. Duke UP, 2016.

Suárez Findlay, Eileen J. *Imposing Decency: The Politics of Sexuality and Race in Puerto Rico, 1870–1920*. Duke UP, 2003.

Thompson, Robert Farris. *Flash of the Spirit: African and Afro-American Art and Philosophy*. Random House, 1983.

Tinsley, Natasha Omise'eke. "Songs for Ezili: Vodou Epistemologies of (Trans) Gender." *Feminist Studies*, vol. 37.2, 2011, pp. 417–36.

———. *Thiefing Sugar: Eroticism between Women in Caribbean Literature*. Duke UP, 2010.

———. "Black Atlantic, Queer Atlantic: Queer Imaginings of the Middle Passage." *GLQ: A Journal of Lesbian and Gay Studies*, vol. 14.2, 2004, pp. 191–215.

Torres-Robles, Carmen. "The Mythification and Demystification of the Jíbaro as a Puerto Rican National Symbol." *Bilingual Review*, vol. 24, no. 3, 1999, pp. 241–53.

Torres-Saillant, Silvio. *Introduction to Dominican Blackness*. CUNY Dominican Studies Institute, City College of New York, 1999.

———. "The Tribulations of Blackness: Stages in Dominican Racial Identity." *Latin American Perspective*, no. 3, 1998, pp. 126–46.

Traylor, Eleanor, et al., editors. *Broad Sympathy: The Howard University Oral Traditions Reader*. Simon and Schuster Custom Pub., 1997.

Tribunal Constitucional Republica Dominicana. *SENTENCIA TC/0168/13*. 23 Sept. 2013.

Valdés, Vanessa Kimberly. *Diasporic Blackness: The Life and Times of Arturo Alfonso Schomburg*. State U of New York P, 2017.

———. *Oshun's Daughters: The Search for Womanhood in the Americas*. State U of New York P, 2015.

Vega, Marta Moreno. "Espiritismo in the Puerto Rican Community: A New World Recreation with the Elements of Kongo Ancestor Worship." *Journal of Black Studies*, vol. 29.3, 1999, pp. 325–53.

Viarnés, Carrie. "All Roads Lead to Yemayá: Transformative Trajectories in the Procession at Regla." *Hemispheric Institute*, 9 Feb. 2021, https://hemisphericinstitute.org/en/emisferica-5-1-traveling/5-1-essays/all-roads-lead-to-yemaya-transformative-trajectories-in-the-procession-at-regla.html.
Vicente, Zamora. "Cachetes." *La Real Academia Española*, Madrid, 2015.
Wanzer-Serrano, Darrel. *The New York Young Lords and the Struggle for Liberation*. Temple UP, 2015.
Wooldridge, Talia. "¡Escuche Las Krudas! Raw, Feminist Rap Music from Havana, Cuba." *Canadian Woman Studies/Les Cahiers de la Femme*, vol. 27.1, 2008, pp. 74–81.
Zenón Cruz, Isabelo. *Narciso descubre su trasero: El negro en la cultura puertorriqueña*. Editorial Furidi, 1975.
Zurbano, Roberto. "For Blacks in Cuba, the Revolution Hasn't Begun." *New York Times*, 23 Mar. 2013.

Index

Abreu, Rosa, 163
academia, 52, 140
Acevedo, 88–89, 96–102, 104, 106–7, 155
   Elizabeth, 4, 88–89, 96
aché, 45, 122–23, 129, 147
   orisha work, 147
   shared, 125
   activism, 40
   cultural, 98, 115
   musical, 135
   spiritual, 3, 13
acts, 17, 22–23, 28, 34–35, 45, 48–49, 56, 58, 64–65, 91–92, 114, 116–17, 122
   ceremonial, 121
   creative, 6, 13
   cultural, 86
   hauntings, 6
Afecto y cutura, 14
affective turn, 14
Africa, 7, 41–43, 46, 49, 73, 76–77, 95–96, 117, 119, 151, 154
African diaspora, 3–5, 13, 17, 21, 47, 53, 69–70, 82, 86, 88, 118–19, 159, 162
African diaspora beliefs, 41
African Diaspora Women's Fiction, 160
African Diasporic Consciousness, 4, 89

Africanized spiritualities, 95, 115
African religious practices, 44, 48, 96
African traditions, 7, 97
African women, 5, 77
   enslaved, 41, 49–50, 54, 89, 132
Afro-Atlantic Religions, 160
Afro-Boricua, 94–95, 107
Afro-Caribbean religiosity, 39, 88
Afro-Caribbean spiritual practices, 39, 88
Afro-Cuban, 115, 117–18, 122, 135, 152
Afro-descendent, 99, 109, 122, 130
Afro-diasporic, 7, 11, 25, 40, 126, 140
Afro-diasporic spiritualities, 10, 12, 82
Afro-Latina Feminisms, 85–107
Afro-Latinidad, 87, 99, 101, 103, 106
Afro-Latinx, 86–88, 93, 141
Afro-Latinx communities, 87, 96, 121
Afro-Latinx women, 1–3, 25, 102, 121
agency, 50–51, 54–55, 74, 131, 140, 152, 156
Ahmed, 13, 18, 67–68, 105–6, 150, 155
Alexander, 17, 21, 64, 70, 77, 155
Algarín, 91–93
Álvarez Ramírez, 110
Americas, 5, 11, 42, 44, 59, 115, 134, 157–58, 163–64
   hemispheric, 11

Analouise Keating, 155
Ana-Maurine Lara, 3, 24, 138
ancestors, 6, 8, 40–45, 49–51, 55–57, 73–74, 76, 78, 86, 95–97, 99–100, 102–3, 105, 139, 147–49
　ritual knowledges and sacred memories of, 72, 119
ancestral knowledge, 40, 96, 120, 139
ancestral memories, 40, 66, 77
anger, 15–16, 55, 91, 96, 99–100, 134
anti-Black sentiment, 60, 69, 87, 98, 100
anxieties, 34, 48–49, 52, 105, 149
Anzaldúa, 13, 21, 75, 77, 131, 155
　Gloria, 144, 157
archives, 18, 22, 25, 39, 41, 49, 53–55, 57, 77, 157–58, 162
　ephemeral, 91, 151
　historical, 75, 103, 144
　unhappy, 106
Arroyo, Jossianna, 36, 156
Arroyo Pizarro, 23–24, 29, 32–34, 38–42, 45, 48–51, 141, 145, 156
art, 3, 95, 103, 124, 156
Arturo Alfonso Schomburg, 90, 164

Baartman, Sarah, 95
Báez, Josefina, 1
BDSM, 51, 55, 148, 157
beauty, 25, 96, 100–1, 128, 148
beliefs, 12, 44–45, 48, 61, 74, 87, 96, 107, 115, 151
Black Atlantic, 66, 147, 150, 164
Black bodies, 29–30, 32, 34, 38, 40, 43, 47–48, 50, 54, 57–58, 104, 132–33, 141, 144
Black Caribbean, 11, 15, 124
Black Cubans, 25, 112–13, 120, 123–24, 130, 153
Black Dominican, 75, 89, 99
Blackface, 32, 48, 71, 145, 160
Black Feminism, 66, 160

Blackness, 32, 34–35, 37–38, 46, 48, 87, 93–95, 98, 100–3, 105–6, 112–13, 145–46, 153, 159, 163–64
　loving, 68
　translating, 87
Black Sovereignty, 13, 73, 160
Black women, 13, 15–16, 39–41, 47, 49, 53, 55, 66, 97–98, 101, 130, 132–35, 140–41, 148
Black Women, Gender, 163
bodies, 1–2, 6–18, 20–25, 34, 36–40, 42–44, 49, 53–57, 62–64, 67, 74, 80, 93, 95–106, 113, 125, 130–32, 137, 143, 146–53
borders, 16–18, 20, 22, 37–38, 45, 67, 69, 77, 79, 81, 87–88, 117–18, 131, 144–46, 149–50
border space, 22, 46, 68, 75, 79
　painful, 17, 50–51, 58, 82, 104
brujas, 79–80, 93–97, 141

Caribbean, 3, 5, 7, 9–10, 13, 15–17, 29, 48, 50, 78–79, 87–88, 96–98, 145, 147, 162–63
Caribe, 16, 35, 38, 67, 145, 158, 160–61
ceremony, 13, 45, 61, 64, 73, 132, 138, 143, 162
　initiation, 129–30
　religious, 104, 121
Changó, 25, 76, 120, 122, 130, 132
Chianita, 27–29, 33, 161
children, 47, 59, 65, 74, 79, 97, 102, 116–17, 122, 128–29, 152
coalitions, 21, 38, 68, 92–93, 107
　intimate, 20
　musical, 107
　poetic, 101
　political, 50, 88
Code Noir, 47–48, 147
colonial, 20, 24, 57, 71, 81, 95, 116–17, 132, 145, 150

Index | 169

colonial difference, 96
colonial discourse, 9, 18
colonial dismemberment, 17
colonialism, 4, 6, 9, 24–25, 35–36, 55, 69, 75, 77, 102, 106, 159, 163
coloniality, 7, 10, 17, 19, 40, 70, 82, 102, 151, 159, 161
coloniality of power, 19, 61, 82
coloniality of power and gender, 66, 69, 74, 95–96, 132, 134–35, 151
colonization, 17, 29, 32, 38, 42, 45–46, 50, 52, 55–56, 95, 99, 147, 151
communities, 1–2, 5–7, 21–23, 33, 46, 67–68, 72, 80, 85–87, 90–94, 101–2, 106, 120–22, 125, 134, 139–41, 150
  decolonial, 150
  displaced, 117
  loving, 67, 139
  sacred, 72
consciousness, 8, 131, 134, 139–40
  critical, 91, 114
  false colonial, 134
Creole Religions, 7, 162
crossings, 17, 21–22, 117, 123, 155
Cuba, 3, 11, 17, 109–15, 117–20, 126–30, 135, 152–54, 156, 163, 165
Cuban Underground Hip Hop, 163
Cuban Underground Hip-Hop Movement. *See* CUHHM
CUHHM (Cuban Underground Hip-Hop Movement), 113–14, 127, 131
Cultural Politics of Emotion, 155
cultural practices, 19, 37, 100, 113, 146

Danticat, 24, 63, 65, 69, 79
decolonial, 4, 57, 63, 85, 130
decolonial love, 4, 18–19, 63–64, 68, 71, 90, 104, 118, 124, 141
deities, 23, 45–46, 65, 80, 121, 129, 131, 148

diaspora, 2, 4–5, 7, 14–15, 17, 23, 25, 86, 88–89, 91, 95, 101–3, 114, 117–18, 155
disidentification, 87
displacement, 21, 24, 66–67, 83, 103, 127
dispossession, 3, 10, 12, 117
Dominican identity, 68, 86, 88, 150
Dominican Republic, 38, 59–61, 63, 67–68, 70–72, 74, 80–81, 87, 89, 96–97, 142, 144, 149, 156, 158
Dominican Republic and Haiti, 5, 79, 155

Edwidge Danticat, 3, 59, 97
Elegguá, 121–23, 132
El Ni'e, 157
emotions, 1, 4, 6, 13–15, 20, 23, 66–67, 87, 91, 137, 139, 143–44, 150
empire, 1, 8, 14, 16, 85, 92, 125, 127, 155
epistemology, 12, 81, 139
erotic, 20–21, 64, 74, 161
Erzulie, 25, 59–83, 116, 129, 149, 157
Espiritismo, 4, 44, 95, 162, 164
everyday life, 1–2, 21, 49, 58, 91–92, 111
exiles, 68, 82, 127
Ezili, 75, 149, 151, 164

fear, 20, 34, 47, 55–56, 105, 140
feminism, 21, 145, 155, 160
  toward a Decolonial, 95, 151, 160
Feminist Spiritualities, 2–134, 137–38, 140, 142
fractal, 10–12, 125
fractality, 4, 10–11

gender, 66, 69, 74, 80, 95–96, 116–17, 119, 132, 134–35, 151, 157, 162, 164
ghosts, 6, 12, 46, 86, 95, 144, 146

Glissant, 81, 159
Grupo OREMI, 126, 163

hair, 88, 94, 99, 101–2, 104, 106, 152
   black, 98, 153
   curly, 101, 152
   good, 153
   kinky, 27
hair straightening, 104, 107, 153
Haiti, 3, 5, 18, 24–25, 59–60, 63, 65, 70–71, 77, 79, 81, 149, 155–58
Haitian descent, 59–60, 62
Haitian migrants, 59, 67, 141
Haitian Revolution, 60, 64–65
Haitian Vodou, 7, 60, 71, 117
happiness, 20, 67–68, 103, 105–6, 155
hate, 15–16, 67, 100
haunt, 52, 55, 79, 83
Havana, 109, 112, 126–27, 163, 165
healing, 1, 4, 45, 69, 79, 120, 132, 144
   spiritual, 4, 44, 63, 71, 74, 80, 137
heart, 1–2, 69, 75, 86, 103, 122–23, 135, 137, 139, 141, 143
hip-hop, 114, 118–19, 126, 158
   underground, 152
humor, 29–30, 48
   racial, 32
   racialized, 34

intimacy, 42, 49, 51, 55–59, 62–63, 73, 132, 139

Journey, 83, 103, 117, 123, 129
Judeo-Christian, 43, 71, 117, 141
Justice, 32, 89, 134

Kariocha, 116, 129
Knowledge, 2, 5–7, 9, 12, 15, 18–22, 117, 119, 121

Labor, 21, 37

lavé tét (washing of the head), 72
Legba, 45, 72, 148
Lesbians, 16, 126
Linear, 3, 8–11, 41, 64, 141
Lorde, Audre, 15–16, 20–21, 96, 124
Love, 1–4, 11, 14–16, 18–22, 42–44, 51, 59, 63–64, 66–71, 74–76, 78–82, 90–95, 96, 101–3, 118–25, 145, 150–54
Lucumí (Cuba), 129
Lwa, 11, 30, 41, 45–46, 57, 60, 62–64, 69, 72–74, 78, 83, 116, 129

Masculinity, 60, 130
Marouan, Maha, 5, 160
Martínez-San Miguel, Yolanda, 16, 38, 145, 150, 153
Memory, 4, 6, 7, 10, 15, 21, 29, 39–44, 51–52, 58, 69, 71, 73–74, 79, 81, 89, 95–97, 99, 101, 114, 117
Metaphysical, 123
Middle Passage, 129, 131
Modernity, 6–7, 9, 14, 17–20, 25, 40, 45, 64, 124, 139, 144
Mohanty, Chandra Talpade, 21
Moraga, Cherríe, 21
Morality, 62

Nation, 62–65, 67–74, 79–82, 89, 111, 114–16
Nationalism, 33, 36–37, 57, 107, 115
Neocolonial, 58
Neoliberal, 33, 52, 68

Ocean, 11, 46, 75–76, 78, 98, 100, 115–16, 128–28, 135
Oppositional, 63, 115
Orisha, 4, 6, 25, 45, 114–21, 125, 128–30, 132, 135
Oya, 65, 80, 121, 128

Patriarchy, 24, 77, 82

Pedagogies of crossing, 17, 21, 24
Pedagogy, 92, 114, 117, 134, 142
Pleasure, 50–52, 54–57, 64, 66

Queer, 13, 50, 61, 64, 75, 78, 106, 115, 129, 130, 132, 134
Queerness, 112

Race, 10, 13, 18, 27, 34–35, 39, 55–56, 68–69, 87, 111–15, 134
Racialization, 10, 87, 104, 106
Reyes-Santos, Alaí, 17, 32, 36–37, 58, 68–69, 72
   Caribbean Women Healers, 138

Sacred, 4, 21, 27, 29, 33, 35, 37, 39, 42, 46, 56–58, 63, 72–73, 116, 119, 121, 125
Sierra-Rivera, Judith, 144, 164
Spirit, 21–23, 33–36, 90–95, 97–98, 102, 104, 113, 119–20, 124, 130, 137–38

Time, 3, 5, 6, 8–10, 13, 21, 24, 40, 51, 56, 70, 120, 137

Time/temporalities, 19, 23–24, 124, 131
Tradition, 1–2, 7, 20, 32, 44, 70, 85, 88
Truth, 91, 120

United States, 1, 3, 11

Vega, Marta Moreno, 1, 12
Violence, 3–5, 12, 22–23, 32–33, 38, 42, 46, 49–54, 57, 63, 65, 69, 72, 74, 77, 79, 81–83, 88, 94, 98, 101, 105, 118, 129–34
Vodou, 4–7, 59–64, 66–73, 76–78, 83, 116–17, 129, 132

Water, 43, 46, 72, 76, 78–79, 96, 117, 121, 127–29
Whiteness, 7, 29, 71, 101, 134, 147
Wholeness, 2, 12, 17, 125
Women of color, 3, 12–13, 16, 19, 63, 69, 134

Yemayá, 44–46, 115–20, 122–23, 125, 127–31, 135
Yoruba, 6, 40, 100, 116, 118–21, 125, 130–31

www.ingramcontent.com/pod-product-compliance
Lightning Source LLC
Chambersburg PA
CBHW030827230426
43667CB00008B/1414